£14.95

Tradir

ae Chains,

# Trading Down

*Africa, Value Chains,
and the Global Economy*

PETER GIBBON AND
STEFANO PONTE

TEMPLE UNIVERSITY PRESS
Philadelphia

Temple University Press
1601 North Broad Street
Philadelphia PA 19122
*www.temple.edu/tempress*

Copyright © 2005 by Temple University
All rights reserved
Published 2005

Printed in the United States of America

⊗ The paper used in this publication meets the requirements of the
American National Standard for Information Sciences — Permanence
of Paper for Printed Library Materials, ANSI Z39.48-1992

Library of Congress Cataloging-in-Publication Data

Gibbon, Peter.
Trading down : Africa, value chains, and the global economy / Peter Gibbon and
  Stefano Ponte.
     p.   cm.
   Includes bibliographical references and index.
   ISBN 1-59213-367-3 (cloth : alk. paper) — ISBN 1-59213-368-1 (pbk. : alk. paper)
   1. Africa—Economic conditions—1960–   2. Africa—Economic policy.
  3. Globalization.   I. Ponte, Stefano.   II. Title.
  HC800.G53 2005
  382′.0967—dc22

                                                                        2004062094

2 4 6 8 9 7 5 3 1

*In memory of Phil Raikes*

# Contents

# Preface

THIS BOOK ANALYZES the effects of some key changes in the global economy on African countries south of the Sahara. Africa has rarely been the main subject of the growing literature on economic globalization. It is either ignored as 'marginal' in the dynamics of global economic change, or is represented as a case study among others. When individual African countries are actually examined in this literature, it is often South Africa that speaks for the continent—hardly the case of appropriate representation. This book fills this gap by putting Africa firmly at the nexus of the economic globalization-development debate. It shows that there are uneven trajectories within the continent, depending on the value chain analyzed and the regulatory structure of the country under study. The kinds of opportunities and constraints that African countries face have also varied in time in relation to changing international trade regimes and global business strategies. There have been cases of marginalization and of increased opportunity; inclusion, and exclusion; new processes of trade integration as well as increased fragmentation; cases of industrial collapse and of technological upgrading; cases of exploitation of local resources (both physical and human) by large corporations and cases of firm-to-firm learning.

Some of the challenges faced by Africa in the changing global economy are entirely new. Others have been modified. In general, the terms of participation in international trade and global value chains (GVCs) have entailed more demanding capabilities and performances. This in turn has generated new winners and losers. The first novelty of this book is that it examines the consequences of these changes through a combination of three areas of thinking and research that have not been previously been confronted with each other. The first is Global Value Chain (GVC) analysis; the second is Convention Theory; and the third is work on Africa's decline and marginalization in the global economy. GVC analysis and convention theory have been applied largely to economic life in the North (and in the case of GVC, to trade between the North and Asia). They have also been elaborated in wholly isolated ways from each other, despite the potential complementarities. Africa's decline and marginalization in the global economy has been discussed mainly in political science analyses of "failed regimes" and in orthodox trade theory in relation to trade "disintegration."

The point of bringing together GVC analysis with a discussion of Africa's contemporary role in the global economy is twofold. First, it enables a broadening of applications of GVC analysis into least-developed and other developing countries and therefore into a range of value chains never previously examined. This in turn allows the testing, refinement, and development of GVC's key concepts of governance and upgrading. Second, it enables a shift of the debate from sterile narratives about African exceptionalism to the diversity of responses within Africa and the link between these and specific dynamics in the global economy.

Convention theory's confrontation with African economic life is similarly provocative. On the one hand, it obliges this body of thought to come to terms with a range of products that it has previously failed to treat. It also highlights the status of conventions as sources of entry barrier to broad groups of producers and not simply as means of arbitrating and justifying the quality of products circulating in Northern economies. On the other hand, it helps Africanist scholarship to recast recent economic developments in the continent in the light of: (1) profound historical changes in the realm of Northern consumption; and (2) the nature of the mechanisms through which the quality of traded products is specified and measured.

Finally, GVC analysis and convention theory add missing dimensions to each others' understanding of economic life. Convention theory enriches GVC analysis' preoccupation with chain governance through a better understanding of the normative dimensions of governance and its consumption-related aspects. GVC analysis enriches convention theory's sociological preoccupation with normative structures as constraints to action through a new approach to the issue of economic power.

The second novelty of this book is that it grounds this combination of GVC analysis, convention theory, and the treatment of Africa's role in the global economy, on a broader discussion of the distinctive features of present-day capitalism and the regulation of international trade. GVC structures are strongly shaped by the strategies of relatively small groups of companies based in the North in the context of changing regulatory regimes. These companies follow specific prescriptions about business strategy, command specific magnitudes of resources, and work within specific conventions of consumption and sets of trade rules. Which types of companies are able to lead GVCs, which prescriptions they follow, and what level of resources they have for doing so, depend on processes unique to the contemporary Northern business environment—and understandable only in relation to its underlying dynamics. The content of the quality paradigms that such actors seek to use, and in relation to which they set supplier specifications, are also strongly influenced by the nature of this environment.

Within this broad framework, we seek to unveil processes of integration and marginalization of African countries, farms, and firms—with a focus on aspects such as entry barriers, shifting power dynamics, mechanisms of governance of value chains, and opportunities for industrial upgrading. A better understanding of the interactions between public forms of governance (international and domestic regulation), private forms of governance (global business strategies, internal dynamics of coordination in value chains), and what falls in between (standard setting networks, label and certification initiatives, public-private partnerships) is aimed at going beyond state-centric approaches to economic development. Yet, GVC analysis was until recently almost exclusively focused on 'internal' dynamics of value chain governance and disregarded the role of regulation in the workings of international trade. This book, although following the GVC tradition, aims at emphasizing the structural limitations within which firms, even multi-national corporations, operate. It also seeks to examine the more cognitive and normative aspects of governance in GVCs—in relation to different corporate cultures, the expectations of financial markets, and different forms of legitimacy and justification of action.

Empirically, this book is based on the analysis of key value chains originating from a number of African countries and ending in Northern economies: citrus (from South Africa), clothing (from Mauritius and South Africa), cocoa (from Ghana), coffee (from Kenya, Ethiopia, Tanzania, and Uganda), cotton (from Tanzania and Zimbabwe), and fresh vegetables (from Kenya and Tanzania). By focusing on agro-food products and labor-intensive manufacturing, the case studies provide the substance for conclusions that apply to least-developed countries (LDCs) generally, and to those in Africa in particular. This compensates for the fact that much GVC analysis has so far been so far focused on more advanced manufacturing sectors and high technology (with the exception of work on clothing and footwear) and on other regions of the world (with the exception of work on fresh fruit and vegetables). The material on the selected GVCs is used mainly for analytical purposes here. More information and empirical details on the specific case studies are available in the publications listed in Table 4.1 and in the edited volume by Fold and Larsen (forthcoming).

As a point of departure, we examine recent transformations in global business and corporate strategies and in the regulative and institutional frameworks that govern international trade. Chapter 1 covers some of the key changes in economic thinking, business strategies, and industrial organization that have taken place at the international level in the last twenty years with specific reference, when appropriate, to the consequences for Africa. This is done in relation to some broad trends that characterize what we call the "age of global capitalism": increased economic globalization (at least in some aspects), corporate financialization and "shareholder value," and the emergence (or re-emergence in some cases) of specific corporate practices and forms of industrial organization. This period started approximately in the early 1980s, but its characteristic trends accelerated in the 1990s and early 2000s. Its defining features are the following:

1. Intensified economic globalization—at least in some respects; globalization skeptics may be correct in pointing out that contemporary foreign-direct investment (FDI) and global trade, far from being comprehensively "globalized," still take the form of flows mostly within and between the so-called "triad" (North America, Western Europe, and Japan). But it is also notable that—since the early 1970s—the tendency for the triad to dominate world exports has been halted or even reversed. Also, exports of merchandise trade from a developing country region *outside* the triad (Asia other than Japan) has increased substantially—not only for basic manufactures like clothing, but also in more technologically sophisticated products.

2. The increasing internationalization of retail activities in Northern countries—mainly as a result of mergers and acquisitions; as recently as the mid-1980s, almost all retailers, even leading ones, served only their domestic markets. World retail sales are today dominated by groups operating not merely across countries, but also across regions—including those regions typically characterized as "emerging markets."

3. The phenomenon of corporate "financialization," or broadening popular participation in corporate shareholding, that has led to a

partial re-orientation of quoted corporations from (mainly) increasing their market share to (also) increasing "shareholder value." Although these phenomena are more relevant to Anglo-Saxon countries, there are signs that similar prescriptions are spreading to other business cultures in Europe.

4. The growing importance of two instruments for attaining "shareholder value" in the context of slow growth of global good and service markets: oligopolistic rent-seeking, and branded marketing.

5. Changes in industrial organization, with the passage from a focus on internal scale economies (related to vertical integration) to one on external economies (via out-sourcing)—and a resulting tendency for "lead firms" to retain control over product definition and marketing, and to out-source manufacturing, supply chain management, and sometimes also inventory management.

6. The rise of "global contract manufacturing;" as lead firms have increasingly redefined themselves as specialists in branding and marketing, certain of their suppliers have chosen to specialize in the manufacture and/or provision of related production services. This allows (some) suppliers to reap the benefits of large economies of scale, to diversify their customer base, and to break away from a "captive" supply relationship.

In Chapter 2, we provide the basic elements for an incorporation of international regulation into the analysis of GVCs. In much of the political economy literature, there has been an implicit assumption that de-regulation means no more than reduction in the amount and encompassing nature of regulation—whereas in fact it means a shift in the type and form of regulation. This has generally involved privatizing regulation and shifting it away from a politically negotiated system, where rules provide the basis for public enforcement, and towards a judicially-regulated system in which rules provide the basis for civil court action and award of damages. This change is also partly reflected in international trade rules, although public enforcement in this case was never a feature of earlier periods of regulation.

In this chapter, we concentrate upon the evolution of the regulative and institutional frameworks that govern international trade. Specifically, we focus on the emergence of a 'new international trade regime' that started with the establishment of WTO in 1994, but that is more recently characterized by a proliferation of bilateral trade agreements.

The observed poorer trade performance of Africa in relation to other developing country groups is especially disturbing in relation to the nature of the new international trade regime. The modest degrees of preferential treatment for developing countries that were present in the pre-1994 trade regime have been diluted in the new regime, whereas the underlying principle of special and differentiated treatment has been re-packaged in terms of equality of opportunity—plus longer periods to meet the compliance conditions of largely Northern country-defined trade rules.

Another element that is often absent from GVC studies relates to how the consequences of changing global business strategies and trade regimes are mediated for producing countries by different types of do-mestic rules and institutional frameworks. This topic, rather than being treated in a separate chapter, is woven into the chapters summarizing our value chain studies. Changes in global business strategies and trade rules do not affect all African countries in the same way. Local-level out-comes are markedly different due to different paths of domestic mar-ket liberalization. Market liberalization has been concomitant with the disappearance of distinctively national regulative or coordinative sys-tems in many African countries—especially in relation to agricultural commodities. National governments are now mostly unable to control or predict crop availability (in terms of volume and timing), and/or quality, or both. Together with the disappearance of the national insti-tutions charged with these types of coordination, this has undermined the effectiveness of attempts by producing countries to revive interna-tional commodity agreements. Consequently, there are no frameworks for managing secular falls in international prices or price instability in domestic markets.

Different paths of liberalization also entail different (public, private, or both) models of sector organization and coordination that have spe-cific implications for price setting and the local management of quality. They have consequences more generally for system performance and the distribution of benefits between actors in different roles in the na-tional segments of GVCs. In many African cases, a tension has emerged between competition and price incentives to producers on the one hand, and input provision and quality control on the other. This tension man-ifests itself in terms of higher shares of the international price being paid to producers, whereas input supply systems are disrupted, quality deteriorates, and generally lower average international unit prices are obtained.

Chapters 3 to 6 elaborate and deploy the GVC and convention theory approaches to understanding the changing role of Africa in the global economy. Chapter 3 delineates some of the key conceptual questions in GVC analysis, providing readers with an introduction to the issues of governance and upgrading in this framework. Chapter 4 examines the historical rise of "buyer-driven" chains. One of the defining parameters of GVC analysis is its distinction between "buyer-" and "producer-driven" value chains, with the implication that the nature of specific categories of lead firms determines both input-output structures and chain geographies. This chapter discusses some of the basic elements—both in the North and in Africa—that facilitated the emergence of buyer-driven chains. Then, it describes the configuration of the selected value chains and the nature of their main actors: lead firms, first-tier suppliers, and second-tier suppliers. Tiering of supply networks is a major trend of recent years, and the gap between first- and second-tier suppliers is, in most cases, almost as large as that between lead firms and first-tier suppliers. This discussion is followed by the analysis of how lead firms exercise "driving" in value chains, with special reference to their relations with first-tier suppliers.

Most first-tier suppliers, like lead firms, are Northern-based. Africa's role in GVCs comes into full focus only when relations between first- and second-tier suppliers are considered. Chapter 5 does so in relation to questions of entry barriers, upgrading opportunities, and marginalization and exclusion experiences encountered by second-tier suppliers. The discussion starts with entry barriers and elaborates two stories arising from our empirical material on Africa: (1) a story of strategies adopted by "lead firms" that raise entry barriers for both first-tier and second-tier suppliers (coffee, clothing, fresh vegetables, citrus); and (2) a story of raised entry barriers for first-tier suppliers, and unchanged or even reduced entry barriers for second-tier suppliers (cocoa, cotton).

These two "stories" have different consequences for developing country producers, processors, and traders in terms of exclusion and marginalization. In the first story, entry barriers for second-tier suppliers are multiple, to some degree mutually reinforcing, and generally rising. In the second story, entry barriers are less numerous and do not necessarily mutually reinforce each other. In principle, it should be easier to negotiate a single entry barrier than multiple ones, even though the rewards may not be high. The fact that some African countries, farms, and firms have had great difficulty in doing so indicates institutional failure and fundamental problems of public policy formulation and implementation. Finally, this chapter turns to opportunities for, and experiences of, upgrading. Upgrading refers here to how second-tier suppliers can access better and/or more stable rewards from participation in GVCs, or can graduate to first-tier supplier status. The analysis traces changes in the reward systems presented to suppliers, and suggests that there have been relatively few examples of clearly successful upgrading in Africa, even of a limited kind.

Chapter 6 incorporates the cognitive and normative aspects of governance addressed in convention theory into the more structural framework of GVC analysis, in order to enrich the theoretical discussion of (private and public) forms of governance in the global economy. This is done through a focus on issues of quality and standards. The chapter starts with the observation that consumption in Northern countries is increasingly characterized by new trends in taste, by greater food and/or user safety awareness, and by social and environmental concerns. This, together with market saturation for goods with commodity traits, has led to product proliferation and differentiation. These trends have also been accompanied by an increased importance for issues of quality control and management, traceability, and certification. As a result, quality standards are proliferating and becoming more specific. They also tend to focus (sometimes exclusively) on production and process methods rather than on the product itself.

The confrontation of convention theory with GVC analysis suggests new ways of understanding these developments [as well as new reflections] on their consequences for economic governance. Consumption is governed quite independently from the governance of value-chains, but lead firms still seek to differentiate their products within the broad boundaries of society-wide prescriptions and justifications concerning what quality consists of. Current trends in the overall composition of quality conventions mean that quality management has become a more important and demanding aspect of value-chain governance. At the same time, control over where and how quality is generated along a chain has also become a key foundation of governance. These trends have emerged in a context where buyer power on the one hand, and shareholder value—based prescriptions about the desirability of outsourcing on the other, provide the basic parameters of value chain driving.

Against this background, lead firms seek to use their power in relation to quality issues by exercising control over the controls that others are expected to implement—rather than by directly managing quality along the full length of a value chain. This propels narratives about quality in the direction of conformity with codified standards, which in turn reinforces the differentiation between first- and second-tier suppliers. However, the extent to which quality can be managed in this way varies considerably from chain to chain, depending on a variety of factors—including how precisely quality comes to be defined, which group of agents within lead firms is involved in defining it, and on the nature of the product traded. This gives rise to a variety of forms of coordination between various segments of the value chain under the common heading of buyer-driven governance. However, new standards, certifications, and codification procedures simultaneously open up opportunities for agents other than lead firms to contest the content of quality prescriptions, prescribe alternative mechanisms of governance, and thus more or less directly challenge buyer dominance.

Chapter 7 sums up the main conclusions of the book. Relative to its position in the global economy half a century ago, Africa has experienced a process of "trading down"—exclusion, marginalization, and location in roles associated with high levels of vulnerability. But the term "trading down" also can be used as a stylized description of the practical business strategies adopted by certain enterprises that have succeeded. These have foci that, although decidedly unappealing in the context of theories of industrial upgrading, appear both viable in business terms and consistent with Africa's basic pattern of factor endowment. The discussion poses the question of whether these spontaneously emerging corporate adjustments point in the direction of a viable and generalizable development strategy. The chapter closes by returning to the implications of the book for GVC analysis and for future research.

This book is based on work carried out between 1999 and 2003 in a research program on "Globalization and Economic Restructuring in Africa" (GLAF) at the Centre for Development Research (CDR), Copenhagen (from 2003, Danish Institute for International Studies). The program was funded with contributions from the Danish Social Science Research Council (SSF) and the Danish Development Studies Research Council (RUF), which we gratefully acknowledge. Besides the authors, the program involved Britt Noehr Jensen, Marianne Nylandsted Larsen, Poul Ove Pedersen, and Lotte Thomsen from CDR; Niels Fold from the Institute of Geography, University of Copenhagen; and Michael Friis Jensen from the Institute of Economics, Danish Royal Veterinary and Agricultural University. We are deeply indebted to our colleagues for their intellectual stimulation, social companionship, and hard work during these years.

We are also particularly thankful to Benoit Daviron (CIRAD-Montpellier), who was our closest external collaborator and most vibrant source of inspiration. Many others participated in one or more of several workshops and conferences that took place during the life of the program, and provided invaluable contributions, feedback, and criticism. Among these, we would like to thank especially Henry Bernstein, Catherine Dolan, Gary Gereffi, John Humphrey, Bruno Losch, Florence Palpacuer. We also thank two anonymous reviewers for their constructive feedback. We also thank two anonymous reviewers for their constructive feedback. The Rockefeller Foundation provided support for a number of workshops that brought the authors together with researchers from Britain, the United States, and elsewhere in the Global Value Chain Initiative (www.ids.ac.uk/globalvaluechains/index.html), generating a stimulating forum for critical theoretical and policy-oriented engagement. Phil Raikes participated in designing the GLAF research program, and was engaged in it until his death in 2001 after a long and courageous struggle with cancer. We dedicate this book to his memory.

# 1    The Age of Global Capitalism

THE OBJECTIVE of this book is to help the reader understand the nature of Africa's current political economy in relation to the broad debate on how economic globalization affects development prospects. To analyze the Africa-globalization-development nexus, it is first necessary to understand some of the central trends and processes that characterize what we call "the age of global capitalism." This implies, at least initially, a focus mainly on Northern countries and changes in their economies. Within this broad framework, this chapter mainly discusses ongoing processes of financial and industrial restructuring and their underlying causes.

This focus reflects our central assumption that Africa has been, and remains, integrated into the world economy on the basis of specific investments, exchanges, and contracts entered into by specific enterprises and individuals. These have taken place in contexts that have been subject to regulation of different kinds—for example, by trade agreements, national economic policies, and international standard setting. However, their more immediate dynamics relate to the emergence of (and interactions between) particular men and women acting in particular markets and the influence of discourses concerning how profit making can be most efficiently organized. These actors, markets, and discourses are all subject to historical evolution and sometimes to revolution. At the beginning of the twenty-first century, they look very different even in comparison to those of two decades ago.

Because Africa's relation to the world economy has turned so persistently on agrofood commodities and minerals, and because the former are the focus of most of the empirical studies covered in this book, we have chosen to illustrate Northern financial and industrial restructuring processes chiefly in terms of developments in the food sector. However, to make certain theoretical points and to show the extent (and limitations) of the applicability of changes in the food sector, the electronics, pharmaceutical, and automotive sectors are also examined.

This chapter begins with discussions of some of the broad trends that characterize contemporary capitalism: economic globalization, "corporate financialization" and shareholder value, and specific corporate practices (especially oligopolistic rent seeking). It then turns to an examination of two central issues for the study of global value chains: how, against this background, lead firms are restructuring their relations to their most immediate (and larger) suppliers and how these suppliers are responding to these processes. Finally, it identifies a number of emerging issues for the analysis of Africa's changing relation to the global economy: the revived importance of economies of scale, the simultaneous demand for large suppliers to exhibit greater specialization and to provide more services, and the implications of these developments for entry barriers.

## ECONOMIC GLOBALIZATION

Narratives concerning economic globalization have gone through two clear phases since they emerged in the early 1980s. In the first decade of the discussion, the dominant form was that propagated by marketing gurus like Levitt (1983) and neoclassical business economists such as Ohmae (1990), who were working for, or in close collaboration with, institutions like the Organization for Economic Co-operation and Development (OECD).[1] The position of these "globalization enthusiasts" was that all critical economic flows—trade, foreign-direct investment (FDI), portfolio investment, lending and borrowing—were becoming more internationalized to an extent and at a pace unmatched during any previous stage in history. They also argued that economic processes and tendencies in different parts of the world were becoming much less open to major local variation and modification. In the case of Ohmae (1990), these positions were complemented by three other arguments: (1) globalization was leading to a net increase in economic benefits, largely through greater competition and thereby greater efficiency; (2) these changes, at least potentially, could benefit all countries equally; and (3) governments could best capture the benefits of globalization by ensuring the greatest possible degree of economic openness.

Since the mid-1990s, this position has been subject to what has been called "death by a thousand qualifications." Several of the most strategic of these were inflicted by Hirst and Thompson (1996). Hirst and Thompson argued that contemporary FDI and global trade, far from being comprehensively globalized, increasingly took the form of flows within and between a triad of advanced economies—North America,

Western Europe, and Japan. Even investment and trade *between* these three blocs was less significant than *within* the first two, whereas flows between each of these groups and the rest of the world were hardly significant and, in most cases, falling in relative importance.

Hirst and Thompson (1996) also asserted that little or no change could be detected in the global distribution of gross domestic product (GDP) since 1970. In the early 1990s, roughly 75 percent of GDP was still generated by the triad, even when including the newly industrialized countries (NICs)—Hong Kong, Korea, Singapore, and Taiwan. Furthermore, they claimed that overall levels of international economic integration, even among countries in the triad, were no greater (and in relation to some indicators, were actually lower) than at two or three earlier times during the twentieth century. Finally, they sought to show that the scope for nation-states to exercise independence in economic policy making was still considerable. Those promulgating such qualifications to the original globalization narrative have been commonly designated as "globalization skeptics." Following Hirst and Thompson's predominantly economic focus of critique, most subsequent contributions have been aimed at refuting claims concerning political globalization (see, for example, Weiss 1998, 1999).

In the rest of this section, an argument will be presented for a partial rehabilitation of the notion of economic globalization, although not in the form asserted by Levitt and Ohmae. This argument is aimed less at saving the concept of economic globalization, which cannot be considered a particularly interesting project in itself, and more at bringing the discussion back to the nature of global capitalism. In the course of rectifying the hyperbole of the globalization enthusiasts, the counternarrative of the globalization skeptics wittingly or unwittingly narrowed the examination of what is going on in the contemporary global economy to measurement of a limited range of headline trends. As noted previously, this measurement seems to reveal a picture of little or no change. However, even a superficial decomposition of some of the apparently static headline trends indicates that they conceal strong subtrends pulling in different directions. Although these may cancel each other out in terms of aggregate data, they are sometimes themselves new and interesting and have broad implications.

The discussion that follows focuses on a specific and interlinked group of subtrends within world merchandise trade as well as on complementary trends in world retail trade. This analysis introduces a number of parameters that will frame later discussion: (1) that trade in manufactures is increasingly dominating merchandise trade generally; (2) that exports of these goods are dominated by a single developing region: Asia other than Japan; (3) that the share of trade in manufactures accounted for by trade in parts and components is rising; and (4) that control over final sale is becoming more concentrated in the hands of a few retail chains.

As the globalization skeptics point out, although world trade/GDP[2] ratios have been rising steadily over the last decades, they are still little higher today than they were at the previous high point of international economic activity (in 1914). Moreover, world trade in aggregate is no more globalized now than it was in the 1910s, in the sense that the trade share of developing countries has stagnated or even declined. At the same time, however, world merchandise trade has become overwhelmingly dominated by manufactures. In 1950, 35 percent of world merchandise trade by value was in agricultural products and 25 percent was in mining products. The share of world trade accounted for by agricultural products steadily subsided to 9 percent in 2001 (all data are from General Agreement on Tariffs and Trade/World Trade Organization; GATT/WTO, various). The share accounted for by mining products rose slightly in the 1960s and 1970s before falling to 13 percent in 2001. Meanwhile, the share accounted for by manufactures has almost doubled, from 39 percent in 1950 to 75 percent in 2001.

Contrary to contemporary wisdom, trade in services has grown less spectacularly and since 1990 has increased its share of world trade only slightly. World trade is thus no longer based on the import of raw materials to Northern countries or even on the exchange of manufactures for raw materials. It is based mainly on the exchange of different kinds of manufactures.

Since the early 1970s, the tendency for the triad to dominate world exports has been halted or even reversed. At the same time, the share accounted for by Asian countries outside of the triad has roughly doubled. The share of world exports accounted for by the triad increased from under 60 percent at the end of the 1940s to 68 percent in 1973. Since that year, it has fluctuated between 61 and 71 percent (1993). In 2001, it was 61.6 percent. Among Asian countries, Hirst and Thompson (1996) include only Japan as part of the triad. Yet, the share of all world merchandise exports accounted for by Asia other than Japan increased from 9 percent in 1963 to 18.3 percent in 2001, having recovered its upward course after a fall as a result of the Asian crisis (GATT/WTO, various).

The relative fall of exports from the triad and the increase of exports from Asia are actually linked. Asia has taken a leading position not only in exports of basic manufactures like clothing but also (and especially since 1990) in more technologically sophisticated products. Table 1.1 shows the share of world exports from Asia for four of the contemporary leading items in world trade. These items together represent over 60 percent of world merchandise trade by value and almost 80 percent of world trade in manufactures.

Three trends stand out from this table. First, from 1990 to 2001, there is a significant rise in the share of world exports accounted for by Asia other than Japan for each of these items. In each case, the more recent shares for Asia other than Japan are higher than those for Japan itself. Second, a majority of all exports of these items, except for textiles, are global rather than being within Asia (including Japan) itself. Third, although its presence in Asian markets has been sometimes growing faster, the extent of the presence of Asia in non-Asian markets has been increasing for all items. On this basis, it is possible to identify a region outside the triad as already being the world's leading manufacturing specialist, and in the process of a transition from being a global specialist in labor-intensive manufactures to becoming one in more capital-intensive manufactures. This important observation is overlooked by globalization skeptics.

Within international trade in manufactures, trade in *manufactured inputs* has seen a very considerable increase. This trend points to the fact that the rise of Asia other than Japan as a center of world manufacturing

**Table 1.1**   Asia other than Japan: share in world exports for selected manufactured products (% of total value: 1990, 2001)

|  | 1990 | 2001 |
| --- | --- | --- |
| Machinery and transport equipment | 9.6 | 19.6* |
| *Proportion exported outside Asia* | *62.7* | *52.8** |
| Office equipment and telecoms equipment | 23.5 | 36.2 |
| *Proportion exported outside Asia* | *67.2* | *51.1* |
| Textiles | 29.7 | 39.8 |
| *Proportion exported outside Asia* | *42.8* | *45.0* |
| Clothing | 43.6 | 45.5 |
| *Proportion exported outside Asia* | *35.5* | *73.4* |

* Figures for 2000 (data for 2001 unavailable).
Source: WTO 2001.

exports has been associated with production of manufactures being undertaken increasingly on an international network or chain basis. Asia's rise as an export center has been associated with imports of components from elsewhere, and domestic manufacturing in the North has also become increasingly dependent on imported components.

International trade statistics are not particularly good at recording or measuring this change. As Milberg (2003) points out, the only industrial classification where official statistics distinguish parts and components from total trade is the classification for machinery and transport equipment. Here, parts and components increased their share from 26.1 percent in 1978 to 30 percent in 1995.[3] Otherwise, the change can be measured only indirectly (through input-output data) and thus with the considerable time lag embodied in this type of data. Campa and Goldberg (1997) report comparable data on imported inputs as a share of total inputs employed in all manufacturing in Canada, the United Kingdom, and the United States (in 1974, 1984, and 1993); Feenstra and Hanson (1999) estimate the share of imported inputs in total incorporation of intermediate goods in U.S. manufacturing (in 1972, 1979, and 1990; see Table 1.2). Although the magnitudes indicated by their data differ, both show a steady rising trend.

There has been a transformation in another aspect of world trade, this time one that is not reported at all in international merchandise or service trade statistics. This is the transformation in international *retail* trade, which has complemented the rise of Asia other than Japan in trade of manufactured goods. A salient feature here is not the emergence of non-Japanese Asian leadership (for global retail leadership is ever more unambiguously with U.S.- and E.U.-based firms), but rather the increasingly international character of retailing itself. As recently as

**Table 1.2**  Share of imported inputs in Northern manufacturing, 1972–1993 (%)

|          | 1972 | 1974 | 1979 | 1984 | 1990 | 1993 |
|----------|------|------|------|------|------|------|
| Canada I |      | 15.9 |      | 14.4 |      | 20.2 |
| UK I     |      | 13.4 |      | 19.0 |      | 21.6 |
| US I     |      | 4.1  |      | 6.2  |      | 8.2  |
| US II    | 6.5  |      | 8.5  |      | 11.6 |      |

I, share of imported inputs in all inputs (Campa and Goldberg 1997); II, share of imported inputs in total use of intermediate goods (Feenstra and Hanson 1999).

the mid-1980s, almost all retailers, even leading ones, served only their domestic markets. World retail sales are today dominated by groups operating not merely across countries but also across regions, including those regions typically characterized as emerging markets. Table 1.3 lists the world's 20 leading retailers by sales, the timing of their first international ventures, and the markets they operate in.[4] The market leader, Wal-Mart, is now the world's largest company by sales and the world's largest private employer.

Of the twenty groups listed, seventeen were operating in at least two countries, sixteen were operating in at least two regions, and eleven were operating in three different regions or more. No fewer than fifteen were operating in emerging market regions. Of the fifteen disclosing overseas sales figures, the median overseas sales level was 17 percent. Of the fourteen for which a year of first overseas investment can be determined, the median year of first internationalization was 1987–1988.

According to Deloitte and Touche, global retail sales in 2000 were around $7 trillion. Assuming a 2 percent growth level during 2001, the twenty-one retailers listed in Table 1.3 jointly accounted for around 12 percent of world retail sales in that year. For a sector that has traditionally exhibited very low levels of global concentration and internationalization, this is unprecedented. Global concentration has clearly been driven upward by the internationalization process, including the movement into emerging markets where growth levels are higher than in the triad. Thus, global relocation of export manufacture, and increasing dependence on imported inputs on the part of global manufacturing that remains in the North, is accompanied by the emergence of a pattern of global marketing whose control is increasingly centralized, but which feeds into a more geographically dispersed pattern of sales.[5]

We are not claiming that the trends identified previously amount to a confirmation of the original claims concerning economic globalization, nor do we deny most of the headline claims made by the globalization skeptics. These trends support mainly the observation that, although globalization is not an accomplished end state, there are nonetheless diverse new trends, new actors, and new links emerging between different trends and actors. Furthermore, although these processes are fragmented, incomplete, discontinuous, and contingent, there are also a few common threads running through them. Against the broad background of global liberalization of markets, these include a deepening of certain forms of economic differentiation and new ways of leveraging them.

**Table 1.3** World's 20 largest retail groups, 2001–2002

| Name | Formats | Country of origin | Year of first international investment | Share of current sales from foreign operations (%) | Regions of foreign operation and share of total sales by foreign region | Total sales 2001 ($billion)**** |
|---|---|---|---|---|---|---|
| Wal-Mart | Discount, warehouses | U.S. | 1991 | 17 | North, Central, and South America; E.U.; E. Asia | 244.5 (2002) |
| Carrefour | Cash and carry, convenience, discount, hypermarket, supermarket | France | 1969 | 44 | E.U. and Eastern Europe, 29%; North, Central, and South America, 8%; E. Asia 7% | 62.1 |
| Royal Ahold | Cash and carry, convenience, discount, drug, hypermarket, supermarket, specialty | Netherlands | 1977 | 86 | North America, 59%, E.U. and Eastern Europe, 19%; Central and South America, 7%; E. Asia 1% | 59.5 |
| Ito-Yokada / 7-Eleven* | Convenience, discount, hypermarket, supermarket, specialty, department | Japan (but 7-Eleven based in U.S.) | Own chains, 2000; 7-Eleven, 1971 | Own chains, 0.5%; 69% of 7-Eleven sales outside U.S. | Own chains, E. Asia; 7-Eleven, all regions | 57.7 (2002) |
| Home Depot | Do-it-yourself (DIY), specialty | U.S. | 1994 | Not available | North and Central America | 53.6 |
| Kroger | Convenience, department, drug, specialty, supermarket | U.S. | None | — | — | 50.1 |
| Metro | Department, DIY, hypermarket, mail order, specialty, supermarket, warehouse | Germany | Not known | 46 | E.U., 29%; Eastern Europe, 14%; Asia and Africa, 2% | 44.2 |

| | Formats | Country | Year | No. | Regions | |
|---|---|---|---|---|---|---|
| Sears | Department, mail order, specialty | U.S. | 2000 | 10 | North America, 10% | 41.1 |
| Target | Department (Dayton Hudson), discount | U.S. | none | — | — | 39.9 |
| Group. des Mousquetaires (Intermarché/Spar)** | Convenience, discount, DIY, hypermarket, restaurant, specialty, supermarket | France | 1988 | Not available | E.U.; Eastern Europe | 36.0 |
| Edeka/AVA | Convenience, discount, DIY, hypermarket, supermarket | Germany | 1991 | 6 | E.U. and Eastern Europe, 6% | 34.2 |
| Costco | Warehouse | U.S. | Not known | 15 | North America, 12%; Central America and Asia, 3% | 32.0 (2002) |
| Albertsons | Drug, supermarket | U.S. | none | — | — | 37.9 (2002) |
| Kmart | Discount | U.S. | none | — | — | 36.2 |
| Tesco | Convenience, hypermarket, supermarket | U.K. | 1994 | 15 | E.U. and Eastern Europe, 9%; Asia, 6% | 34.4 (2002) |
| Rewe | Cash and carry, convenience, department, discount, DIY, hypermarket, specialty, supermarket | Germany | 1993 | 20 | E.U. and Eastern Europe, 20% | 33.5 |
| Safeway/Casa Ley*** | Supermarket | U.S. | 1981 | 14 | North America, 10%; Central America, 4% | 35.8 (2001/1999) |
| J C Penney | Department, drug, mail order | U.S. | Not known | 2 | Central and South America, 2% | 32.0 |

Continued

**Table 1.3** World's 20 largest retail groups, 2001–2002 (Continued)

| Name | Formats | Country of origin | Year of first international investment | Share of current sales from foreign operations (%) | Regions of foreign operation and share of total sales by foreign region | Total sales 2001 ($billion)**** |
|---|---|---|---|---|---|---|
| J Sainsbury | Convenience, hypermarket, supermarket | U.K. | 1987 | 17 | North America, 17% | 26.5 (2002) |
| Tengelmann | Discount, DIY, drug, hypermarket, specialty, supermarket | Germany | 1972 | 56 | North America, 38%; E.U. and Eastern Europe, 18% | 25.4 |
| Auchan | Convenience, DIY, hypermarket, restaurant, specialty, supermarket | France | 1981 | 47 | E.U., 34%; Eastern Europe, Central and South America not disclosed, Asia and N Africa, 13% | 23.4 |

* Ito-Yokado owns a majority of the shares of 7-Eleven.

** Groupelment des Mousquetaires owns a majority of the shares of Spar. It also holds large minority shareholdings in Rona (Canada, sales C$1.2 billion) and in Grupo Eroski (Spain, sales € 4.6 billion). Only the figures from Spar are included in the total given in the table.

*** Safeway owns half of the shares of Casa Ley (Mexico), whose sales data from 1999 (its last reported figures) are added here to Safeway's 2001 sales for North America. The group has no relation to the U.K. retailer of the same name.

**** Where figures were given in € , the exchange rate applied is that at 31st December for the year concerned (in 2001, $1 = € 1.12; in 2002, $1 = € 1.06 (source: http://www.oanda.com/convert/fxhistory)

***** Different figures given in different versions of accounts.

Source: Company annual reports and accounts.

## CORPORATE FINANCIALIZATION AND SHAREHOLDER VALUE

Two of the most profound differences between the age of global capitalism, especially in its Anglo-Saxon embodiment, and the capitalism of even two decades ago are the linked phenomena of corporate financialization and the doctrine of shareholder value. The emergence of these phenomena follows from the liberalization of national and international financial markets, including equity markets. They coincide with a broadening popular participation in corporate shareholding and the corresponding rise of institutional investors, such as pension funds and investment trusts (especially so-called delegate funds).[6]

According to Williams (2000), corporate equity is now owned by over 40 percent of households, both in the United States and Britain. Financial assets accounted for 61 percent of total British household assets in 1995, as opposed to only 46 percent in 1975. At the same time, it is the institutions aggregating household assets that have come to dominate the stock market. The proportion of total U.S. stock held directly by individuals has fallen from 90 percent in the 1950s to 48.6 percent in 1995 and further down to a little over 40 percent in 2001 (Crotty 2002). The figure for the United Kingdom in 2000 was only 16 percent (down from 20.3 percent in 1995; *Financial Times*, February 21, 2003).

Corporate financialization refers directly to two resulting tendencies. The first is for large increases in the market value of equities and in the market capitalization of listed companies. The total market capitalization of U.S. listed companies, for example, rose from a long-term average of 50 percent of GDP in the 1980s to 185 percent in 1999. Even after the bear market of the subsequent years, it remained at 128 percent in 2002 (*Financial Times*, February 21, 2003). The second tendency is for much greater levels of market volatility arising from higher levels of turnover in share ownership. Crotty (2002) states that the turnover rate in U.S. stock market ownership rose from around 20 percent a year in the late 1970s to 50 percent a year in the early 1990s and to 100 percent a year by 2000.[7]

The shareholder value doctrine refers to the consequences of financialization for corporate behavior. Although rapid growth of, and resulting price inflation in, equity markets expands the opportunities for listed companies to raise large amounts of capital in these markets, most make relatively little use of this possibility. Instead, as in the past, they prefer to finance investment either by borrowing or out of retained earnings. Thus, corporate behavior should not be much affected by share values. But the costs of almost all types of borrowing are based on credit ratings derived from share price performance. Thus, equity comes to exercise control over the totality of corporate finance. On this basis, it influences corporate behavior in the direction of aiming to improve the share price (Grahl 2001). Shareholder value is also promoted as a rationale through the almost universal trend for senior managers to be remunerated through equity and stock options. The share of the pay of U.S. listed companies' CEOs that derived from exercised stock options rose from 22 percent in 1979 (and around 50 percent during the 1980s) to an average of 63 percent during 1995–1999 (Crotty 2002).[8]

According to Lazonick and O'Sullivan (2000), the spread of the shareholder value doctrine has led to a reorientation of quoted corporations away from competition on the basis of productivity-improving innovations and increasing product market share. Financial markets assess corporate performance primarily in terms of purely financial performance, especially the return on capital employed (ROCE). U.S. and U.K. markets have even evolved a common market standard in relation to financial performance (12 to 15 percent ROCE; Froud et al. 2000). Corporate ROCEs at or above this level are rewarded with higher market values for their equities, enabling shareholder value to be realized when these equities are sold.

Although this standard is only infrequently attained in practice, it has acted as a stimulus for directors and managers to seek radical solutions to the problem of attaining or sustaining a high level of return on capital. For Lazonick and O'Sullivan (2000), this is most easily attained by corporate restructuring in the form of downsizing. The rationale of downsizing is to concentrate on (or acquire new) activities thought to have high ROCEs while stripping out or selling off those thought to have low ones. High ROCE activities are thought to include product definition, design, branding, marketing, retailing, and lending for consumption. Low ROCE activities are thought to include manufacturing, assembly, and distribution. Other restructuring doctrines advocate withdrawal from manufacturing, reducing investment in emerging technologies, and refocusing on services with lower fixed asset ratios (Dupuy and Lung 2001). In almost all cases, there are subtexts concerning employment, wage levels, and employment rights, such as reduction or casualization of employees, pegging of rewards at all levels to performance, and weakening of rights.

The corporate financialization/shareholder value argument captures an extremely important aspect of contemporary capitalist development—and one that has clear implications for industrial organization and for the international division of labor. However, the processes it describes are probably interpreted best as "stylized facts" rather than as empirical generalizations. Taking only the shareholder value part of the argument (which is more relevant to the subject of this book), two sets of qualifications need to be introduced.

First, assuming that the corporate internalization of the shareholder value doctrine is both widespread and comprehensive, it is not clear why downsizing or corporate restructuring alone should be considered the most obvious ways to increase ROCE. For example, gaining higher returns on some existing assets on the basis of greater economies of scale would appear to be equally consistent with improving ROCE. Indeed, such strategies have also been widely pursued by companies that are oriented toward shareholder value.

This has been most obviously the case in relation to the so-called "cash cow" strategy. According to this strategy, firms in mature sectors can still most easily increase earnings in product markets on the basis of attaining market leadership in specific, already strong, lines or formats. At least initially, this approach implies greater investment in marketing and the selective adoption of aggressive pricing policies. Market leadership allows higher margins not only on the basis of economies of scale,[9] but also permits oligopolistic price setting and the exercise of buyer power in relation to suppliers.

A central problem with the notion that all shareholder value–oriented companies will pursue strictly financial solutions to maximizing ROCE lies with its implication that, within all these companies' managements, a financial(ist) discourse dominates. In reality, it is more likely that there is a plurality of discourses reflecting the different professional and occupational backgrounds and interests of different groups of managers. Kädtler and Sperling's (2002) work on competing technical and financial discourses within management in auto manufacturing, and Gibbon's (2002a) parallel discussion of competing "retailerist" and financial discourses among U.K. clothing retailers, demonstrate that the shareholder value doctrine is translated into corporate decision making only via internally contested processes that usually lead to some modifications.[10]

The second qualification to the shareholder value argument concerns how widely it can be applied in geographical terms. The widespread literature on differences between business systems or varieties of capitalism (cf. Dore, Lazonick, and O'Sullivan 1999; Hall and Soskice 2001;

Whitley 1999) highlights varied institutional structures and traditions (promoting entrepreneurship in the narrow sense in the United States, as opposed to technological innovation, for example, in Germany) as well as differences in broader economic and social policies (neoliberal vs. corporatist). Reflecting this, relative to the Anglo-Saxon countries, smaller proportions of mainland Europe's population own shares, institutional investors play a smaller role in listed companies,[11] shares change hand less frequently, and share price counts for less, both in company credit ratings and in senior management remuneration. Although the set of managerial doctrines associated with the term shareholder value (stripping out overhead costs, identifying and concentrating on core competences, implementing supply chain rationalization programs) are present in mainland Europe, they are so far not part of the everyday discourse of most public companies in the way that they are in the United States and United Kingdom (Froud et al. 2000; Kädtler and Sperling 2002; Morin 2000).

One aspect of these differences is that the ownership structures of non-Anglo-Saxon–based large companies tend to be dominated by banks rather than by delegate management funds and other types of private institutional investors.[12] The former are also typically creditors and have more modest expectations concerning both optimal levels of returns on loans/investment and how rapidly it is possible to reach such optimal levels. Correspondingly, they tend to have longer-term and closer relations with corporate management. Another result is that hostile mergers and acquisitions (M&As), a key mechanism of Anglo-Saxon corporate restructuring, are difficult to accomplish even if they are desired. Underlying this are also differences in corporate law. U.S. corporate law has some notable (antitrust) peculiarities, discouraging investment by banks in nonfinancial corporations, restricting returns from cross-corporate shareholding, and constraining intrasectoral cooperation between firms. In contrast, German corporate law, through the institution of supervisory boards, protects companies from the influence of so-called floating (short-term minority) shareholders. In many other non-Anglo-Saxon countries, other types of institution play a similar role. According to Guillén (2000), Anglo-Saxon countries accounted for 79 percent of all hostile M&As in OECD countries during the period 1990–1998.

Although, in general, shareholder value–type prescriptions play less of a role in corporate strategy in the non-Anglo-Saxon world, evidence is emerging that even in countries where corporate and broader institutional structures appear to be most at variance with the Anglo-Saxon model, what might be termed an incremental form of shareholder value has emerged. Recent studies of the German pharmaceutical and automotive sectors (Jürgens 2002; Vitols 2002) underline this trend. In German pharmaceuticals, the three leading players of the early 1990s (Bayer, Hoechst, and BASF) were integrated into production of chemicals and in some cases also polymers. By 2002, Hoechst had sold off its chemical interests and merged with Rhone Poulenc to form a new life sciences company based in France (Aventis). BASF had sold off its pharmaceutical interests to concentrate on chemicals. In both companies, a visibly stronger emphasis on financial performance and planning had emerged. Even in Bayer, whose public commitment to the corporatist Rhineland capitalism model was strongest of all, a financial specialist was appointed as CEO, and the central pillars of the business as a whole (pharmaceuticals, chemicals, agrochemicals, and polymers) were split into separate legal entities. Finally, in 2003, Bayer decided to spin off most of its chemicals and polymers business and to focus on pharmaceuticals (*Financial Times*, November 8, 2003).

Meanwhile, the main traditional exemplar of the German model in the auto sector, Volkswagen, also experienced incremental changes in the same direction. Although still retaining much of its component manufacture in-house, this has been a separate legal entity since 1997. Financial targets, first introduced in 1993, were revised in 2000 to include ROCE objectives, reductions in prices of materials, and reductions in fixed costs. In the same year, Volkswagen undertook a share buyback scheme to try to push up its share price. Both Jürgens (2002) and Vitols (2002), moreover, emphasize that a number of these initiatives actually followed prompting from their long-term partners in the banking sector and that two key banks (Deutsche Bank and Allianz) have been increasingly critical of German firms' traditional focus on sales growth and of their lack of a clear sectoral focus.[13]

## Saturated Markets and Oligopolistic Rent Seeking

Liberalization of global financial markets dates from the 1980s with the opening of Northern country stock markets to foreign participation. It accelerated and spread to developing countries in the wake of the 1994 General Agreement on Trade in Services (GATS) of the WTO which covers financial services (see Chapter 2). The combination of these changes with near-universal removal of restrictions on foreign exchange transactions led to a massive increase in international private capital flows and to portfolio flows becoming their largest component.

This liberalization underwrote important aspects of corporate financialization and the rise of the shareholder value doctrine. However, all three occurred against a background of levels of economic growth that were low in relation to the recent past. Global real GDP[14] grew at an average of 5.4 percent per annum in the 1960s, 4.1 percent in the 1970s, 3.0 percent in the 1980s, and only 2.3 percent in the 1990s (Maddison 2001).[15] In the first three years of the 2000s, growth averaged around 2.1 percent. In other words, increasing global opportunities for trade, investment, and financial mobilization have coincided with global goods and services markets apparently approaching saturation level. In practice, this has added to the credibility of the shareholder value doctrine and has helped make oligopolistic rent seeking the most popular instrument for squeezing more out of less.

The main feature of current forms of oligopolistic rent seeking, as explained earlier, has been the cash cow strategy adopted by retailers and supermarket chains. This approach seeks to attain market leadership—and thereby greater economies of scale—where product lines or formats are already strong. This entails (1) more aggressive marketing and (selectively) pricing in order to establish or defend market leadership, (2) oligopolistic price setting where competition can be avoided, and (3) exercising greater buyer power in relation to suppliers. In a number of key sectors, this strategy has been successfully used as a lever to overcome the constraints on corporate growth implied by saturated markets and also to differentiate more clearly, and on a new basis, an élite of lead firms. This argument will be illustrated in this section mainly on the basis of a further elaboration of developments in retailing (and, more specifically, food retailing) that were introduced earlier in the chapter.

During the last two decades, global retail markets have grown at almost exactly the same rates as GDP. In OECD countries, retail markets have grown somewhat more slowly than GDP. *Food* retail markets in the OECD have grown even more slowly, reflecting not only a global economic slowdown but also the workings of Engels' law—that, as incomes rise, food tends to account for an ever-diminishing share of household expenditure. Competition in this environment has been increasingly premised on the assumption that low-growth businesses require above all scale, both directly to attain the textbook rewards of greater scale economies, and also to use the resulting market leadership as a lever to increase margins in a series of other ways that will be discussed later.

To attain market leadership in the form of greater scale, leading retailers have sought to expand their floor space by building bigger stores (larger supermarkets and hypermarkets), acquiring the stores of competitors (via M&As), and by extending their operations geographically, both nationally and internationally. However, in most Northern countries, a combination of tight property markets and planning restrictions has limited the opportunities for upscaling and geographical expansion in recent times. This has been reflected in increased attention to M&As and to internationalization as growth strategies. U.S. market concentration increased markedly in 1998 with Albertson's acquisition of American Stores and Kroger's of Fred Meyer. In England and Ireland, the period 1993–1998 witnessed five major food retail M&As (Tesco's takeovers of William Law, Stewards, and Quinnsworth; Somerfield's of Kwik Save; and Rewe's of Budgen's).[16]

An important feature in recent M&As is that they have extended to emerging markets. Wal-Mart, Carrefour, Royal Ahold, Auchan, and Casino have all moved into Latin America since 1995, almost without exception on the basis of M&As.[17] Tesco, in contrast, has moved into Asia (particularly Thailand and South Korea), where it has established sales worth almost US$3.4 billion in less than five years on the basis of a combination of M&As and partnerships with local players. A similar pattern has been followed in the company's expansion into central Europe, where it is now the largest operator.[18]

A similar proliferation of takeovers by multinational corporate retailers has not yet occurred in Africa, although supermarket chains are also becoming increasingly important here in various countries, especially in southern and eastern Africa. In urban areas of these countries, modern retail stores are gradually displacing small shops and public markets. Sometimes this has been followed by acquisitions by larger South African chains.[19] According to Weatherspoon and Reardon (2003), it is likely that Northern retailers will move into Africa within the next decade.

Many, but not all, of the M&As described in this section have been directed toward increasing the numbers of large supermarkets and hypermarkets owned by a company. Where this has been the case, it has been associated with a drive to attain market leadership through widening product ranges. Whereas conventional supermarkets stock around 5,000 separate products, hypermarkets normally carry in excess of 20,000. Within food retail, there has been a steady expansion into new fruits and vegetables (and combinations of them) and a rapid one into chilled and ready-made meals. At the same time, many larger supermarkets now carry offerings of clothing (especially children's and women's clothing), medicines, and newspapers/magazines, all relatively rare a decade ago.[20] Rates of introduction of new versions of existing products have also increased in pace. According to Baas, van Potten, and Zwanenbery (1998), more than 20,000 new products had been introduced globally into supermarket channels in 1996, of which 13,000 were food items.

Although supermarkets and hypermarkets dominate food sales in many E.U. countries,[21] other nontraditional formats have also recently grown in significance, including discount stores and a new generation of convenience stores and outlets (for example, stores at petrol stations). As Table 1.3 illustrated, the quest for market leadership has also led many formerly single-format actors to build portfolios encompassing all the main formats. The ability of a relatively restricted number of retail groups to execute a range of these strategies (increasing floor space, M&As, internationalization, widening product range, multiformatting) on a simultaneous basis has led to high levels of market concentration, particularly in the E.U. (see Table 1.4). At the national level, U.S. food retail is considerably less concentrated,[22] although levels of market concentration within specific U.S. regions are comparable to the E.U. average.

Market leadership is enabling the world's leading supermarket chains to earn oligopolistic rents in three distinct areas: (1) on some sale prices, (2) through own-label products,[23] and (3) in relation to suppliers. There is evidence to suggest that the third of these is the most important source of rents. During its recent examination of the grocery part of the British supermarket trade, the U.K. Competition Commission (2000) ran a series of regression analyses on the impact of existing economies of scale on supermarket margins. It found that the largest effect was in respect to supplier prices obtained. The Commission also made a detailed examination of supermarkets' retail pricing. Not surprisingly, it found a direct relationship between degrees of local market concentration and retail price levels. Where only a single group from the top five was present in a specific local area, the prices it charged were considerably in excess of the prices that it charged for the same items in areas characterized by higher levels of competition. Second, it also found that, while there was extremely aggressive price competition nationally between chains on a limited range of items, on a majority of items sold there was very little variation in price. In other words, the retail market had both natural monopolistic pockets and, implicitly at

**Table 1.4**  Market share of top 5 food retailers by country (1999)

| Country | Share of top 5 (%)* | Share of top 5 (%) ** | Market leaders |
|---|---|---|---|
| Austria (top 4 share) | 74.3 | 59.9 | Billa/Rewe, Intermarché/Spar, Metro, Hofer/Aldi, Adeg/Edeka |
| Belgium (top 4 share) | 70.8 | 64.0 | GIB, Delhaize le Lion, Colruyt, Louis Delhaize, Aldi |
| Denmark | n/a | 77.6 | FDB, Dansk Supermarked, Dagrofa, Aldi, Samkøb |
| France | 58.1 | 77.0 | Carrefour, Intermarché, Leclerc, Auchan, Casino |
| Germany | 80.3 | 63.1 | Metro, Rewe, Edeka/AVA, Aldi, Tengelmann |
| Greece | n/a | 44.0 | Carrefour, Makro/Metro, Sklaventis, Veropoulos, Alpha Beta |
| Italy | n/a | 29.8 | Coop Italia, Rinascente/Auchan, Carrefour, Metro, Esselunga |
| Netherlands | 51.8 | 68.1 | Royal Ahold, Laurus, Makro/Metro, Aldi, Dirk van der Broek |
| Portugal | n/a | 63.0 | Carrefour, JMR, Auchan, Makro/Metro, Intermarché |
| Spain | n/a | 57.0 | Pryca-Carrefour, El Corte Ingles, Alcampa, Erosi, Mercadona |
| Sweden | n/a | 95.8 | ICA/Ahold, KF, D&D, Axel Johnson, Bergendahl |
| U.K. | n/a | 49.9 | Tesco, J. Sainsbury, Asda/Wal-Mart, Safeway, Somerfield |

Sources: *Corporate Intelligence; **mm.eurodata.

least, a degree of collusive oligopoly that existed irrespective of varying levels of natural monopoly (see also Vorley 2003).

Market leadership levels also appeared to support at least some of the success of supermarkets in promoting higher-margin own-label products at the expense of lower-margin bought-in brands. According to one market research source,[24] own-label sales represented half of all sales by the largest five U.K. supermarkets in 2002. The Competition Commission (2000), using another source (TNS Retailer Sharetrack), gives own-label shares of 31.9 percent in 1995 and of 35.3 percent in 1999. Market leadership allows supermarkets to increase sales of these products directly and indirectly. Directly, the general reputational benefits of market leadership can be managed in a way that also improves the reputation of these products. Also, high sales volume by itself helps in financing the diversification of own-label sales into new areas (new items and premium ranges). Indirectly, but probably more significantly, market leadership generates enhanced buyer power in relation to suppliers. This in turn allows own-label products to be ordered and sold at a discount. This raises the more general question of buyer power, to which we now turn.

## BUYER POWER AND STRATEGIC OUTSOURCING

The U.K. Competition Commission (2000) calculated that in the United Kingdom, a grocery retail market share of 8 percent or higher was sufficient to be able to sustain noncompetitive buying practices in relation to the U.K. supplier base. As a result, those lacking this relatively low level of market share were unable to compete on retail price. The exercise of buyer power is also based on the disparity between the relative importance of leading retailers for most suppliers on the one hand, and of most suppliers for leading retailers on the other hand. A sample of just over 100 leading suppliers examined by the Commission found that their top five U.K. retail customers accounted for an average of 68.5 percent of their total U.K. sales (for fresh fruit and vegetable suppliers, the proportion was even higher). The largest U.K. retailer (Tesco) typically represented 20 to 30 percent of sales alone. But Tesco's own largest grocery supplier accounted for only 2.7 percent by value of its total intake. Tesco had only eight suppliers (of a total of 2,600) whose share of total intake exceeded 1 percent and only 230 with a share higher than 0.1 percent.

According to the Commission, buyer power was used to extract concessions on price, to enforce nonstandard (and in certain cases predatory) contractual terms, and to leverage significant changes in the traditional division of labor between retailers and suppliers. On price, the Commission noted that discounts were typically sought or simply imposed in the context of increases in volumes, or adoption of new product lines, or when promotions were planned. Base prices paid to suppliers by leading retailers appeared to be significantly lower than those paid by other retailers and wholesalers. Taking the average prices paid to leading suppliers for a range of items by the largest 24 U.K. grocery retailers as 100, the five largest retailers paid on average 97.8 percent of this amount. Retailers and wholesalers who were not part of the top 24 paid 105.9 percent.

Promotion-related discounts and up-front lump sum payments, made by suppliers to retailers agreeing to run promotions, are possibly more significant for retailers' earnings than the gains associated with base price reductions. Public awareness of the magnitude of some lump sum payments emerged in the wake of the Royal Ahold accounting scandal of 2002–2003, when it was revealed that a large proportion of what had been recorded as the profits of its U.S. food service operation were actually payments of this kind.[25] In the wake of the Ahold scandal, the section of Wal-Mart's 2003 *Annual Report* on significant accounting policies listed the following kinds of payment under payments from suppliers: warehousing allowances ("allowances provided by suppliers to compensate the Company for distributing their product through our distribution systems, which are more efficient than most other available [ones]"; volume discounts; and "allowances... for specific programs including markdown protection, margin protection, new product lines, special promotions [and] specific advertising" (p. 36). Payments under the first two categories were booked as deductions from costs of sales, whereas those from the third group were booked as profits. The accounts gave details only of what stood in the different accounts where these sums are held on the day of annual financial reporting.[26]

The main reported variations in standard contractual terms enforced by leading U.K. retailers as a group, and the frequency with which they were enforced, are indicated in Table 1.5. In addition to special payments by suppliers (including one case where a supplier was told to make three separate cash payments within a short period of time—including one of £100,000—as contributions toward profits), the Commission listed other ways in which power appeared to have been exercised in highly predatory ways. In one, a first-tier vegetable supplier was instructed to delist two growers from *all* its customers, on the grounds that the growers had declined to trade with the supermarket in question.

Retailers' efforts to change the division of labor with suppliers are to-day underwritten by shareholder value doctrines concerning the desirability of outsourcing of non–core functions. However, in practice these efforts emerged as early as the 1980s, following retailers' recognition that expanding floor space in Northern countries was becoming very costly. Against this background arose efforts to maximize floor space productivity, codified in the doctrine of Efficient Consumer Response. This doctrine encompasses the incorporation of information technology into supply and distribution (as a minimum in the form of bar-coding and electronic funds transfer), requirements that suppliers meet higher

**Table 1.5**  Frequency in variation of standard contractual terms by top 24 U.K. grocery retailers, according to leading suppliers

| Practice | Never | Rarely | Sometimes | Fairly often | Often | No answer |
|---|---|---|---|---|---|---|
| Delay payment by 15 days over terms | 44 | 33 | 18 | 2 | 2 | 2 |
| Delay other amounts by more than 15 days | 32 | 34 | 22 | 7 | 4 | 2 |
| Break other contractual terms | 39 | 30 | 12 | 4 | 0 | 16 |
| Change quality requirement without adequate notice | 58 | 25 | 11 | 0 | 0 | 7 |
| Change other requirements without reasonable notice | 35 | 19 | 26 | 7 | 2 | 11 |
| Threaten delisting without reasonable cause | 21 | 42 | 32 | 2 | 0 | 4 |
| Require charitable contributions | 32 | 16 | 37 | 9 | 4 | 4 |
| Require discounts or other payments when profits from product fail to meet expectations | 26 | 25 | 30 | 11 | 5 | 4 |
| Require buying back of unsold goods | 47 | 35 | 11 | 4 | 0 | 4 |
| Make deductions to returned goods to cover wastage | 54 | 23 | 12 | 2 | 4 | 5 |
| Impose slotting charges | 49 | 11 | 18 | 5 | 10 | 7 |
| Charge for shelf space | 49 | 19 | 18 | 4 | 7 | 4 |
| Charge for listing | 37 | 19 | 25 | 9 | 5 | 5 |

*N* respondents: 101.
Source: U.K. Competition Commission (2000).

standards of reliability and accuracy for deliveries, and, at least in some cases, sales-based reordering of inventory (that is, orders are generated by suppliers themselves rather than by retailers).

Sales-based reordering, also known as model stock replenishment or supplier-managed inventory (SMI), was first introduced in 1988 by Wal-Mart. It entails suppliers holding open a minimum capacity for a customer over a 6- to 12-month period and continuously supplying variable volumes against orders that are automatically generated from sales data, and therefore modified by the week, the day, or even every 12 hours. On the one hand, this gives the supplier some security of capacity utilization, both in the sense that agreements cover reasonably long periods and that procurement (or production) for stock can be undertaken on a relatively low-risk basis. On the other hand, it gives the buyer much more. If the system functions as planned, the risks of being left with unsold stock or, conversely, of incurring stock-outs (running out of stock in high demand) are eliminated. So too are the working capital costs of carrying inventory, since these are transferred to suppliers, as are the cost of all ordering errors and incorrect sales forecasts. The transfer of these risks can be assured by buyers' insistence that sales take place on a so-called consignment basis. This means that the legal title to merchandise is not transferred until the moment of sale by the retailer.[27]

The extent of the presence of SMI programs in the grocery retail sector is limited, according to some sources, as a result of the sheer number of different items sold by supermarkets and the resulting complexity of the required data systems. However, this may be changing fast as leading players like Tesco (2003) today claim that all the product lines they sell are on replenishment programs. In any event, as will be seen elsewhere in this book, SMI has spread to other branches of retail as well as to other sectors.

The final element of the Efficient Consumer Response doctrine has been more widely adopted than SMI, even though it may be seen in some respects as building on it. This is the outsourcing of category or commodity management to so-called lead suppliers (also known as first-tier suppliers). *Category management* means planning and execution of all functions except marketing and ringing up the sales for a given group of products (for example, all snacks, all fresh vegetables, all citrus fruit). It entails a retailer selecting a small number of suppliers—sometimes only one—to act as category captains. These are made responsible for analyzing data on customer preferences, identifying the best means of satisfying these preferences in terms of product range/selection, determining the most effective way that suppliers can provide the relevant products (and often who these suppliers should be), making proposals on the allocation of store space in terms of product presentation, developing new products, and so on.[28]

The outsourcing of category/commodity management is part of a much broader, cross-sectoral transition in which corporations are becoming less vertically integrated. This transition is encouraged and validated by the shareholder value doctrine, but as Feenstra (1998) and Langlois (2003) have pointed out, it also has roots in contemporary changes in the nature of markets. According to these authors, the long period of domination of vertically (and horizontally) integrated forms of industrial organization was one in which a mismatch existed between technological development (in the form of high-throughput production and relatively efficient systems of transport and communication) and market integration. Markets (including supply markets) were smaller, less continuous, and more fragmented, and market institutions were patchy in their coverage and lacked depth. Under these conditions, the economies of scale and scope made feasible by technology could be realized only if corporations bypassed at least some supply markets and aggregated other (demand) ones. In contrast, the present period is one of integration and thickening of markets, allowing a more market-based supply chain and more focus on marketing single products.

Although it is hard to disagree with this analysis, it is also necessary to reassert that demand conditions play an important role in determining industrial organization forms, independently of more qualitative aspects of market development. The recent rise of strategic outsourcing emerged against a background where a high level of concentration in end-market share in many sectors has coincided with a flattening in demand in almost all markets. As Hopkins and Wallerstein (1986, 1994) have shown, throughout the history of capitalism a rough association has prevailed between periods of economic boom and trends toward vertical integration, and conversely, between periods of economic stagnation and outsourcing. If the present period is exceptional in its extent and degree of outsourcing, it is because of the contrast between the massive increase in buyer power and the relatively limited growth of demand.

Two distinct, but sometimes combined, responses by suppliers have emerged in response to the new strategic outsourcing environment that retailers have created. One is (global) contract supply—including global contract manufacturing. The other is the emergence of new variants of product differentiation and/or branding. In the next section, we examine them in this order.

## SUPPLIER ADJUSTMENT IN THE WORLD OF CATEGORY MANAGEMENT

### Contract Manufacturing/Supply

One of the most important contributions to the analysis of the emergence of global contract manufacturing is Sturgeon's study (2002) of the differences in buyer-supplier relations in industrial and high-tech manufacturing between the early 1980s and the late 1990s. Sturgeon argues that, unlike the two prevalent models for outsourcing in the earlier period ("Toyotaism" and the "Third Italy"),[29] contemporary forms of outsourcing often encompass core manufacturing processes rather than simply the provision of components. He also argues that companies that outsource today make little direct investment (financial or managerial) in the companies that they outsource to. Coming up to speed is the responsibility of the supplier alone. The long-term trust relations depicted in academic accounts of Toyotaist and Third Italy–style outsourcing are now largely absent. Commitments rarely apply for longer than a year or two and there is relatively little intensive personal interaction between owners/managers of contracting and contracted companies.[30] There is, moreover, an absence of captive (or exclusive) supply relations of the Toyotaist type, where the buyer's *quid pro quo* for assisting in the technological upgrading of the supplier was to reserve the benefits of this technology exclusively for him/herself.

According to Sturgeon (2002), a qualitatively new kind of supplier has come to the fore: specialized manufacturing companies that also provide some related services. Sturgeon borrows the expression "global contract manufacturer" from the terminology of the electronics sector to describe this new category of supplier. His main examples are also borrowed from the electronics sector (companies such as Solectron, Flextronics, and SCI). Rather than following the common invocations of the 1980s to move up the value chain (from own-equipment manufacture, through own-design manufacture, to own-brand manufacture),[31] lead suppliers today are concentrating their attention (and investments) on developing generic manufacturing competences across a range of related product categories. For the more successful of these companies, these competences are in core manufacturing areas rather than component or subsystem supply. The most successful companies combine a single base manufacturing process (and by implication a standardized labor process) with a broad product range.[32] In addition, this new generation of suppliers is characterized by its global presence. Supplier globalization is necessary partly because of residual trade barriers in some important end markets (requiring, for example, minimum local content levels).[33] Also, their lead firm clients market globally and require engineering, manufacturing, and logistics in multiple locations. Finally, supplier globalization is necessary because retaining competitiveness in relation to other suppliers requires global sourcing of subsystems, components, and subcomponents.

The broader background to this trend comprises new demand for core manufacturing services. This emerged as a result of the movement of the most powerful firms within the industrial and high-tech manufacturing sectors in the direction of presumed higher ROCE activities, including those associated with demand management (for example, the definition of new product markets; see Lüthje 2001). In explanation of why global contract manufacturers chose to specialize in supply rather than follow the latter path, Sturgeon goes on to demonstrate that, under certain conditions, contract manufacture may be more profitable than a movement toward downstream functions.[34]

If electronics is the most obvious example of the rise of global contract manufacturing, there is no shortage of other sectors exhibiting the same tendencies. This phenomenon is described in some detail for the pharmaceutical sector by the (somewhat inappropriately titled) Director of Manufacturing at GlaxoSmithKlein (Tyson 2000). The rise of global contract manufacturing in this sector is said to date from the period 1993–1999. Its genesis comes from a decision by the leading players in this sector to concentrate their resources on research and development and marketing. Their reason for doing so was that competition in the sector has become redefined around a generation of new breakthrough (or blockbuster) products—often in previously neglected areas of medicine—on which oligopolistic rents could be earned for a period of five to ten years (Prozac, Viagra). This development is also connected to the tendency for pharmaceutical companies to delink from chemicals and refocus around life sciences, often on the basis of M&As as discussed earlier in relation to German companies.[35]

Global contract manufacturers have also emerged in the automotive sector, although in this case only Ford among the leading companies has actually gone as far as outsourcing final assembly. Nonetheless, other

traditional automakers have also started to concentrate more on vehi-
cle design, the aftermarket, and financing auto purchasing. As a result,
the supply of modules and module systems (groups of related modules
such as seats, cockpits, dashboards, and climate control systems) has
been outsourced to financially independent (but still internal) supply
companies or to former traditional first-tier component suppliers. First-
tier suppliers are currently expected not only to supply broader manufacturing services, but also to organize second-tier component sourcing,
take care of local content requirements, and take over module design
(Sturgeon and Lester 2002).

There has been a similar evolution in relation to the food production
sector, where the main clients for manufacturers and other suppliers
consist of food retailers and the catering/fast food industry. In this sector, the leading food multinational corporations (Kraft/Philip Morris,
Nestlé, Pepsico, Unilever, Tyson Foods, ConAgra, General Mills,
Danone, Sara Lee, H.J. Heinz, Kellogg) have globalized their manufacturing activities. At the same time, they have also shifted from exclusively branded production to a mixture of branded production and
production for retailer chains' own-label products. However, their main
efforts have been directed at narrowing their own branded food product
ranges and at achieving clearer branded market leadership in specific
product categories (usually on the basis of M&As). These companies
have themselves started outsourcing the production of specific items
to contract manufacturers—whose existing main businesses comprise
supplying large players in the catering/fast food sector and retailer
chains with own-label products. Well-publicized U.S. examples include
Kraft/Philip Morris outsourcing the production of around half of their
Nabisco product range and ConAgra outsourcing its Beatrice Cheese
range to Schreiber Foods.[36]

A few companies in the fresh produce supply subsector also have
a global status, most notably the giant banana traders Chiquita, Dole,
Fresh Del Monte, and Fyffes. The role of these groups is similar to that of
large brand name food manufacturers. They largely produce in-house[37]
and sell to large retail chains and independents (via wholesalers) under their own brand names. Fresh vegetable contract suppliers tend
to be smaller in scale and less internationalized. The same is true for
(non-banana) fruit contract suppliers, except that most of these have
either joint production ventures in two or three producing countries or
originate in producing countries themselves. Two of the largest U.K. contract citrus suppliers, Thames Fruit and Muñoz-Mehadrin, have whole

or partial ownership links with Spanish (and in the latter case also Israeli) producers.[38]

The largest U.K.-based contract supplier of fresh vegetables is Geest (turnover £7 billion in 2001), a company that until the mid 1990s grew flower bulbs and fresh produce and traded these as well as bananas from ACP countries[39] through U.K. wholesale markets. The group started a fresh prepared salads business in 1972, but this was its main activity only from 1995–1996 when the wholesale and banana divisions were disposed of. Geest today produces only own-label products (salads, ready-made meals, soups, fresh pasta, pizza, pizza breads, desserts, and prepared fruits) for large supermarkets and for the Pizza Express chain. Geest's internationalization dates from the takeover of a ready-made meals business in Belgium and of a South African prepared fruits company in 1995–1997 and has continued with acquisitions in France. The leading customer of its E.U. business is the main Netherlands subsidiary of Royal Ahold (Albert Heijn). Yet, its overall levels of internationalization are low: non-U.K. sales account for only 7 percent of turnover and direct procurement of fresh produce occurs only in the United Kingdom, France, Iberia, and South Africa.

According to Sturgeon and Lester (2002), the global contract manufacturing/contract supply phenomenon has undergone a further change since the late 1990s. This followed from heightened customer requirements for product development, which in turn lead to a process of internal differentiation among contract manufacturers themselves. This has been especially the case in electronics, where the five leading manufacturers had already achieved a global market share of 38 percent by 1999. Because these five companies are based in North America, Sturgeon and Lester argue that the geographical proximity of the main design/engineering facilities of contract manufacturers to the headquarters of lead customers is an important variable in influencing differentiation. This is because greater involvement (or involvement at an earlier stage) in design implies a need for much more intensive and frequent interaction.

A second factor favoring North America–based companies is that—as a result of the North American Free Trade Agreement (NAFTA)—they have maintained low-cost rapid response, build-to-order, and configure-to-order production capacity within relatively short distances of leading end customers. The same leading five contractors are also dominant in the E.U. market, where a European version of the NAFTA precondition is replicated (access to low-cost skilled labor in Eastern Europe).

The differentiation of a group of more qualified contract manufac-turers/suppliers can be noted in other sectors too. In his discussion of contract manufacturing in pharmaceuticals, Tyson (2000) states that GlaxoSmithKline has now started formally to distinguish so-called dif-ferentiated from merely qualified suppliers. Although the latter are de-scribed as cost-effective producers of high volume products, the for-mer are producers capable of launching stage process developments. By implication, cost is a less important performance parameter for stage process developers, which implies that they can be profitably located in higher wage locations.[40] The companies discussed earlier in relation to contract manufacture/supply to large retailers are headquartered, or at least strongly represented, in the countries where these retailers are also headquartered (or ones immediately neighboring them). Against the background of the growing dominance of Asia other than Japan in trade of manufactured goods, this suggests that outsourcing networks are undergoing a dual development. On the one hand, the management of these networks—and the provision of higher-value services in relation to them—is being geographically concentrated in Northern countries. On the other hand, production functions within them (especially routine ones) are located with greater frequency in developing countries.

## Brand Development

In the sectors discussed in this chapter so far, the large-scale multi-national corporations (MNCs) that were formerly branded manufactur-ers, but which now have withdrawn at least partially from manufacture in favor of product development and marketing, in many cases have also undertaken a fundamental restructuring of their branded offerings. The main objective has been to assert market leadership, and thereby earn oligopoly rents, on products and lines where market share is already high. A secondary objective has been to establish market leadership in respect to emerging areas of demand, either on the basis of extension of existing brands or by launching new ones.

The central role of branding in oligopolistic competition was al-ready recognized explicitly by Schumpeter (1943) and, at least implic-itly, around the same time by Chamberlin (1946) and Robinson (1953). Schumpeter noted the association between product differentiation and oligopolistic competition and the latter's capacity to award such differ-entiation with rents via premium prices and dampened demand fluctu-ations (repeat sales).[41] Subsequently, as markets in Northern countries reached saturation point and growth slowed, branding became arguably the leading form of product differentiation. As vividly described by Klein (2000), the 1980s and early 1990s were a period of spectacular brand proliferation when brands were launched for an ever-increasing range of products and when unbranded space steadily dwindled. At the same time, important changes took place in means of branding and consequently in brand narratives, with a virtual disappearance of the once-dominant emphases on surnames and discourses concerning reliability and consistency in favor of an invocation of ever-more intangible psychographic qualities (above all, personal identity). This reflected the fact that tangible qualities had become increasingly difficult to earn rents on, mainly due to the greater availability of cheaper own-label alternatives. It reflected also a tendency, at least in Northern countries, for brand loyalties themselves to become weaker and more transitory.

Changes in the rationale and effectiveness of branding implied higher marketing costs. Against the background of the expanding influence of the cash cow doctrine, as well as a recognition of the implications of category management (major reductions by retailers in the range of brands they were willing to carry), branders have adapted by focusing on a smaller number of more promising brands. Internal brand culling became a common strategy, combined with the acquisition of competing brands in areas where branded market leadership was considered possible. In the food sector, the most spectacular brand cull was carried out by Unilever in 1999 with a reduction from 1600 to 400 branded product lines.[42] Similar culls have been carried out by most of the other large players, most recently by H.J. Heinz, which in 2002 sold all its pet food and tuna brands to Del Monte (as well as its private-label soup business). This left Heinz with a series of brands in meal enhancers,[43] frozen foods and snacks that were all number one or two in their category. Asked in an interview whether this left Heinz in a position where it could still generate economies of scale, the company's CEO replied: "scale is category-related. We are a very powerful company with leadership in many categories" (*Financial Times*, June 17, 2002).

Intensified M&A activity—and complementary disposals—has been the foundation of increasing brand-related concentration within the food sector. During the late 1990s, one food product category after another became dominated by a tiny handful of players. Pasta and industrial bread, for example, has become dominated internationally by the Italian company Barilla and by the U.S. company Sara Lee. Barilla's internationalization began with the opening of a French subsidiary in 1979, but really took off only during the 1990s with the acquisition of locally owned producers in Greece and Scandinavia and the opening of a mill and pasta plant in the United States (allowing the company to build on its existing 9 percent of the U.S. market share). This was followed by the takeover of the European Union's leading industrial bread producer Kamps (Germany) in 2002.

The U.S. industrial bread market has also reached a high level of concentration following Sara Lee's takeover of the Earthgrains company in 2002.[44] Similar trends can be noted in ice cream and pet food. In ice cream, the duopolistic positions of Unilever and Nestlé have been reinforced through the acquisitions of Ben & Jerry by Unilever and of Schöller, Mövenpick, and the U.S.-based Dreyer by Nestlé, all in 2002–2003. Pet food has seen a similar strengthening of duopoly, with Nestlé's takeover of the U.S.-owned Ralston Purina and Mars' of the French-owned Royal Canin in 2002.[45] A similar intensification in M&A activity can be noted in the other sectors discussed here, notably in pharmaceuticals. According to PriceWaterhouse Cooper's annual reviews of the pharmaceutical sector, there were at least 334 pharmaceutical M&As in 2000 (worth $61 billion) and 374 in 2001 (worth $71 billion).

At the same time as brands are being culled, a degree of controlled brand extension/proliferation has been undertaken in new product markets and/or to adjust to new underlying consumption trends. In the food sector, this has occurred most notably in relation to organic products, where all the major players have either launched new products or have acquired organic food brands (see also DuPuis 2000).[46]

## CONCLUSION

Three issues of central relevance for Africa's evolving place in the international division of labor have been raised in this chapter. The first is the effects and broader implications of the *(re-)emergence of economies of scale* as a key source of advantage and differentiation in the global economy. This re-emergence runs in direct opposition to a generation of predictions within political economy known as "Post-Fordism" (see Chapter 3). It has occurred against the background of a combination of financialization, flat demand, and unprecedented levels of market integration and corporate concentration. Economies of scale are the key to earning oligopolistic rents in this context, both in relation to global marketing and to bargaining with suppliers. The implications for suppliers, and for supply chains more generally, have not been directly addressed in this chapter, nor can they be automatically deduced from the arguments developed in it. But one implication is that the logic of economies of scale is likely to apply to suppliers/supply chains too—and that the ability to realize them will be an important source of differentiation in these chains. This may apply to countries/regions (in relation to density/frequency of individual suppliers of a given size) just as much as it does to individual suppliers themselves.

A second issue concerns *supply chain reorganization* in the context of corporate restructuring in end markets. As described in this chapter, while this restructuring has by no means followed financialist prescriptions to the letter, it has moved in the direction of dropping certain (previously thought of as) core functions. This is most obviously the case with branded marketers and the manufacturing function, but also applies to retail in relation to category management, which seems to imply an outsourcing of supply chain management and sometimes also inventory management. Some of the implications of this restructuring have been traced in relation to first-tier suppliers where apparently contradictory dynamics are emerging. On the one hand, such suppliers are moving in the direction of greater specialization (for example, in manufacture/production on an increasingly global basis). On the other hand, they are despecializing to provide more services. In certain sectors, notably pharmaceuticals, this contradiction has been resolved via a process of first-tier supplier differentiation—whereby a premier league of manufacturer–product/process developers has emerged. The issue arising from this line of development concerns its broader upstream (toward the producer) implications. What do these restructuring processes (and their different variants) mean for the overall size, shape, and nature of supply bases? Are demands for higher levels of specialization or broader ranges of competences (or both) being cascaded upstream, and if so how systematically? Is the result likely to be greater concentration, greater differentiation, or something else?

A third issue emerging from this chapter, and one that links the previous two issues, is that of *entry barriers*. Entry barriers are a particularly sensitive issue for Africa (and African suppliers) because of its weak resource base and the large number of its natural obstacles to integration in the global economy (distance, communications). If demands for greater scale, specialization, and capacity for enhanced levels of service provision were fully transmitted throughout the whole length of supply chains, Africa's participation in the global economy would be seriously affected.

Exploring the issues raised here requires analyses of a different kind to those presented in this chapter. As the differences between developments in food/grocery retail, pharmaceuticals, electronics, and automobiles described here suggest, tracing changes upstream from end markets requires a sector-by-sector and value chain–by–value chain approach. It also requires a methodology capable of identifying relevant actors at all stages of a given chain, as well as of tracing their interactions on the basis of establishing an overall pattern or dynamic of chain governance. Before turning to a discussion of the methodological tools that allow this kind of study (GVC analysis), we first place the developments discussed in this chapter in relation to the changing role of Africa in international trade and to the emergence of a new international trade regime that followed the creation of WTO in 1994.

# 2    The New International Trade Regime

GLOBAL VALUE CHAINS (GVCs) are subject to exogenous regulation as well as to endogenous processes of governance. Exogenous regulation has a number of dimensions, of which the most important are regulation of markets in producing and consuming countries and international trade regulation. Markets in different producing countries, and in different consuming ones, may all be regulated according to distinct principles. Furthermore, the principles according to which domestic markets are regulated may differ strongly from the ones in which international market regulation occurs. Recently, however, a relatively high level of convergence has emerged, with trends toward deregulation in producing and consuming country markets and regulation of a new kind in international ones. The new type of international regulation is aimed, ostensibly at least, at removing what orthodox economists call "distortions" in both international and national markets. Historically, this level of convergence is a novel phenomenon. In this chapter, we focus specifically on new forms of regulation in international trade. Deregulation in consuming and, especially, producing countries will be analyzed in the context of specific value chain discussions in the following chapters.

Mechanisms for regulating international markets (or specific countries' relations to them) are known in the literature as "trade regimes." This term implies a more or less complex system of interlocking rules and institutions—although it does not necessarily imply that such systems are internally coherent. It is commonly agreed that the creation of the World Trade Organization (WTO) in 1994 signaled the emergence of a new multilateral trade regime. Many of the post-1994 rules are entirely new, at least in relation to international trade. Together with the set of rules inherited from the old General Agreement on Tariffs and Trade (GATT), they form a system in a much more explicit and comprehensive way than was ever the case in past multilateral trade agreements.

One of the new aspects of the WTO regime is precisely that many of its agreements are aimed directly at securing convergence or coherence between domestic and international systems of market regulation. In other words, they deal not only with traditional border issues like tariffs but also with issues previously considered to be entirely domestic in character, although perhaps also having consequences for trade. The current convergence rests on more than some new international rules, however. It is linked, with different degrees of causality, to (1) the rise of the so-called Washington Consensus in Northern policy-making circles from the early 1980s,[1] (2) the fall of the Soviet Union later in the same decade, (3) the growing economic dependence of most countries on trade—and therefore also on major trading partners and their policy preferences, and (4) the rise of "buyer drivenness" and related economic interests in the major trading nations (see Chapters 3 and 4).

Although the WTO is clearly one of the central elements of the new international trade regime, its rules and institutions make up only part of it. Alongside WTO's multilateral provisions are an ever-growing number of bilateral agreements,[2] institutionalized in free trade arrangements of different scope and content. The growth in the number of such agreements reflects increased competition for market domination between leading trading countries and blocs. It also reflects efforts by these countries and blocs to use their economic power to extract concessions from junior trading partners concerning domestic market deregulation, over and above those already achieved through the WTO. Insofar as there is a source of incoherence in the new international trade regime, it is the result of what Bhagwati and others (Bhagwati, Panagariya, and Krishna 1999) call the ever-expanding "spaghetti bow" of such free trade agreements. The result is an encirclement of multilateral agreements and institutions by an array of inconsistent and sometimes conflicting sets of preferences, exceptions, and conditionalities. Driven by a dynamic of competition, some of these agreements have come to present opportunities for African countries that are blocked at the multilateral level. Others introduce new obstacles over and above those found in multilateral agreements, at least in comparison to earlier generations of bilateral agreements.

This chapter focuses on the post-1994 international trade regime and some of its consequences for developing countries in general and for Africa in particular. It argues that many of the new WTO rules make the growth of trade and exports from the continent more rather than less difficult. Most of the traditional trade barriers that African countries have always faced remain, although sometimes in new guises that are less easy to recognize. At the same time, the new agreements and mechanisms inaugurated in 1994 either tend to create new barriers of market access or to remove the possibility of using key instruments to mitigate them. These issues are tackled on the basis of three main discussions. First, some basic market trends in the trade of sub-Saharan African countries are outlined, with a particular focus on the 1990s. Next, the nature of the international trade regime prior to 1994 is sketched, at the multilateral level as well as the bilateral levels insofar as these concerned Africa. The chapter then turns to the post-1994 regime in its multilateral and bilateral aspects.

Just as in the analysis of global capitalism in the last chapter, the discussion that follows is largely descriptive. It suggests links between trade regime changes and the evolving nature of Africa's insertion in specific value chains—and the global economy more broadly. However, its objective is not to derive Africa's economic situation from a general theory of contemporary economic organization. Rather, it is to cast light on Africa's position from a number of different directions and work toward developing a set of more modest, empirically based, regional understandings of contemporary economic reality.

## Trends in Africa's International Trade

Any serious discussion of Africa's international trade has to begin with caveats concerning data. Two difficulties present themselves at the outset. The first is the quality and regularity of reporting of trade data by African countries themselves. Quality is very poor, even in countries like South Africa.[3] Moreover, reporting is often years out of date. For this reason, recent studies of African trade conducted by institutions like the International Monetary Fund (IMF), the World Bank, and the African Economic Research Consortium (AERC), all use the reported data of a group of Africa's trading partners. Because the partners concerned account for over 90 percent of world trade, these data can be considered to have a high degree of validity and reliability concerning the continent's global trade. Nonetheless, it necessarily leaves some trade unreported, particularly that between African countries themselves.

A second issue is that the common (trading partner–based) database used by these organizations does not appear to stretch back prior to 1980 or currently extend beyond 1998. Discussion outside of this period therefore has to be based on other sources. In what follows, GATT/WTO statistics have been used for some longer-term and more global comparisons, whereas data reported in work by the IMF, World Bank, and AERC have been used as the main source for sub-Saharan Africa during the period 1980–1998. Finally, it should be noted that most of the GATT/WTO data resorted to below use the category of Africa rather than of sub-Saharan Africa and thus include North African trade. The distortive effect of this inconsistency does not seem to be great, however. For the period 1983–1998, the basic story that these data tell is much the same as that described in more detail for sub-Saharan Africa in other sets of data.

The following trends in African trade are considered in the next paragraphs: (1) levels of export growth, (2) levels of integration with leading trading countries, (3) levels of export diversification by product and by level of processing, and (4) levels of involvement in GVCs for manufactured goods.

## Levels of Export Growth

In absolute terms, African (including North African) exports grew fairly rapidly from 1963 to 2000 (see Table 2.1). However, this represented a much slower rate of growth than that for world trade generally. As a result, Africa's share of world exports dropped by around two-thirds over the period as a whole, falling from 5.7 percent in 1962 to 2.4 percent in 2000. Other regions have also lost considerable shares, but in no other case has this trend been continuous over the whole period.

Table 2.2 presents more detailed data on levels of growth for three broad non–oil product groups for a sample of fourteen sub-Saharan countries[4] during the period 1980–1998. These show sharply lower levels of export growth in sub-Saharan Africa than in the rest of the world for both food and manufactured products for the period 1980–1993. In 1993–1998, export growth rates for this sample of sub-Saharan African countries were much closer to those of the rest of the world and for food products they were higher. Yet, this does not seem to have been enough of an improvement for African export growth rates to equal those of the rest of the world for the longer period of 1990–2001. WTO (2002) data give an African annual export growth rate for agricultural products generally of 2 percent (rest of the world 3 percent) for this period and an annual growth rate for manufactures of 5 percent (rest of the world 6 percent).

**Table 2.1**   World merchandise exports by region and selected economy (% of total), 1948–2000

|  | 1948 | 1963 | 1983 | 1993 | 2000 |
|---|---|---|---|---|---|
| Total merchandise exports (US$ billion) | 58 | 157 | 1,835 | 3,641 | 6,186 |
| North America | 27.3 | 19.3 | 15.4 | 16.8 | 17.1 |
| Latin America | 12.3 | 7.0 | 5.8 | 4.4 | 5.8 |
| Western Europe | 31.5 | 41.4 | 38.9 | 44.0 | 39.5 |
| Central and Eastern Europe and the former USSR | 6.0 | 11.0 | 9.5 | 2.8 | 4.4 |
| Middle East | 2.0 | 3.2 | 6.8 | 3.4 | 4.2 |
| Africa | 7.3 | 5.7 | 4.4 | 2.4 | 2.4 |
| (value in US$ billion) | (4.2) | (8.9) | (80.7) | (91.0) | (141.0) |
| Asia | 13.6 | 12.4 | 19.1 | 26.3 | 26.7 |
| Japan | 0.4 | 3.5 | 8.0 | 10.1 | 7.7 |
| "6 Asian tigers"* | 3.0 | 2.4 | 5.8 | 9.0 | 10.5 |

* Taiwan, Hong Kong, Korea, Malaysia, Singapore, Thailand.
Source:   GATT/WTO, various.

## Levels of Integration

Economists are divided as to the significance of the trends just described. One common line of argument is that of Sachs (see, for example, Sachs and Warner 1997), who argues that Africa's trade performance is disastrous on all counts. A more cautious position is advanced by Rodrik (1999) and others, who maintain that the decline described should be read in the context of Africa's levels of income, population, distance from market, and general socioeconomic development. If these factors are controlled for, then African trade performance is much closer to the average.[5] Even if Rodrik's position is accepted (as it increasingly appears to be), there remain important questions to be asked about trade performance. These concern differences in performance *within* Africa and issues of trade integration. According to Subramanian and Tamirisa (2001), the critical aspects of trade integration in Africa concern its market orientation and its internal composition. Market orientation is crucial because trade with large Northern economies is more likely to be associated with technology transfer than trade with less developed ones. Internal composition is crucial because greater integration in intraindustry and higher value-added dimensions of trade

**Table 2.2** Rates of export growth of sub-Saharan Africa (SSA) sample and rest of the world (1980–1998, annual average, %)

| | 1980–1985 | | 1985–1990 | | 1990–1993 | | 1993–1996 | | 1996–1998 | |
|---|---|---|---|---|---|---|---|---|---|---|
| | SSA sample | All non-SSA | SSA sample | All non-SSA | SSA sample | All non-SSA | SSA sample | All non-SSA | SSA sample | All non-SSA |
| All nonoil | −6.9 | 1.2 | 8.0 | 16.6 | −4.6 | 3.3 | 13.9 | 12.6 | 0.6 | 2.5 |
| All food | −4.4 | −1.4 | 1.6 | 12.3 | −2.0 | 2.2 | 16.8 | 10.8 | 0.9 | −2.5 |
| All manufactures | −6.1 | 2.7 | 12.8 | 17.6 | 0.0 | 3.9 | 16.1 | 13.0 | 1.6 | 3.3 |

Source: Ng and Yeats (2001).

are more likely to provide the contexts and learning experiences for transferred technologies to be consolidated.

As far as differences in trade performance within Africa are concerned, Subramanian and Tamirisa (2001) examine the trade data of the partners of an overlapping but somewhat larger sample of sub-Saharan African countries[6] than that used by Ng and Yeats (2001). Controlling for the same factors as Rodrik (1999), they conclude that, in 1980, sub-Saharan trade was indeed normal (typical in terms of export levels and composition). Thereafter, performance sharply diverges between anglophone and francophone countries. Francophone Africa's exports fall to 52 percent below normal by 1997, whereas anglophone Africa's remain normal. However, if Mauritius is shifted from the anglophone to the francophone category (as arguably it should be),[7] then both groups of countries perform below normal. More important, given Subramanian and Tamirisa's central argument, trade with Northern countries grows much slower in comparison to trade with other countries. Even in the case of anglophone African countries, trade with the North grew at less than 1 percent annually, although in aggregate it grew at 2.1 percent. Despite probable under-reporting, trade within the region still shows up as the only area of relatively dynamic growth for both groups of countries.

Levels of African trade integration with the North can be considered also on the basis of two other sets of statistics on direction of trade. Table 2.3 traces the historical trend in the market share of imports from Africa as a whole into three major Northern (groups of) countries between 1963 and 2001. Table 2.4 examines changes in the direction of exports for selected years between 1985 and 1998 for Ng and Yeats' sample (2001) of sub-Saharan African countries. Both sets of data confirm the declining role of Africa as a trade partner with the North, in both

**Table 2.3**   African shares of total imports into Western Europe, North America, and Japan (1963–2001, %)

|  | 1963 | 1973 | 1983 | 1993 | 2001 |
|---|---|---|---|---|---|
| Western Europe | 7.6 | 5.7 | 6.6 | 3.1 | 3.0 |
| imports from sub-Saharan Africa | 5.1 | 3.7 | 3.2 | 1.6 | 1.6 |
| North America | 3.8 | 3.6 | 4.7 | 2.3 | 2.0 |
| Japan | 3.9 | 4.5 | 2.6 | 1.6 | 1.3 |

Source:  GATT/WTO, various.

**Table 2.4** Average share of sub-Saharan African exports by type of country and region of destination (selected years 1985–1998, %)

| | Industrial countries | Of which France | Of which U.K. | Of which U.S. | Developing countries | Of which Africa | Of which Asia |
|---|---|---|---|---|---|---|---|
| 1985 | 64.7 | 8.6 | 8.4 | 16.7 | 26.2 | 13.5 | 4.9 |
| 1990 | 66.7 | 9.6 | 6.1 | 16.3 | 14.1 | 7.3 | 3.7 |
| 1995 | 57.7 | 7.3 | 5.7 | 17.8 | 26.6 | 9.2 | 6.5 |
| 1998 | 56.7 | 6.9 | 5.4 | 16.5 | 25.8 | 10.0 | 11.9 |

Source: Calculated from Ng and Yeats (2001).

absolute and relative terms, although they cast some doubts on the notion of consistent growth of intra-African trade.

## Levels of Export Diversification and of Concentration by Product and Level of Processing

The last two decades have witnessed a shift in African exports away from their traditional focus on mining products/fuels and toward manufactures (see Tables 2.5 and 2.6). However, because the movement toward manufactures has been far less marked than in other regions (particularly East Asia), it is still associated with a tiny and actually declining share for Africa in world exports in this category. Africa's share of exports of manufactures stood at 0.9 percent in 1990 and 0.8 percent in 2001 (WTO 2002). In contrast, Africa's levels of export concentration in fuels and other mining products remain exceptionally high.

Although indicating that diversification has been very limited, these tables probably understate sub-Saharan Africa's export concentration. According to Ng and Yeats (2001), if one goes to more detailed industrial sector-related data (the four-digit Standard Industrial Classification level), then the average share of the top three four-digit categories in the total exports of each country in their sample was 69.9 percent in 1990 and 67.4 percent in 1998. For least developed countries (LDCs)

**Table 2.5** Merchandise exports of Africa and the world by product group (1980–2001, %)

|  | Africa (1980) | Africa (1988) | Africa (2001) | World (2001) |
|---|---|---|---|---|
| Agriculture | 14 | 20 | 15 | 9 |
| Mining products | 67 | 50 | 59 | 13 |
| (of which Fuels) |  |  | 51 | 10 |
| Manufactures | 7 | 18 | 26 | 74 |
| (of which Iron and Steel) |  |  | 1.6 | 2.2 |
| (of which Chemicals) |  |  | 3.6 | 9.9 |
| (of which Office Machinery and Telecoms) |  |  | 0.7 | 13.8 |
| (of which Automotive) |  |  | 1.4 | 9.4 |
| (of which Textiles) |  |  | 1.0 | 2.5 |
| (of which Clothing) |  |  | 5.1 | 3.3 |

Source: GATT/WTO, various.

**Table 2.6** Merchandise exports of sub-Saharan Africa by product group (1985–1998, %)

|      | All foods | Agricultural raw materials | Fuels | Ores and minerals | All manufactures | Miscelleneous |
|------|-----------|---------------------------|-------|-------------------|------------------|---------------|
| 1985 | 14.8      | 4.6                       | 55.4  | 12.7              | 11.5             | 0.9           |
| 1990 | 13.2      | 6.3                       | 46.0  | 16.6              | 17.4             | 0.6           |
| 1995 | 16.9      | 7.1                       | 38.9  | 12.7              | 23.1             | 1.3           |
| 1998 | 18.9      | 6.2                       | 33.8  | 13.6              | 26.5             | 0.8           |

Source: Calculated from Ng and Yeats (2001).

in particular, levels of concentration tend to be extreme, with exports focused on a narrow group of primary commodities. UNCTAD (2001) data on the exports of 26 sub-Saharan African LDCs[8] show an average level of concentration on primary commodity exports of 86.3 percent in 1997—a level basically unaltered since 1980 (when it stood at 89.2 percent). The primary commodity exports of these countries encompassed eleven different mineral and thirteen different agricultural products, plus seafood, timber, and meat/livestock. But an average of only 2.7 commodities from this list were being exported by each country.[9]

According to Ng and Yeats (2001), even within the categories of food and minerals/fuels, sub-Saharan Africa countries (and not just LDCs) have generally failed to detectably move up the value-added ladder away from primary commodity exports. They provide a breakdown (see Table 2.7) of the share of the exports of four product groups *including manufactures* between primary, intermediate, and final products. These data suggest an unchanged level of dependence on primary products during the 1990s. Thus, we conclude that there is no support for the proposition that progress has been made toward processed commodities.

## Integration in Global Value Chains for Manufacturing

A final dimension of trade performance that links the issue of integration with that of levels of processing of exported goods is performance in intra-industry trade. Intra-industry trade, which can be read broadly as an indicator for global production sharing and integration in global value chains for manufactured products, is one of the most dynamically expanding areas of global trade (see Chapter 1). International trade data show shares of parts and components in total manufacturing exports to

**Table 2.7**   Structure of African countries' exports by level of processing (1990 and 1998)

| Product | Processing stage | Share of all African exports of product category (%), 1990 | Share of all African exports of product category (%), 1998 |
|---|---|---|---|
| Food | Primary | 83.5 | 82.9 |
| | Intermediate | 6.5 | 7.1 |
| | Final | 10.0 | 10.0 |
| Ores/Minerals | Primary | 27.0 | 32.0 |
| | Intermediate | 60.9 | 48.7 |
| | Final | 12.1 | 19.3 |
| Mineral fuels | Primary | 97.4 | 97.4 |
| | Final | 2.6 | 2.6 |
| Manufactures | Primary | 54.2 | 44.7 |
| | Intermediate | 31.1 | 35.9 |
| | Final | 14.6 | 19.4 |

Source:   Ng and Yeats (2001).

be a high and generally rising share of all manufacturing exports for more industrialized developing countries such as Brazil, Chile, Korea, Turkey, and Taiwan. For this group of countries, the share in question averaged 43 percent of manufacturing exports in 1990 and 45 percent in 1998 (Ng and Yeats 2001). For their sample of sub-Saharan African countries, the averages were only 7 percent and 10 percent for the same years.

In conclusion, Africa's export trade over the last half-century has been characterized by a low rate of growth. After 1980, this rate has been low even in relation to the continent's general level of economic development. Africa's export trade has been also characterized by a degree of disintegration from Northern markets and isolation from more dynamic developments in the composition of international trade. It remains highly focused on a narrow range of primary commodities, and although export of manufactures is increasing in importance, this is largely confined to products with low levels of processing.

## THE INTERNATIONAL TRADE REGIME PRIOR TO WTO

As recently as the beginning of the 1980s, the international trade regime had a number of features that made it quite different from the one that exists today. At the multilateral level, the General Agreement on Tariffs and Trade (GATT), the forerunner of WTO, included OECD countries but not—for most of its life—a majority of developing ones. Most of its members signed up to all its agreements, but this was not a requirement. These agreements confined themselves almost exclusively to border issues such as duties and tariffs. At the same time, GATT was accompanied by a series of international commodity agreements for coffee, cocoa, sugar, natural rubber, and tin. In essence, these were multilateral contracts over price and supply conditions between the main exporting and importing countries. At the bilateral level, there were a relatively small number of free trade arrangements (mainly radiating from the E.U.) and two important preferential trade arrangements for developing countries, the Lomé Convention (in relation to the E.U.) and the UNCTAD Generalized System of Preferences (GSP). This section will describe the "old" trade regime on the basis of a more detailed outline of each of these elements.

## The General Agreement on Tariffs and Trade (GATT)

GATT came into being in 1947–1948 with twenty-three contracting parties who agreed to conduct trade with each other according to a specific set of basic rules. According to Srinivasan (1998: 53), the most important of these were those of most favored nation, national treatment, and the prohibition in principle of all border measures other than duties, taxes, and other charges on external trade. According to the most favored nation rule, each contracting party should give every other party the same treatment (as far as trade measures were concerned) as it gave to its most favored trading partner. According to the national treatment rule, each contracting party should extend to foreign actors the same treatment it gives to its own domestic actors (e.g., for taxation purposes). The third rule can be taken as an injunction to convert all nontariff barriers into tariffs or to remove them completely. Implicit in Srinivasan's presentation is that reciprocity, the principle that all parties to an agreement should grant each other the same preferences as they themselves received, was not a fundamental principle of GATT.

By 1986, GATT had expanded—but still embraced only 65 countries. Most developing countries did not become members, initially in the hope that they would get a powerful multilateral organization directly linking trade and development issues, and later because membership offered them few direct benefits. The core activity of GATT was a series of negotiating rounds aimed at reducing tariffs on products that were of main interest to Northern countries. Textiles and clothing negotiations remained entirely at the bilateral level (albeit from 1961 onward within the general framework of the Multifibre Arrangement). Agricultural trade was, in effect, excluded entirely from GATT deliberations.

Over the years, a series of issue-specific agreements or disciplines were also established, under which signatories committed themselves to adopt identical trade-related policies. The number and range of disciplines underwent a significant increase at the conclusion of the Tokyo Round in 1979 when agreements were ratified on, among others, export subsidies, countervailing duties, technical barriers to trade, and government procurement. But a central feature of GATT was that contracting parties could remain party to the General Agreement without having to become signatories to all, or even any, of its subagreements. Many developing country members, for example, never signed up to the agreements on export subsidies or on government procurement.

Rounds of tariff reduction and rulesetting were preceeded by political negotiation and horse-trading, aiming at reaching a consensus. These principles were extended into the GATT dispute settlement mechanism, whose role was seen as one of rebalancing agreements found to be working one-sidedly, as well as correcting anomalies identified after negotiations were completed. Complaints could be made, but defendants could block the formation of panels or the promulgation of panel decisions. Most stages of the mechanism lacked standard terms of reference, and GATT itself had little involvement in the functioning of dispute procedures or, more broadly, in the promotion of arbitration.

Most economists, reflecting on the experience of GATT, currently agree that it was a forum where political compromise prevailed over the enforcement of rules. They also agree that the trade policy objectives of leading Northern countries were shaped by more than trade interests in the narrow sense (Michalopolous 2001; Finger and Nogués 2002). The United States, for example, was restrained in its pursuit of national trade interests by the foreign policy objectives of uniting Europe to prevent further wars and of containing the influence of the Soviet Union. The latter objective, which was also shared by European powers and Japan, led to a pragmatic rather than doctrinaire response to the concerns about the international trading system raised by developing countries.

In principle at least, GATT accepted developing countries' own definitions of their problems in relation to the international trading system. That is, development was seen in terms of overcoming specific structural problems, notably those of industrializing within an already established pattern of international specialization and of managing economies where the balance of payments position was heavily dependent on the price of primary commodities. As early as 1954/1955, the original articles of GATT were revised to allow developing countries to implement import controls to deal with balance of payment problems, adopt physical and tariff restrictions on imports to lend protection to infant industries, and remove Northern countries' rights to veto such restrictions. This was followed by declarations and new articles (in 1961 to 1964) legitimizing nonreciprocal preferential trade arrangements for developing countries. A waiver for the most far-reaching of such arrangements, the Generalized System of Preferences, followed in 1971.

The early and mid-1970s, with the boom in primary commodity prices and the political shock of U.S. defeat in Vietnam, represented a high-water mark for the influence of developing countries in the multilateral trading system. Yet, the achievements of this period were still partial and ambiguous. Northern countries never became bound by firm commitments to make changes to their own trade barriers that would specifically benefit developing countries. Hence, during the entire GATT period, there was little or no progress made on issues such as tariff escalation[10] or reduction of Northern countries' nontariff barriers, such as rules of origin (the rules determining which country a product may be deemed as originating from). On the other hand, Northern countries pursued market access issues almost exclusively in relation to each other and allowed the institutionalization of a system of producing country oligopolies for a range of commodities—with apparent GATT blessing.

## International Commodity Agreements

At the same time as GATT was revising its articles to allow developing countries to use import controls, the first international commodity agreement (that for sugar) was being signed, also with explicit GATT consent (under Articles XXXVI and XXXVIII). Consultations on a cocoa agreement began within FAO in 1956, and two further international agreements covering tropical export crops were introduced later, for coffee in 1962 and for natural rubber in 1980.[11]

The geopolitics of these agreements was based on fear in Northern countries over security of access to supply, particularly in the context of global bipolarity and the uncertain allegiance of a growing number of developing countries, coupled with a certain wish to give developing countries a greater stake in the capitalist system. The economic background of these agreements was twofold. Economists like Prebisch (1950) and Singer (1950) argued strongly that developing countries deserved compensation for the long-term decline in the barter terms of trade of primary commodities relative to manufactures. Others, such as Keynes (1942/1980), argued that unstable commodity prices had critical importance in relation to importing country inflation levels, short-term movements of capital, and thereby economic cycles generally (see also Hone 1973). The tension between these two arguments was to be incorporated into the Agreements themselves.

Prebisch's arguments (1950) were to become institutionalized in UNCTAD, as he became the first secretary-general of the organization in 1964. Subsequently, UNCTAD endeavored to promote other agreements, and to secure long-term funding for those that existed already, via setting up a Common Fund for Commodities. Agreement was reached to create this Fund in 1976, but it only came into existence almost a decade and a half later.

The four agreements covering tropical export crops to which African countries were party are presented in Table 2.8. Both producing and consuming country governments were parties to the agreements. Recommended or support prices were established and defended, either on

**Table 2.8**  International commodity agreements for tropical export crops

| Commodity | Title and start year | Price control mechanism | Years when economic provisions were operational | Number of years during which average price exceeded recommended level | Number of African producing country signatories |
|---|---|---|---|---|---|
| Sugar | ISA, 1954 | Export controls | 1954–1961, 1969–1973, 1978–1984 | 10 years | 7 |
| Coffee | ICA, 1962 | Export controls | 1964–1971, 1980–1984, 1987–1988 | 13 years | 22 |
| Cocoa | ICCA, 1972 | Buffer stocks | 1973–1979, 1981–1989 | 8 years | 8 |
| Natural Rubber | INRA, 1980 | Buffer stocks | 1980–present | Entire period | 2 |

Source:  based on Mshomba (2000).

the basis of setting producing country export quotas or via the financing of centrally held buffer stocks. As Table 2.8 shows, price levels above the recommended price were achieved for a substantial majority of the lives of the coffee and rubber agreements and for around half the life of the cocoa and sugar agreements.

According to Hermann, Burger, and Smit (1993, cited in Mshomba 2000), at least one of the agreements (the ICA) persistently raised prices by 24 to 30 percent over what would have been market-clearing levels. The relative success of the ICA regime was due not only to the participation of consuming countries in the negotiations and administration of quotas, but also to the existence of producing country export monopolies or state-run auctions. However, none of the agreements in question (apart from INRA),[12] were continuous in character or able to survive to the end of the 1980s. Bates (1997), Daviron (1996), Gilbert (1996), and Mshomba (2000) all mention two complementary reasons for this. First, securing agreement between, or even the participation of, all major suppliers was a continuous problem. For example, in its later years ICA was plagued by disagreements between Latin American and African producers over the allocation of quotas. ICCA lost much of its influence when Côte d'Ivoire, the world's leading producer with 20 to 30 percent of the market, pulled out between 1980 and 1986 to pursue a policy of block dealing (selling large volumes to individual traders through a single contract). Second, securing the consent of major consuming countries was an ongoing and growing problem. In the cases of both coffee and cocoa, this was linked to the continuing fragmentation of the geography of production and the steady increase in the number of producing countries with significant export levels that were not part of the agreement. This led to a widening spread between the prices paid for commodities traded between parties to the agreements and the prices paid by those outside the agreements (see also Chapter 5).

Whatever the reasons for the collapse of the agreements, it is clear that this led to major and long-term declines in prices—and thereby in producing country incomes (Table 2.9).[13]

The long-term nature of these declines appears to refute the notion that they were simply a function of the release onto the world market of stocks that had been artificially withheld to support the recommended prices under the agreements. Nor are they simply a function of the secular declines in terms of trade for primary commodities during the same period. World cotton prices, for example, show a far less steep decline over the same extended period covered in Table 2.9.[14]

**Table 2.9**   Export prices of coffee and cocoa in the wake of the collapse of ICA and ICCA (1990 prices = 100)

|  | Average price (final 6 years of agreement) | Average price (first 6 years after collapse) | Average price (second 6 years after collapse) |
|---|---|---|---|
| Coffee (economic provisions of ICA ended 1988) | 182.3 | 109.8 | 145.3 |
| Cocoa (economic provisions of ICCA ended 1989) | 151.7 | 98.6 | 103.7 |

Source:   GATT/WTO, various.

## The Generalized System of Preferences (GSP)

The Generalized System of Preferences (GSP) was promoted by UNCTAD from its foundation, but became institutionalized in the form of a set of offers only in 1971–1976. The objective of the GSP was to facilitate global reductions in tariffs for developing country exports, without general obligations to reciprocate for developing countries. For LDCs, the resulting preferences were supposed to be deeper and more all-embracing than for other developing countries. However, only eleven Northern countries or country groups implemented GSP, and all did so in different ways and without binding the resulting offers in the GATT.[15]

The preference margin provided to developing countries by GSP was, at least theoretically, quite significant. But because Northern countries already zero-rated most primary commodities for tariff purposes, real preference margins were high only for industrial goods. As a result, the main beneficiaries of GSP tended to be Asian countries with strong manufacturing bases. In 1997, China, Indonesia, India, Thailand, and Brazil accounted for 60 percent of all GSP trade (China alone accounted for 28 percent; Arnau 2002). Furthermore, even for these countries, GSP did not open all doors to all countries. Products such as textiles and clothing, footwear, and certain agricultural goods were mostly excluded from the offers, while others faced quantitative ceilings. GSP compliance procedures were also exacting in terms of product rules of origin and of bureaucratic capacity to obtain national eligibility. Moreover, certain countries offering GSPs excluded specific developing countries from the scheme on political grounds (most notably, the U.S. excluded China). Nonetheless, there is evidence that GSP played an important role in the promotion of developing country exports, particularly those of semi-industrialized Asian countries. According to Arnau, during the period 1976–1991, GSP imports into OECD countries grew at 14.5 percent annually—while total imports grew at only 8.9 percent.[16]

## Preferential Trade Agreements (PTAs) and the Lomé Convention

The GATT period was characterized by a number of bilateral preferential trade agreements (PTAs). However, their coverage was relatively limited and their evolution lacked a clear pattern. Between 1949 and 1994, 109 PTAs were notified to GATT (Sapir 2000). The European Union was probably party to half or more (no precise breakdown of these by hub country/group of countries is available). Those that had the European Union as a party fell into three broad groups: (1) reciprocal trade agreements with countries that were thought to have a chance of joining the European Union in the short-to-medium term; (2) nonreciprocal Economic Partnership Agreements with selected North African and Middle Eastern countries (Algeria, Morocco, Tunisia, Egypt, Jordan, Lebanon, and Syria); and (3) nonreciprocal agreements with more than 70 sub-Saharan African, Caribbean, and Pacific (ACP) developing countries—the Lomé Convention. Apart from the Lomé Convention, there were no E.U. agreements stretching beyond Europe and the Mediterranean. Most remaining Preferential Trade Agreements were regional in character and spread over both the developing and the developed worlds. The United States was party to only two such arrangements prior to the implementation of NAFTA in 1994 (free trade agreements with Israel in 1985 and Canada in 1989), and Japan to none.

The Lomé Convention, signed in 1975, created an arrangement between the European Union and a large group of developing countries that were mostly former British, French, Portuguese, or Spanish colonies. Forty-seven of these countries were located in sub-Saharan Africa and thirty-nine were LDCs. Under this arrangement, exports from ACP countries (with some exceptions) could enter the European Union at zero or highly concessional tariff levels. At the same time, ACP countries could continue to levy tariffs of their choice on imports from the European Union. In addition, two commodity funds were established (STABEX and SYSMIN),[17] under which the European Union compensated ACP countries for lower-than-expected commodity earnings.

A number of important agricultural goods were excepted from these preferences. Most nontropical agricultural exports were subject to (usually seasonal) physical quotas, whereas others—mainly nontraditional temperate-zone products—were granted only partial mitigations of duty. Four agrofood products (bananas, rum, sugar, and beef/veal) were subject to separate protocols that specified given quotas to be admitted duty-free or near duty-free, or to be guaranteed a regulated internal E.U. market price.[18]

The most important restrictions in the Lomé Convention applied to industrial goods, which were embodied in the Convention's regulations on rules of origin. Under these rules, a product could be considered to be an export of a beneficiary country only if: a transformation within the country had taken place between tariff headings and there had been a minimum of 60 percent domestic value addition. Rules of origin for clothing were even tighter. A process criterion (two distinct stages of production had to be undertaken in the beneficiary country) was applied, and third country raw material content could not exceed 15 percent of the ex-factory price of an exported good. In other words, in the case of clothing, weaving or spinning had to take place in the country of origin (or in another beneficiary country) for the product in question to command duty-free status. The U.S. GSP rules of origin, by contrast, demanded that only 35 percent of the value added embodied in a clothing item needed to originate in the exporting country.

In part because of these restrictions, the Lomé Convention is usually considered to have been the least effective of the elements of the old international trade regime that sought to balance the interests of developed and developing countries. E.U. imports from ACP countries grew at a much slower rate than total imports. As a proportion of E.U. trade, they actually fell sharply.[19] The only exporter to fully industrialize on the basis of the Convention was Mauritius,[20] where sufficient resources were generated in the locally owned sugar sector to finance a full backward integration for textiles and clothing. Even in this case, Lomé preferences were partly eroded by GSP ones.

## The New International Trade Regime

As indicated earlier, a distinctively new international trade regime has come into being in the last decade. The central pillar of this regime is WTO, which in effect replaced GATT in 1994. WTO differs from GATT in a series of fundamental ways. Because its membership has been extended to include a large majority of developing countries, as well as some transition economies, it now covers the great bulk of world trade. It also incorporates a much wider set of agreements than GATT, dealing with domestic as well as border issues. As the result of being launched as a single undertaking, all its member countries are obliged to be party to all its agreements. The principle of reciprocity of trade preferences plays a clearer and more central role than it did in GATT. Finally, the essentially political logic of the GATT process, based on consensus building around the drawing up of new rules and subsequent decisions to rebalance them, has been replaced by a juridical logic—at least as far as rebalancing is concerned.

A second feature of the new regime is that WTO stands increasingly alone at the multilateral level. The international commodity agreements have all disappeared (except for that on natural rubber). The GSP has been relegated to a marginal role. Instead, the trade regulation landscape has become cluttered by a host of Preferential Trade Agreements and offers. These have radically increased in number, in country coverage, and in scope (what border and domestic issues they seek to regulate). As far as developing countries are concerned, there is no generalized provision of special and differentiated treatment within these agreements. Instead, where this treatment is provided at all, it is reserved to LDCs[21] and occurs on the basis of unilateral offers rather than agreements.

In relation to WTO Agreements themselves, there are still remnants of special and differentiated treatment for developing countries generally and a substantively greater degree of special and differentiated treatment for LDCs. However, in neither case are the specific *structural* problems of developing countries taken as a starting point for determining this treatment. Rather, WTO Agreements are guided by the perspective that developing countries are simply at a lower stage of development, which will be overcome by being allowed more time to catch up. For developing countries that are not LDCs, this treatment (multilaterally as well as bilaterally) is within a framework of full reciprocity.

## The World Trade Organization (WTO)

The new agreements that became incorporated into the WTO as a result of the Uruguay Round covered agriculture, textiles and clothing, intellectual property rights (TRIPs), investment (TRIMs), services (GATS), customs valuation, and sanitary and phytosanitary standards (SPS).

In addition to inaugurating these agreements, the Uruguay Round entailed a generalization to new signatories (not just new members, but GATT members who had earlier declined to sign) of expanded versions of Tokyo Round agreements on export subsidies, technical barriers to trade, countervailing duties, and government procurement. It also extended to all countries the obligation to bind tariffs. At the same time, a mechanism was introduced to ensure domestic legal system conformity to these agreements, in the form of a country-by-country trade policy review mechanism.

In the WTO, developing countries still receive some form of special and differentiated treatment, but mostly on the basis of temporary exemptions from some provisions of new agreements and longer implementation periods. In general, as a result of the reciprocity principle, they are now expected to have national trade regimes exactly as open as Northern countries ones—within a period of five to ten years. Longer and deeper forms of infant industry protection, the use of import quotas, and the practice of opting out of specific agreements were all prohibited. This was done on the basis of arguments against industrial protectionism, in particular its disincentives to export, the opportunities it creates for rent seeking, and its discrimination against agriculture.

It is now generally agreed that developing countries were attracted to the single undertaking as a condition of WTO membership (entailing assent to all these agreements and the downgrading of special and differential treatment) by the opportunities apparently on offer to negotiate much better market access for their agricultural and textile/clothing products.[22] These expectations were to be badly disappointed. Developing countries were also apparently attracted by the reform to the dispute settlement mechanism (DSM), which in principle provides legal protection to all countries whatever their size or level of development. This improved protection was to be based on a greater role for jurisprudence in decision making and on the adoption of a so-called negative consensus rule governing the acceptance of complaints and the adoption of rulings.[23] As far as the net costs and benefits of the DSM for developing countries are concerned, these hopes ended up being illusory too. Developing countries' delayed recognition of the full implications of what they signed up to, and the lack of substantial progress in the areas of agriculture and textiles and clothing, sewed a harvest of bitterness.

In what follows, brief sketches will be provided of the main areas where developing countries' expectations were high (agriculture, textiles and clothing, and DSM), followed by the main areas where their expectations were neutral or low to begin with, but where they were unprepared for the full consequences of what was negotiated (TRIPs, TRIMs, GATS, and SPS).

*The Agreement on Agriculture*    The 1994 Agreement on Agriculture required multilateral reductions in farm subsidies and increases in market access. Members agreed to reduce export subsidies by a minimum of 20 percent from their 1986–1988 levels by 2000 and to reduce aggregate levels of domestic support by 80 percent over the same period. Agricultural subsidies in the form of support to specific production volumes or physical areas were to be phased out completely, although direct payments under production-limiting or environmental/rural development programs were exempted. Members also agreed to convert all nontariff barriers to bound tariffs. Existing tariff items were to be reduced by a minimum of 15 percent, whereas new bound tariffs expressing earlier nontariff barriers were to be reduced by 36 percent by 2000 by Northern countries and by 24 percent by 2004 by developing ones.[24] Finally, all countries agreed to take no new actions related to countervailing duties until 2000 (later extended to 2005).

The leading Northern providers of agricultural subsidies, the European Union and the United States, have actually increased levels of public support to agriculture since the Agreement was signed. According to OECD (2001), net public support to agriculture for OECD countries as a whole rose to 40 percent of the value of total farm receipts in 1999. In 2000, subsidies accounted for 39 percent of the total value of E.U. production and 22 percent of the value of U.S. production (Hoekman and Anderson 2001).

In general, OECD agricultural tariff levels also remained unchanged, at around 40 percent (OECD 2001). The European Union and United States engaged in what became known as "dirty tariffication" (Finger and Nogués 2002; Hoekman and Anderson 2001). Bindings of new tariffs were made at levels so high that, even after agreed reductions had been undertaken in 2000, tariff rates still remained above the real levels of effective protection of a decade earlier. This proved possible as no formula for translating nontariff barriers into tariffs was bound into the Agreement. As a result of the complete failure of Northern countries to honor the spirit of the Agreement, developing countries were unable to expand their share of global agricultural trade. On the contrary, as a result of subsidized exports, the combined share of the European

Union and United States in world agricultural exports rose slightly from 49.8 percent in 1980 to 51.8 percent in 2001 (GATT/WTO, various).

*The Agreement on Textiles and Clothing (ATC)*   For two decades prior to the birth of WTO, international trade in textiles and clothing fell under the auspices of a framework known as the Multifibre Arrangement (MFA), which laid down parameters for bilateral compacts covering export restrictions on producing countries in relation to specific importing countries. The main Northern country users of such compacts were the European Union, United States, Canada, and Norway, although many developing countries also used them. Under the different bilateral agreements, restricted items were specified and physical quotas were attached to them. Exports above the level of these quotas were punished by higher rates of duty. In return for filling quotas, however, exporting countries could earn incremental increases in quota levels (in the case of the United States, these averaged around 5 to 6 percent per year).

The WTO Agreement on Textiles and Clothing (ATC) entailed the full integration of quota-bound items into general tariff schemes by importing countries by 2005 according to a step-by-step timetable. It also provided a corresponding timetable for increases in quota levels for items remaining restricted during the life of the Agreement. Finally (under Article 6), it provided a mechanism until 2005 for importing countries to use safeguard measures when it could be demonstrated that a particular product was being imported in quantities "likely to cause serious damage to the local industry of the importing country".[25] A WTO Textiles monitoring body was set up to police the use of these measures.

The Agreement on Textiles and Clothing required that quota-using countries should list all the product items to which they applied quotas in an Annex. This list would then form the base from which the agreed step-by-step integration would occur. It seems that the Northern country users of quota inflated their lists of items under quota by including large numbers of product categories that had never been restricted (Reinart 2000; Tang 2000). Then, they offered almost wholly nonrestricted items for integration during the first phase of planned liberalization. In the two subsequent phases, the United States and European Union freed a much higher percentage of items from quota, but the cumulative shares of total import volume subject to integration still remained less than half what were agreed (Table 2.10). Furthermore, despite China's entry into the WTO in 2001, the articles of its accession agreement provide its trading

**Table 2.10** Integration of the Multifibre Arrangement into the GATT/WTO by Northern countries

| Stage of integration and date by which stage must be completed | Amount by which quotas must be increased over existing rates of increase (%) | Cumulative minimum volume of restricted imports that must be integrated (%) | Cumulative volume of restricted imports actually integrated (%) | | | |
|---|---|---|---|---|---|---|
| | | | E.U. | U.S. | Canada | Norway |
| I, 1 January 1995 | 16 | 16 | n/a | n/a | n/a | n/a |
| II, 1 January 1998 | 25 | 33 | 4.7 | 1.3 | n/a | 100 |
| III, 1 January 2002 | 27 | 51 | 20.0 | 19.5 | n/a | n/a |
| IV, 1 January 2005 | n/a | 100 | n/a | n/a | n/a | n/a |

Sources: Tang (2000); Raghavan (2000).

partners with the right to use safeguard actions against it until 2008 and in certain cases until 2013. Of the quota-using Northern countries, only Norway has fulfilled its obligations under the Agreement.

There were thirty-eight safeguard actions under Article 6 during the first three years of the Agreement's life, of which about two-thirds were brought by the United States. However, the Textile monitoring body made few recommendations in favor of the United States, leading the country to take a series of antidumping actions and to route its complaints through the dispute settlement mechanism instead (see later). The United States also introduced tougher rules of origin for Multifibre Agreement clothing imports in 1996. Since 1998, Latin American countries appear to have been the main users of safeguard actions.

A number of developing countries (except for large and low-cost producers, such as China and India), whose exports into the European Union or United States have been bound by quota, believe that they stand more to lose from the successful implementation of the Agreement than they do from its failure. This is because they share the widespread belief that the main effect of a phasing out of quotas will be a shift of world production to China, at their expense.[26] A number of the countries that pressed strongly for the full implementation of the Agreement on Textiles and Clothing in its early years, and who raised its nonimplementation as an instance of unfair trade, have subsequently fallen quiet.

*The Dispute Settlement Mechanism (DSM)*　At the time of its unveiling, the new dispute settlement mechanism was widely seen as strengthening the rule-based nature of the WTO and, on the basis of greater formalization, giving weaker countries greater protection against unilateral actions by stronger ones (such as those authorized by Section 301 of the 1988 U.S. Trade Act).[27] This formalization included the following: (1) making panel decisions binding if they were confirmed by a new specialized and professional appellate body, (2) providing standard terms of reference for panels and the body itself, (3) introducing time limits for the different stages of the making and processing of a complaint, and (4) providing additional opportunities for arbitration. In addition, provision for "special and differentiated treatment" for developing countries was built into the mechanism, in the form of an obligatory presence of developing country panelists in cases involving developing countries, legal assistance to developing country defendants by the WTO Secretariat, and a requirement that panels indicate how they have taken the special and differentiated treatment provisions of particular agreements into account in their deliberations.

As widely predicted, the new DSM was used more often than the old one. Whereas 216 complaints were brought before GATT from 1980 to 1994, 281 were brought before WTO from 1995 to 2002. However, contrary to hopes (if not predictions), developing countries have been involved in the new DSM more as defendants than as complainants. According to Schaffer (2003), developing countries are one-third less likely to file complaints under WTO than under GATT, whereas the number of cases against developing countries has risen from 19 percent to 33 percent. Yet, recent developments also suggest that some developing countries are becoming more active and bold in using the DSM against major trading partners (i.e., Brazil's cotton and sugar cases against the U.S. and the E.U. respectively).

Schaffer (2003) states that the increase in the number of WTO rules and the juridicalization of the DSM are among the main reasons for this turn of events. In a context where avoiding infringement of WTO rules has become more difficult and resource demanding, developing countries (and especially LDCs) are more likely to have complaints brought against them than to act as complainants, as they lack resources. At the same time, the DSM itself has taken on juridical characteristics. Thus, these resource imbalances are replicated by others reflecting of real-world civil law systems. Initiating and prosecuting complaints (not to mention defending them) is burdensome. Those who lack the capacity to use the system therefore bring few cases, and when cases are brought against them, they tend to concede defeat before the case reaches a more costly stage of proceedings.

Schaffer (2003) adds that the content of the emerging WTO jurisprudence is also problematic for developing countries. The United States has been party to over half all disputes as either complainant or defendant and to almost 90 percent of all cases if we include those where it has taken third-party status. The United States has intensively used trade lawyers in these cases. Thus, emerging WTO law has come to be based on the Anglo-Saxon common law tradition. This involves appeals to precedent and to the detail of the facts of specific cases. Appeal to generic principles, as in other legal traditions, has been specifically rejected by the appellate body on a number of occasions. Arguably, an institutionalization of the use of generic principles would have much better served the interests of developing countries. Moreover, as a certain legal tradition gains ground, those countries most familiar with it enjoy an additional advantage. Access to U.S. or British legal expertise (at the cost of US$250 to $1000 per hour) has become necessary to competently pursue or defend a complaint, further raising the threshold at which litigation becomes worthwhile.

*The Agreement on Trade-Related Aspects of Intellectual Property Rights (TRIPs)*   The TRIPs Agreement globalizes the protection of trademarks, patents, and copyrights, as well as of geographical indications for wines and spirits.[28] It does so by obliging all members to introduce national systems of legal protection that eliminate the rights of member governments unilaterally to determine areas of nonpatentability, patent duration, and rights of patent holders. It further widens the definition of what can be patented to include software, production processes, product varieties, and product parts. In addition, it protects rental rights for sound recordings and films. The only areas where national governments retain discretion are in relation to medicines and choice of systems for intellectual property protection for living objects (plants and animals). In cases of national medical emergency or exclusively noncommercial medical use, members may decline to observe patents for relevant drugs, but only for domestic market use. In regard to living objects, they may choose between patenting and another *sui generis* system, most obviously that of the International Union for the Protection of New Varieties of Plants (UPOV), which provides some exceptions to patent law in respect to farmers' and breeders' rights.[29] Enforcement of TRIPs is, in the first instance, through the WTO TRIPs Council's rolling review of member country legislation. Special and differential treatment is restricted to longer phase-in periods for developing countries (six years) and LDCs (ten years), and to a nonbinding provision that Northern country members provide developing ones with assistance for implementation.

The immediate logic for global extension of patent protection is to increase substantially patent holders' sales in countries where markets had been dominated by (mostly local) companies selling either copied products or ones that closely resemble those under patent elsewhere.[30] No rationale has ever been provided for TRIPs in terms of increasing the openness of the international trading system. Instead, apologists for the Agreement have claimed that it will extend to all countries incentives to invest in and develop knowledge-based industries. In addition, by providing higher levels of protection universally, it will supposedly increase the pace of global accumulation of knowledge, with predicted spill-over effects for poor countries (Srinivasan 1998: 52–53).[31]

**Table 2.11**  Short-run net transfers following from TRIPs (US$ million)

| Gains | | Losses | |
|---|---|---|---|
| United States | 1,277 | India | 1,129 |
| Germany | 496 | Brazil | 439 |
| France | 292 | Canada | 317 |
| Italy | 116 | Spain | 144 |
| Switzerland | 101 | Mexico | 126 |
| Netherlands | 58 | United Kingdom | 126 |
| Sweden | 57 | Norway | 37 |
| Japan | 52 | Austria | 36 |

Source:  McCalman (2000).

A more obvious prediction is that, because of the overwhelmingly skewed nature of the global distribution of patents in favor of Northern countries (particularly the United States, Switzerland, France, and Germany),[32] a significant short-term transfer of resources to them from developing countries is likely to follow. Efforts to model the effects of TRIPs tend to confirm this, not only for static but also dynamic effects. One such attempt (McCalman 2000) examines a sample of twenty-seven countries, of which five are developing ones (India, Brazil, Mexico, South Africa, and Korea). Table 2.11 reports the short-run net transfers involved, holding constant the differences in patent registration between countries. Table 2.12 provides an index of long-term gains and losses,

**Table 2.12**  Index of long-run gains and losses from TRIPs, relative to income

| Gains | | Losses | |
|---|---|---|---|
| Switzerland | 1.12 | India | 1.16 |
| France | 0.63 | Portugal | 0.63 |
| Germany | 0.59 | Norway | 0.44 |
| United States | 0.50 | Greece | 0.42 |
| Sweden | 0.49 | Brazil | 0.38 |
| Netherlands | 0.40 | Ireland | 0.38 |
| Italy | 0.38 | Mexico | 0.35 |
| United Kingdom | 0.25 | South Africa | 0.28 |

Source:  McCalman (2000).

allowing for increased patenting, in relation to national income levels. The latter table thus measures the consequences of TRIPs for economic differentiation between countries rather than the net benefits or losses. The only surprises are the presence of some Western European countries among those experiencing net losses in the short term and relative losses in the longer term, and the fact that Switzerland, France, and Germany stand to make the major relative gains. All five developing countries in the sample are net losers in the short term and relative losers in the longer term—in the case of India on a dramatic scale.

A series of other concerns have also been raised concerning likely adverse effects of TRIPs for developing countries, most notably the possibilities it opens for Northern countries to gain ownership of plant varieties endogenous to developing countries and the difficulties that developing countries without pharmaceutical industries face in importing cheap copied drugs after 2005, even when faced by national emergencies. Although these concerns are genuine, another that has been less discussed may actually be as significant. This is the implications for global industrial concentration of the increased returns to research and development that seem to be a consequence of TRIPs. The institutionalization of securer rents for innovation embedded in TRIPs is likely to benefit most those firms with the largest research and development capacities. This is likely to speed up industry concentration, depress competition in the longer term, and thus amplify already enhanced capacities to charge oligopoly prices. It is developing countries and enterprises in them who, as price takers, will feel the effects most strongly.

*The Trade-related Investment Measures (TRIMs) Agreement*    Prior to the 1990s, most developing countries used investment codes or sets of conditions either to prevent incoming foreign companies from engaging in restrictive business practices or, more ambitiously, to impose development-related obligations on them. The form of restrictive business practice causing most concern was transfer pricing, carried out to allow the reporting of corporate income not in the country where it was actually made, but rather in the country of operation where the corporation concerned faced the lowest tax obligations. Investment codes typically sought to reduce transfer pricing, as well as to impose certain domestic economic policy objectives on incoming firms: foreign exchange generation requirements, import-export balancing, and specific local content levels for exports.

Under the TRIMs Agreement, members are explicitly prohibited from using any of these three types of conditions on the grounds that they constitute restrictions on trade. Other types of TRIMs (such as other types of export performance requirement or mandatory technology transfer) are not explicitly banned, but may be now open to challenge. The TRIMs Agreement thus represents the culmination of a process of foreign firms acquiring new rights while shedding obligations. This process includes the failure by developing countries to get the United Nations to adopt a global Code of Conduct for transnational corporations and the dismantling of the U.N. Centre on Transnational Corporations.

Work by Morrissey and Rai (1995) and Morrissey (2000) concludes that, because the WTO embodies no compensating response to the potential trade-disturbing activities of transnational corporations, the economic impact of implementing the TRIMs Agreement is likely to be negative for developing countries. This negative impact is also likely to increase over time, as the potential rent losses entailed rise in tandem with the growing importance of foreign direct investment (FDI) in international flows. Although the elimination of export requirements is ambiguous in its consequences, the elimination of both import restrictions and local content requirements directly implies increases in imports, deteriorations in trade balances, and falling local production and employment.

*The General Agreement on Trade in Services (GATS)*   The General Agreement on Trade in Services (GATS), like those on TRIPs, TRIMs, and SPS (see below), has explicit implications for systems of domestic market regulation. This follows from the fact that tariff barriers in the form found in merchandise trade are difficult or impossible to impose for services and that trade in services is therefore regulated through domestic laws. GATS lays down a set of rules covering all trade in services. These include a requirement for domestic market transparency and entail that members making offers and commitments to open specific areas of service provision must recognize the principles of national treatment and market access. Services are in principle exempt from GATS coverage only if they are supplied in the exercise of government authority, on a noncommercial basis, and not in competition with other service providers. These expressions are yet to be fully clarified.

Although TRIPs, TRIMs, and SPS had a big bang character—that is, members undertook to implement them in their entirety at the time of their signing (with some time-limited exemptions for developing countries)—GATS resembles earlier generations of multilateral trade agreements. Members can offer specific degrees of market opening for specific service sectors according to their own timetables. They can also decline to make any offers for particular sectors. However, the Agreement also embodied commitments by members to extend coverage progressively over time.

GATS aspires to cover not only all service sectors but also all aspects of trade in services. These include (1) cross-border supply without in-country supplier presence, (2) consumption outside the country of residence, (3) in-country commercial presence by foreign suppliers, and (4) temporary migration to provide a service. During the Uruguay Round, comprehensive sectoral agreements emerged in only two main areas, namely computer products and telecommunications. Efforts to obtain agreements on financial services and maritime services made little progress.

Hoekman (1996) provides an index of 1994 levels of commitment by type of country and type of commitment (in terms of sectors covered) in relation to the full list of categories of services drawn up by the Group of Negotiation on Services. According to this source, high-income countries made commitments on market access for 49 percent of service sector categories and on national treatment for 53 percent. Developing countries made commitments on 11 percent of service sector categories for market access and 13 percent for national treatment. On the one hand, developing countries have been able to forestall what they perceive as the more negative possible consequences of the GATS Agreement. On the other hand, the principle of sector-by-sector opening means that they have no guarantee of gaining access to markets for the provision of services in which they may have a comparative advantage. It is notable that neither of the service sectors opened for international competition by Northern countries during the Uruguay Round was labor intensive in character, where developing countries would enjoy such an advantage.

*The Agreement on Sanitary and Phytosanitary Measures (SPS)*   The WTO Agreement on Sanitary and Phytosanitary Measures (SPS) is ostensibly designed to prevent governments from using food, animal health, and plant safety measures as technical barriers to trade. For purposes of controlling imports, members may use only such food and plant safety measures that are based on sound science and that are backed by risk assessments. The requirement for risk assessment is waived if the measures simply restate standards laid down by three international bodies: the Codex Alimentarius for food safety, the International Office of Epizootics for animal health, and the International Plant Protection Convention for plant health.[33]

Members also have to change their own SPS frameworks to conform to the Agreement. They must establish notification points to receive information on the SPS measures of their trading partners and inquiry points to provide information about their own SPS rules. They also need to set up internal conformity mechanisms and procedures for conducting risk assessments. The costs and human resource requirements of conforming to the Agreement, in terms of its implications for domestic regulation (refining domestic standards, introducing risk assessment procedures, retraining personnel, and restructuring public agencies), are considerable. It is not clear how many developing countries—if any—have managed to fully conform to the SPS Agreement. Moreover, the relevance of such complex systems and procedures to meeting main domestic food safety concerns of developing countries is weak (M. F. Jensen 2002a). However, the main area of developing country concern in relation to sanitary and phytosanitary standards is the nature of Northern country and international standard-setting processes. Most obviously, standards (including means of assurance) generally reflect Northern country food safety concerns, if only because developing countries are poorly represented in the work of the three bodies mentioned earlier. In recent years, partly as a result of the proliferation of food safety scares in Northern countries (E. coli, mad cow disease, salmonella), there has been an escalation in these standards. At the same time, international organizations pay little or no attention to the issue of establishing simpler equivalents to the prescribed means for assuring them.

Several observers (Henson and Loader 2001; M. F. Jensen 2002b; Unnevehr 2000) observe a drift of conformity assurance practices, particularly in the European Union, from product testing to process conformity. This drift has been explicitly sanctioned in the Codex Alimentarius. Intentionally or unintentionally, process-based assurance involves a passing of the burden of monitoring costs from buyers to suppliers, with strong implications for entry barriers to supplier roles. Furthermore, it may require restructuring of production processes and supply chains. Thus, at the same time as they are faced with escalating costs of in-country regulatory conformity, developing countries are also faced with an institutionalization of more restrictive entry barriers in their export markets. As in the case of TRIPs and TRIMs, special and differentiated treatment in the context of the SPS Agreement essentially concerns longer time frames for implementation and nonbinding commitments by Northern countries to provide technical and financial assistance.

## Preferential Trade Agreements (PTAs) in the new regime

By 2002, 243 Preferential Trade Agreements (PTAs) had been notified to the WTO (Tharakan 2002), more than double the total in 1994. This number is still spiraling: more than twenty new sets of talks were underway or were proposed in the second half of 2002 alone (*Financial Times*, November 1, 2002; November 19, 2002). The WTO estimates that almost half of world trade now takes place within PTAs. For some major trading countries or groups of countries, this share is much higher. In the case of the European Union (including intra–single market trade), it rises to two-thirds. The European Union also has the largest number of such agreements, although the United States is catching up. The region where most rapid movement is taking place is Asia.[34]

There are three main reasons behind this development. The first concerns the relatively slow pace of movement in multilateral trade negotiations since 1994, in a context where some countries are seeking to push the trade liberalization agenda at a higher pace. The second concerns the political economy of trade policy in the leading trading countries and blocs, around which these webs of agreements center. In the case of the United States, Shoch (2001) argues that, while the strong dollar of the early- and mid-1980s was associated with narratives of deindustrialization and demands to curb the rising tide of imports, the late 1980s saw trade-related stress spread to formerly competitive high-technology sectors. This was a result of their failure to penetrate certain export markets, in a context of increasing dependence on economies of scale. This period also saw a new form of politicization of U.S. trade policy, with the democrats becoming an anti–free trade party. Against the background of a falling dollar and a falling trade deficit in the early 1990s, a consensus could be gathered around global market liberalization. Subsequently, this consensus could be obtained only for a more focused version of mercantilism, which in turn was easier to force through in bilateral trade agreements than multilateral ones. The underlying strength of protectionist pressures is underlined by the fact that the only U.S.-initiated PTA that seeks to embrace other major exporting countries (the Free Trade Agreement of the Americas) also seems likely to be that which involves the lowest level of mutual commitments.[35] The third reason behind the proliferation of PTAs concerns the motives of the countries with whom the leading trading nations and blocs are making agreements. As these countries see new PTAs signed in one region after another, they perceive their existing preferences to be eroded, thus creating incentives for them to conclude new deals (Nielsen 2003).

There are a multitude of types of PTA, but for purposes of this discussion they can be divided into two basic categories. The first is reciprocal PTAs and the second is nonreciprocal ones. These will be discussed in turn.

*Reciprocal PTAs of the European Union*    In addition to its own single market, the European Union has reciprocal arrangements with Mexico, South Africa, Morocco, Tunisia, and Israel and the Palestinian Authority. It has a customs union with Turkey and preferential agreements with most nonmember countries in Central and Eastern Europe. Negotiations with most of the other Mediterranean countries (except Syria) are in the process of being completed, and an E.U.-Mediterranean Free Trade Area is due to come into existence in 2010. The European Union is meanwhile negotiating PTAs with Chile, Mercosur (Argentina, Brazil, Paraguay, and Uruguay), and the Andean Pact countries (Colombia, Ecuador, Peru, and Venezuela), and it has started negotiations on a regional basis with signatories of the Cotonou Agreement (see later).

Some common features of these agreements are that they cover not only trade in goods and services but also export subsidies, capital flows, property rights, safeguard measures, dispute settlement, customs valuation, and preshipment inspection. In a number of cases, most obviously export subsidies, they go beyond WTO provisions by incorporating E.U. Competition Law standards. Second, they are consistent with the E.U. stance in the WTO of making only paper concessions in relation to agricultural trade.[36] In this respect, they circumvent WTO requirements that Free Trade Arrangements are permitted only if they cover substantially all trade, by defining *substantially* in terms of 90 percent of all trade. This allows up to 30 percent of agricultural trade to be exempted. Hence, in the case of the E.U.–South Africa Free Trade Agreement, the European Union opened up only 62 percent of its agricultural trade for duty-free South African imports (and this only by 2010–2012), plus giving tariff reductions on a further 11 percent. Its Free Trade Agreements with Mediterranean countries likewise still incorporate seasonal restrictions on entry of fresh produce and recommended price provisions. Third, they all continue to incorporate E.U. stringent rules of origin for manufactures and make provision for regional accumulation only in forms that are more restrictive than under Lomé.[37]

Because of the areas of trade that they exclude and the rules of origin that they apply, and because most partners to these agreements already enjoy some kind of preferences into the European Union, the trade creation and broader economic development effects of these Agreements in partner countries are likely to be low. McQueen (2002) describes Computable General Equilibrium (CGE) model–based simulations for a variety of the new generation of PTAs of the European Union. The GDP growth effects for developing countries, assuming full implementation, range between +0.44 percent (South Africa) and +3.3 percent (Tunisia) *over a twelve-year period.* Growth effects in the European Union itself are larger.

In 2002, the European Union launched Economic Partnership Agreement (EPA) negotiations with Africa, Caribbean, and Pacific (ACP) countries, scheduled under the Cotonou Agreement of 2000. The European Union had decided not to renew its earlier (Lomé Convention) agreements with the ACP countries, ostensibly because they contravened WTO rules on reciprocity and nondiscrimination (i.e., discrimination in the Convention against developing countries that were not ACP members). The framework for the new agreements is supposed to be regional and to include ACP LDCs as well as non-LDCs. At the same time, LDCs could theoretically benefit from the European Union's "Everything But Arms" offer (see later) even if they do not enter EPAs.[38]

At the conclusion of Phase I negotiations in 2003, very little agreement was reached on general principles. Discussion was dominated by a difference in principle concerning the objectives of EPAs. The ACP countries expressed the view that agreements should be structured with a view to promoting poverty eradication and sustainable development by incorporating resource flows from the outset. The European Union expressed the view that these objectives would follow naturally from trade liberalization and that resource flows be sequenced accordingly. A second area of divergence was over provision for additional flexibility over and above WTO rules, especially in relation to linking the phase-in of tariff reductions to reaching specific development goals. Hence Phase II negotiations commenced in November 2003 without a legally binding Phase I agreement having been reached.

*Reciprocal PTAs of the United States*    In 1994, the United States implemented the North American Free Trade Agreement (NAFTA) with Canada and Mexico. Subsequently, it has ratified Free Trade Agreements with Jordan, Chile, and Singapore. By April 2004, it had concluded negotiations on agreements with Morocco, Australia, and a group of countries in Central America (Nicaragua, Costa Rica, El Salvador, and Guatemala). It was also in the process of negotiating a Free Trade Agreement of the Americas (FTAA) embracing all Northern and Latin American countries except Cuba, an accelerated implementation of the Asia-Pacific Economic Cooperation (APEC) arrangement (involving twenty-one Pacific Rim countries) and agreements with the Southern Africa Customs Union (SACU) and Bahrain.[39]

There are striking similarities between the content (or proposed content) of these agreements and those of the European Union. However, in relation to areas like trade in services, capital flows, property rights, safeguard measures, and dispute settlement, the U.S. agreements typically go further than the E.U. ones. It is U.S. policy for provisions on investment and services to be based on the so-called negative list principle. That is, rather than volunteering sectors for market opening, as under GATS, parties are expected to table areas where this opening should not take place (and thereby provide clear arguments for the reasons). The United States also pushes for provisions on capital flows to be extended to general restrictions on capital controls and for an elimination of all conditions (not merely trade-related ones) on foreign investment.[40] U.S. agreements also typically allow for a continuation of restrictions on U.S. market entry for agricultural goods and textiles and clothing, at least in indirect forms.[41] The refusal of the United States to allow discussion of its own agricultural export subsidies within the FTAA negotiations has been a sticking point. U.S. rules of origin for clothing under NAFTA are even more restrictive than those insisted on by the European Union in its own PTAs.[42]

Little modeling of the economic effects of the U.S. agreements and proposed agreements appears to have been carried out, but ex-post data on NAFTA suggests that it has had some significantly positive effects for Mexico (when taken in conjunction with the large devaluation of the peso, with which the implementation of the agreement coincided). Mexican exports to the United States increased from $39.9 billion in 1993 to $131.4 billion in 2001. For a time, Mexico overtook China as the leading exporter of clothing to the United States, and the number of clothing workers in Mexico increased from 231,000 in 1994 to 762,000 in 1998.

There has also been a significant level of FDI- and locally based invest-ment in the textile sector in the country, to allow trade preferences to be fully taken advantage of (and to be combined with reduced lead times; Gereffi, Spener, and Bair 2002). However, employment growth in cloth-ing has been more than offset by job losses in agriculture, imports have grown at a similar rate as exports, and Mexico's trade balance with the United States has remained negative (as it was prior to NAFTA). Finally, Mexican GDP growth marginally declined in the five years following implementation, compared to the five years prior to it (Audley et al. 2003).

*Nonreciprocal PTAs*   The first and most extensive nonreciprocal PTA, the Generalized System of Preferences, is still in existence, in the form of six national schemes. These are all due to expire between 2004 and 2007 and their future is unclear. There is evidence that their value has been reduced by the rise of new preferences at multilateral as well as bilateral levels.[43] Trade under the GSP has actually fallen in nominal terms since 1995.

The European Union retains some older non-reciprocal PTAs but only on an interim basis. Its only new nonreciprocal initiative is its Everything But Arms (EBA) offer of February 2001. This applies only to LDCs, but it covers all forty-nine (not only ACP) LDCs—although ACP LDCs are expected to join the EU Economic Partnership Agreement rather than opt to become Everything But Arms beneficiaries. On the one hand, Everything But Arms unilaterally removes tariffs and quotas on all ex-ports from these countries to the European Union except weapons. This is implemented with immediate effect for all products except for sugar, bananas, and rice, where there are five- to eight-year phase-in periods. On the other hand, the offer does not change the E.U. standard rules of origin—and in some respects, it even toughens them.[44] Discussion about the likely consequences of Everything But Arms has focused mainly on its possible trade diversion effects with regard to sugar, beef, bananas, maize, and rice (Page and Hewitt 2002; Stevens and Kennan 2001). These authors conclude that the main effects are likely to concern sugar pro-ducers, where Caribbean non-LDCs are likely to lose market share in favor of ACP LDCs. They also argue that the scale of increase in LDC exports is not likely to be large.

The United States has three nonreciprocal PTAs, both dating from 2000 and both intended to last eight years. The first is the Africa Growth and Opportunity Act (AGOA). AGOA gives duty- and quota-free access to a number of exports from those sub-Saharan African countries fulfilling a series of economic policy, political, and security conditions laid down by the United States. As of spring 2004, thirty-eight African countries were designated as beneficiaries. The largest preference advantage conferred, in relation to the GSP of the United States, is for clothing (averaging 17 percent of the landed price). As in the case of its reciprocal PTAs, the standard rule of origin for clothing in AGOA is "yarn forward" (spinning as well as knitting/weaving and assembly have to be carried out in the exporting country or in another beneficiary country). However, this rule of origin was suspended until October 2004 for low-income beneficiary countries. For the time being, the applied rule of origin requires only assembly to have been carried out in the beneficiary country. Raw materials from any third country may be used. Following the recategorization of certain countries in a second version of the Act passed in 2002, this waiver applied to all beneficiaries except Mauritius and South Africa. These preferences are applied only for volumes below 7 percent of total U.S. clothing imports.[45]

The second U.S. nonreciprocal PTA, the Caribbean Basin Trade Partnership, is an offer broadly paralleling AGOA but covering the Caribbean Community and eight other Central American countries. In this case, it replaces an existing offer (the Caribbean Basin Recovery Act) and represents an improved preference in terms of rules of origin. These rules are now the same as in AGOA, but there is no waiver for lesser-developed beneficiary countries on the yarn forward provision. There are also individual country caps by volume on the preference. The third U.S. offer, the Andean Trade & Drug Eradication Act, is a more restrictive offer than AGOA and CBTA in terms of country and product coverage. It applies to only 14 percent of U.S. tariff lines by value and excludes clothing.

Initial work on AGOA, reported in more detail in Chapter 5 (see also Gibbon 2003), suggests a major surge of clothing exports by a group of anglophone countries in eastern and southern Africa, but excluding Mauritius and to a large extent South Africa. The export surge is based mainly on FDI, especially by Far Eastern enterprises. Domestically owned enterprises, which form a large majority of companies in Mauritius and South Africa, were less likely to benefit from AGOA because their business models and overhead structures were geared to very different end markets (domestic in the case of South Africa, the European Union in the case of Mauritius). This outcome is somewhat ironic, as Mauritian exporters were one of two leading lobbies that campaigned in favor of AGOA in the United States. The other lobby consisted of certain U.S. sourcing companies (notably MAST Industries) and retailers seeking to establish new, more competitive sources of supply into the U.S. market.[46] Outside of clothing, African gains under AGOA have been minimal (Brenton and Ikezuki 2004).

## Conclusion

The trade regime of the pre-WTO era recognized the structural problems faced by developing countries and provided some opportunities to mitigate them. Developing countries could opt out of multilateral agreements that were not to their advantage, could form cartels to sell commodities, and obtained some nonreciprocal preferences for their exports of manufactures. Yet, opt outs were often used to pursue unrealistic domestic policies, the commodity agreements rested on the highly fragile consent of consuming countries, and nonreciprocal preferences for manufactured goods were often undermined by restrictive rules of origin.

In principle, the new trade regime creates conditions under which better trade opportunities for developing countries could be institutionalized. Having much more of a mandatory and rule-bound character than GATT, WTO should have led to improved market access. In practice, however, gains for developing countries remained small, propelling the ill feeling that has plagued the Doha Round. Currently, the main implications of WTO for developing countries are to be found in its requirements that they open their own markets and internalize Northern country standards in respect to patent recognition, investment regulations, and food safety standards. Special and differential treatment for developing countries has been incorporated into the new system in terms of temporary exemptions to uniform agreements rather than a toleration of a distinct set of agreements and preferences. Thus, developing countries have lost much of the space for autonomous decision making that they enjoyed earlier, even if this space was often poorly used.

It is against this background that one can make sense of the apparently increasing differentiation in trade performance between African countries and the rest of the world. The new international trade regime, like public policy generally, has redefined the pursuit of equality not in terms of modest degrees of distinct treatment for the disadvantaged as prior to 1994, but rather in terms of equality of opportunity. Like other such redefinitions, the outcome is to allow for much greater play for differences in endowments, from classic factor endowments to new ones like intellectual property holdings and access to lawyers.

For African countries, in particular LDCs, there are still some opportunities in the new regime. These tend not to be found in WTO itself, but rather, arise as an outcome of intensified competition between major trading blocs in their elaboration of bilateral agreements and offers. In this process, the generic preferences of the General System of Preference have been steadily eroded. But some of the new offers (notably AGOA) do incorporate significant improvements in preferences for a few products that African LDCs should have a comparative advantage in. The drawback of these new opportunities is that they are unilateral, time limited, and hedged by conditions. As the WTO process stalls and intra–trading bloc competition increases, the hope is that there will be more such concessions in more permanent forms.

In the next chapters, we explore both opportunities and difficulties that participation in GVCs offers to African countries, farms, and firms in the context of the new international trade regime. In doing so, we seek to integrate the discussion of governance of the global economy that we have presented so far in two separate "boxes": one for public forms of governance, as in domestic regulation and international trade agreements; and one for private forms of governance in relation to corporate strategies, firm organization and interfirm relations.

# 3    Global Value Chain (GVC) Analysis

## Main Features

THE APPROACH known as global value chain (GVC) analysis first appeared in the literature under the term global commodity chain (GCC) analysis. The notion of a commodity chain, "a network of labor and production processes whose end result is a finished commodity" comes from Hopkins and Wallerstein (1986, 1994), where it is used to discuss a variety of international chains for agricultural (and timber) products, from the beginning of the early modern era. Hopkins and Wallerstein (1994) see all firms (and specific processes, referred to as boxes) as being involved in commodity chains as either producers of inputs to others or users of inputs from others. These basic structures are said to persist through historical cycles of economic expansion and contraction. During periods of expansion, the more profitable boxes of a given chain are subject to less concentration (demonopolization). During periods of contraction, fiercer competition weeds out the weaker firms, and these boxes are subject to higher degrees of concentration (monopolization). Both phases are characterized by technological change and/or redefinition of the organizational boundaries of boxes. During expansionary phases, chains are typically extended and become more vertically integrated. During phases of contraction, chains tend to become vertically disintegrated into layers of contractual relations to reduce labor and transaction costs. Hopkins and Wallerstein (1994) argue that these changes, rather than being interpreted as novel (as in the literature on post-Fordism), are part of a cyclical pattern that has repeated itself several times in the past few hundred years.

If Hopkins and Wallerstein introduced the notion of commodity chains, the beginning of *global* commodity chain analysis as a relatively coherent paradigm can be traced to a collection edited by Gereffi and Korzeniewicz (1994). Although the book starts with a brief version of Hopkins and Wallerstein's argument (1994), Gereffi and most of his collaborators are concerned specifically with industrial commodity chains. They largely ignore the long-term historical/cyclical context and focus on the emergence of a new global manufacturing system in which economic integration goes beyond international trade in raw materials and final products to encompass centrally coordinated but internationally dispersed production of many of the activities along the chains of given commodities or manufactured products. Thus, the internationalization of manufacturing chains is seen to be related to an externalization of functions that were previously carried out "within the organizational boundaries of vertically integrated corporations" (Gereffi, Korzeniewicz, and Korzeniewicz 1994, 7).

As highlighted in Raikes, Jensen, and Ponte (2000), global commodity chain analysis is also related to the French empirical tradition of *filière* (chain) studies, which has its origin in technocratic agricultural research and sees the filière as a neutral and purely empirical category. These studies are mainly restricted to agriculture in developing countries and were heavily influenced by the needs of the colonial and postcolonial French state, because state (agricultural) development policy in former French colonies was commodity centered and required a matching analytical framework. Thus filière analysis is applied overwhelmingly to agricultural commodities and without any specific time frame. Although GCC analysts attempt to work under a unified theoretical framework, no such effort is made in filière analysis, which includes several different schools of thought or research traditions, each adhering to its own theoretical underpinnings and posing its own research questions. Therefore, whereas the global commodity chain approach is centered on contributions from a distinct school of thought, the French filière approach is a loosely knit set of studies with the common characteristic that they use the filière (or chain) of activities and exchanges as a tool and to delimit the scope of their analysis.[1]

The global commodity chain approach started to attract wide attention in the mid-1990s. At that time, most case studies concerned manufacturing. Gereffi himself mainly applied the GCC framework to analyzing exports of clothing from East Asian countries (more recently from Mexico and the Caribbean) to the United States. Other GCC and related studies analyzed tourism (Clancy 1998), services (Rabach and Kim 1994), footwear (Schmitz 1999), electronics and other commodities imported by Japan from Mexico (Kenney and Florida 1994), and automobiles and auto components (Barnes and Kaplinsky 1999).

In its original formulation, Gereffi identified three key dimensions of commodity chains: their input-output structure and geographical coverage, their form of governance, and their institutional framework (Gereffi 1994, 1995).

1. The term *input-output structure* and the geographical coverage of commodity chains were used mainly descriptively to outline chain configuration.

2. The term *form of governance* introduced the key notions of entry barriers and chain coordination. The GCC literature originally distinguished broadly between "producer-driven" and "buyer-driven" types of governance. Producer-driven chains were said to be found usually in sectors with high technological and capital requirements, where capital and proprietary know-how constitute the main entry barriers to lead firm status. In these chains, producers tend to keep control of capital-intensive operations and subcontract more labor-intensive functions, often in the form of vertically integrated networks. Buyer-driven chains were said to be found in generally more labor-intensive sectors, where market information, product design, and marketing/advertising costs set the entry barriers for would-be lead firms. In these chains, production functions are usually outsourced and key actors concentrate on branding, design, and marketing functions.

3. The institutional framework surrounding the chain was meant to delineate the conditions under which lead firms subordinate agents through their control of market access and information, both technological and regarding markets. Under the rubric of institutional framework, Gereffi also discussed how subordinate participation in a global commodity chain could provide indirect access to markets at lower costs than individual small-scale producers would otherwise face, and how technological information and "learning by doing" allow (the more favored) producers to move up the chain hierarchy (also known as upgrading). This suggested that participation in a global commodity chain is a necessary, but not sufficient, condition for subordinate agents to upgrade. Participation also involves acceptance of terms defined by key agents or institutions, especially for those aiming to progress toward higher (technology, value-added) positions in the chain (see Gereffi 1999).

In recent years, the global commodity chain literature has abandoned the term *commodity chain* and has taken up that of *value chain* in its place. The latter is thought to better capture a wider variety of products, some of which lack commodity features. As a result, the global commodity chain approach is now known as global value chain (GVC) analysis. The concept of value chain has been known in the literatures on industrial organization, business studies, and management for a while. Porter's (1985, 1990) concept of value chain emphasizes the interconnected and sequential nature of economic activity in which each link adds value in the process. His notion of a value chain, however, is designed primarily as a heuristic tool to allow individual firms or countries to understand which in-house and external steps their activities depend on and how they can improve their competitiveness by capturing more effectively those steps associated with the greatest generation of value added.[2] By contrast, the political economy use of value chain takes its point of departure not in the activities surrounding a specific firm or country, but in the full range of activities, *including coordination,* that are required to bring a specific product from its conception to its end use and beyond. This includes activities such as design, production, marketing, distribution, support to the final consumer, and governance of this entire process. The concept of *global* value chain refers to configuration of coordinated activities that are divided among firms and that have a global geographical scale.

The use of the term *chain* suggests a focus on vertical relationships between buyers and suppliers and the movement of a good or service from producer to consumer. This entails an analysis centered on flows of material resources, finance, knowledge, and information between buyers and suppliers. Processes of coordination and competition among actors operating in the same function or segment of a particular market are given less attention in GVC analysis. Furthermore, along with the production network and commodity system/networks literatures (Dicken 2003; Ernst 2000; Friedland 1984, 2001; Henderson et al. 2002; Hughes 2000; 2001; Raynolds 2002, 2004; Smith et al. 2002), GVC analysis focuses on more explicit structural elements of production, distribution, and consumption than on the social/cultural/symbolic relations among actors (Appadurai 1986; DuPuis 2000; Granovetter 1985; Marsden, Banks, and Bristow 2000; Marsden et al. 1996; Murdoch 1995; Murdoch, Marsden, and Banks 2000). Until recently, GVC also stopped its analysis normally at the retail level, thus was largely silent on issues of consumption and after-use disposal/recycling (on consumption, see Fine

2002; Goodman 2002; Marsden, Flynn, and Harrison 2000). It has also been criticized for not paying enough attention to labor relations at the site of production. But the latest generation of GVC contributions have started to weave into their analyses both material and symbolic aspects of exchange, to tackle issues of social embeddedness, to cover horizontal aspects such as gender and labor relations, and to extend their reach by analyzing consumption as one of the key dimensions of governance (see Barrientos, Dolan, and Tallontire 2003; Daviron and Ponte forthcoming; Leslie and Reimer 1999, 2003; Rammohan and Sundaresan 2003).[3]

## GOVERNANCE

At the nexus of GVC analysis lies the contractual linkage of formally independent firms, whether as the result of the outsourcing of previously integrated functions carried out by multinational corporations or through the contractual subordination of suppliers previously linked through open market transactions. While one of the attractions for Northern firms of outsourcing to developing countries is seen as cheap labor, a more important one is seen as organizational flexibility for lead firms. Thus, GVCs do not depend on incorporating cheap labor for their existence. Gereffi, Korzeniewicz, and Korzeniewicz (1994) follow Porter (1987) in finding cheap labor a lower-order (dead-end) factor in competitiveness for the subordinate firm, compared with higher-order factors like "proprietary technology, product differentiation, brand reputation, customer relations and constant industrial upgrading" (Gereffi, Korzeniewicz, and Korzeniewicz 1994, 6). From this angle, GVCs also constitute an organizational basis for developing country firms' participation in international trade. It is also a starting point for developing country firms to attempt improving their position within GVCs (in other words, to upgrade). Therefore, GVC membership can be seen as providing access to social capital and thus valuable competitive assets in the global economy. However, given that such advantages are contingent on belonging to a value chain (and acceptance of the strict terms imposed for this), they can also be seen as a means to exclude actors unwilling to accept the conditions and the increased costs that tend to accompany them, at least in the short run. This further underlines the power of key agents and their capacity to incorporate less powerful actors to perform unwanted value-added activities, or alternatively to exclude them.

In his original formulation, Gereffi (1994, 7) linked governance to issues of authority and power relationships within GVCs and distinguished between two types of GVCs on the basis of the nature of their lead firms, which was in turn elaborated in terms of the "location of their key barriers to entry" (ibid.). In producer-driven chains—for example, the automobile and aircraft industries—barriers to lead firm entry are located in large-scale, high-technology production facilities involving heavy investment and scale economies, and manufacturers are the lead agents. Most producer-driven chains are characterized by production to order (often order by the state, the military). Where they are not based on production to order, because of the "lumpy" investments that they require, they are dependent on publicly managed demand. Thus, suppliers are often tied together rather than internally competing. They also tend to be located close to the sites of end production. Therefore, the geographic division of labor is less pronounced than in buyer-driven chains.

*Buyer-driven chains* in Gereffi's formulation (ibid.) differ from producer-driven chains in that they have low barriers to entry in production. Instead, producers are subordinated to lead agents controlling design and marketing, specifically those controlling international brand names and retailing, where barriers to entry are high and profits concentrated. In this context, production becomes a low-profit and noncore function that is externalized to a competitive and decentralized system of subcontractors. The majority of these are typically located in developing countries and are often ranged in a multistage but also multiquality array with the lowest technology, quality, and value added located in the countries with the lowest wages. New brand-name "producers without factories" are organized entirely on this basis. Such buyer-driven structures are typical in clothing, footwear, toys, and fresh fruit and vegetables.

The initial stimulus for further discussions on governance issues in GVCs beyond the buyer-driven and producer-driven typology came from work by Sturgeon (2001, 2002) on the electronics industry. As seen previously, in the early GVC literature, outsourcing of manufacturing functions was typically interpreted as an instance of externalization of low-profit and noncore functions upstream that is peculiar to buyer-driven chains—although increasingly relevant in some producer-driven chains as well. Sturgeon questioned this interpretation. He argued that the functions externalized by brand-name firms to global contract manufacturers are not necessarily low profit and that they do not entail a captive position of suppliers. As explained in Chapter 1, global contract manufacturers have become prominent in electronic products, and they are also emerging in the auto parts industry, food processing, and pharmaceuticals. In the agricultural sector, they are an important part of the cocoa/chocolate complex, where branded chocolate manufacturers are increasingly outsourcing the supply of cocoa intermediate products (see Fold 2001). What should be noted here, though, is that in both the cases of the electronics industry and cocoa, the functions that were outsourced by lead firms were low profit at the time this happened. They became more profitable as a result of subsequent technological changes that created opportunities for scale economies.[4]

A related observation about the producer-driven versus buyer-driven dichotomy that was raised in the late 1990s was that some value chains exhibit the tendency to move from one category to the other. In some producer-driven chains such as automobile, computer, and consumer electronics, producers are increasingly outsourcing portions of component manufacture; sometimes they even outsource supply-chain logistics and final assembly, while keeping control of promotion and marketing of the brand names on which market access is based—a trait of buyer-driven chains. This may be linked to the fact that the state is withdrawing from demand management functions, and thus lead firms in producer-driven chains are becoming more focused on it. Furthermore, Gereffi himself (2001a, 2001b) conceded that the dichotomy does not adequately explain some of the characteristics of service chains and some of the changing features of chain governance that relate to e-commerce operations. This has led Gereffi at one point to explore the possibility that another category of governance is emerging, the infomediary-driven chain.[5]

Finally, it has been observed that the category of buyer covers a variety of types of lead firms who may drive chains in different ways. Buyers include retailers, branded marketers, industrial processors, and international traders. Levels of drivenness tend to be higher in chains led by retailers, branded marketers, and industrial processors (clothing, footwear, bananas, other fresh fruit and vegetables, coffee, cocoa) than in those led by international traders (cotton, fish, cashew nuts; see Fold 2001, 2002; Gibbon 2001a; Ponte 2002b).

Such debates have led to efforts to refine definitions of governance in GVCs in terms of how certain firms set, measure, and enforce the parameters under which others in the chain operate (Humphrey and Schmitz 2002a). In other words, governance is now seen by some GVC analysts as the process of exercising control along the chain through the specification of what type of product needs to be supplied, in what quantity and when, how it should be produced, and at what price (ibid, 6–7). When a group of firms in a particular functional position (or positions) in a value chain is able to shape who does what (and at what price, on the basis of which standards, to which specifications, and on the basis of which delivery schedules) along the chain, they are said to be in a "lead firm" position. This approach focuses on "inter-firm relationships and institutional mechanisms through which non-market coordination of activities in the chain is achieved" (ibid.).

On this basis, Gereffi, Humphrey, and Sturgeon (2004) have gone on to formulate an analytic framework that yields governance classifications that go beyond (and seem to replace) the original distinction between buyer-driven and producer-driven chains. They develop a matrix with three independent variables that can each take two values (high and low). These variables are the following: (1) the complexity of the information and knowledge required to sustain a particular transaction, (2) the ability to codify and transmit efficiently this information between the parties, and (3) the capabilities of the supply base in relation to the requirements of the transaction (ibid., 6). The matrix yields eight combinations, three of which are ruled out in practice as inherently improbable. This leaves five possible categories of governance (ibid., 5):

1. Market: spot or repeated market-type interfirm links characterized by low informational complexity, ease of codification of information, and high supplier capabilities; both parties' costs of switching to new partners are low.
2. Modular: interfirm links involving somewhat more specialized suppliers who finance part of production on the part of the customer, but whose technology is sufficiently generic to allow its use by a broad customer base; characterized by high informational complexity, ease of codification, and high supplier capabilities.
3. Relational: interfirm links involving multiple interdependencies, often underwritten by close social ties; characterized by high informational complexity, low ability to codify information, and high supplier capabilities.

4. Captive: interfirm linkages involving one-way dependency of suppliers, high levels of supplier monitoring, and high costs of switching for suppliers; characterized by high informational complexity and ease of codification, but low supplier capabilities.
5. Hierarchy: classic vertical integration; characterized by high informational complexity, difficulty of codification, and low capabilities among independent suppliers.

According to Gereffi, Humphrey, and Sturgeon (ibid., 6–7), *market* relations are dominant when transactions are easily codified, product specifications are simple, and suppliers have the capability to produce without much input from buyers. *Modular* value chains arise when the ability to codify specifications extends to complex products and when suppliers have the capacity of using generic manufacturing competences to supply full packages and modules, lowering the need for buyers to monitor and control design and production processes. *Relational* value chains arise when product specifications cannot be easily codified, products are complex, and supplier capabilities are high; this leads to the exchange of knowledge between buyers and suppliers within the framework of a certain degree of mutual dependence that may be regulated through reputation, social ties, and/or proximity. *Captive* value chains arise when there is ability to codify complex product specifications, but the capability of suppliers is low; this leads to a higher degree of monitoring and intervention by the buyer and to a transactional dependence of the supplier. Finally, *hierarchy* appears when product specifications cannot be codified, products are complex, and competent suppliers are not available; as a result, the buyer has to develop design and production skills in-house. In this framework, as value chains move from market to hierarchy, the level of explicit coordination increases—and with it the power asymmetry among actors (ibid., 8).

Although this framework captures some important elements that influence the *forms of coordination* between actors in different functional positions in a GVC, it has only limited explanatory power to determine the overall form of governance. GVCs may be characterized by different forms of coordination in different segments of the same chain. In the coffee value chain, for example, market relations characterize the link between retailers and roasters, modular relations the link between roasters and international traders, and hierarchy (vertical integration) is often observed at the interface of the international trader–exporter functions. In producer countries themselves, the coffee trade is organized on the basis of a mixture of hierarchical, market, and relational links. Yet, the overall value chain is clearly buyer driven, and coffee roasters play the lead role in determining the functional division of labor along the chain (see Ponte 2002b). In other words, roasters define the key terms of participation directly for their immediate suppliers and indirectly for other actors further upstream.

Moving beyond issues of classification of governance types, it is important to note that one of the main features characterizing governance in buyer-driven GVCs today is enforcement of specifications and allocation of functions along the chain on a more indirect basis than hitherto. Increasingly, lead firms are devising forms of "hands-off" governance that are exercised on the basis of setting of precise standards, modularization of production specifications, and/or codification of suppliers' knowledge requirements. These specifications are then left to first-tier suppliers to implement further upstream. As we will see in Chapter 6, this often results in paradoxically tighter forms of coordination emerging between first-tier and second-tier suppliers and beyond. In this way, lead firms may govern GVC without directly controlling it in its entirety (or even in large segments).

The analytic framework proposed by Gereffi, Humphrey, and Sturgeon (2004) has the advantage of highlighting issues related to the complexity of transactional information and the importance of their codification for the existence of hands-off relationships. What it does not achieve, though, is a clear distinction between immediate forms of coordination and overall forms of governance. By focusing on make or buy decision-making processes, and thus a transaction cost or microlevel approach to power, the framework misses the larger picture. It also portrays governance in terms of a dehistoricized vocabulary of logical possibilities, whereas buyer drivenness and producer drivenness are also illuminating historical categories. As argued by Palpacuer (2000), there is a need to differentiate between coordination mechanisms and power relations in the analysis of chain governance. A narrow approach to governance focuses on the agglomeration of individual interfirm relationships at various points in a chain. A broader approach (as originally intended by Gereffi) examines relations of power as manifested in issues of drivenness, asymmetrical ability to take make or buy decisions and consequent asymmetrical flexibility to shift between partners (see Chapters 4 and 5). In this perspective, governance is what links the functional division of labor along a chain to a specific allocation of resources and distribution of gains (Kaplinsky 2000).

One of the strongest qualities of the GVC approach in its earlier formulations (as GCC) was indeed precisely its inclusion of power in economic relations and transactions and a willingness to recognize aspects of power excluded from other analyses of international production and trading relations. Besides capturing the link between increased entry barriers to lead firm positions and increased externalization of low-profit functions (outsourcing), Gereffi's (1994) original treatment of power drew attention to other important changes in the organization of value chains that have taken place since the mid-1960s. These range from the movement away from vertical integration and large Fordist firms to the adoption of various mechanisms, such as downsizing, just-in-time, and more comprehensive contractual structures, by which multinational corporations cut labor costs and the cost and risk of investment, while maintaining or even increasing their control over subordinated labor processes.

On the one hand, one of the problematic aspects of using the concept of power is that, once introduced into an analysis and however well and clearly defined, it has a tendency to be seen by critics in all-or-nothing terms. In fact, however, the distinction between buyer-driven and producer-driven chains does not prevent GVC analysts from registering that different degrees of power do exist. This applies not only to different types of buyer (e.g., large-scale retailer vs. international trader), or to different concrete cases in the same type of buyer (e.g., Wal-Mart vs. KMart), but also to different categories of supplier. For example, there exist a hierarchy of firms under contract, producing different types and qualities of clothing for different markets and occupying different positions in the supply chains for them. Gereffi's concentric ring diagram (1994, 111) shows that suppliers to élite high-profit markets are concentrated in the North and in the larger or more advanced developing countries, whereas the more discount the final market, the lower the wage and level of advancedness of the producing country. Moreover, within each market there are preferred suppliers with more stable contracts, and others, less preferred, that produce for lower prices and/or less certain market access (often as subcontractors to preferred suppliers). Further elaboration of the specifics of such hierarchies will be carried out in the following chapters.

A second problem with the Gereffi, Sturgeon, and Humphrey (2004) framework is that, in seeking to devise a formal model with some degree of predictive power, it retains the blindness of external regulative conditions that represented a central weakness of the original global commodity chain approach (see earlier discussion of this in Raikes, Jensen, and Ponte 2000). Lead firms do not operate in an institutional and regulatory vacuum. The areas where the analysis of governance in GVCs requires strengthening most are not only acknowledgement of coordinative pluralism within broader frameworks of drivenness, but also of the broader institutional frameworks in which lead firms operate. In GVCs where public regulation and trade policy instruments are important, the reshaping of institutional frameworks may occur through lobbying public agencies or influencing negotiation processes (for example, in relation to tariff modifications and quota allocations). Where product definition, quality standards, and what is considered to be "fit for trade" are key concerns, lead firms may concentrate efforts on promulgating the adoption of standards that they already use (or have devised). This may happen both in the form of embedding standards in regulation and in the promotion of voluntary standards that are likely to become *de facto* mandatory—at least for those firms willing to operate at the global level or even just to participate in a specific value chain.

Thus, governance in GVCs involves more than how firms decide whether to make or buy something (a classic preoccupation in the industrial organization literature), and more than how they relate with their immediate suppliers and buyers. For example, the governance of the global clothing industry is also related to the Multifibre Arrangement, AGOA, and NAFTA rules (see Gibbon 2003). At the same time, governance is not just an effect of changing trade agreements and public regulation either, as trade analysts would have it. Hence, trade liberalization does not necessarily lead to fully open markets or perfect competition. Decisions made by lead firms exclude some categories of actors even if there is no trade barrier involved. So far, these two spheres of governance of international exchange of goods and services have been kept relatively separate. This book attempts to describe their interlinkages in a number of sectors characterized by a combination of buyer drivenness and high levels of public regulation.

The external regulation of GVCs has an additional critical dimension. This is public only in an informal sense and is institutionalized not in a set of rules agreed by governments but rather in a set of habits of thinking and acting internalized by individuals. The goods and services traded within GVCs embody value in two senses: first, in the sense that they are the outcomes of specific production processes whereby value is added, and second, in the sense that they are commonly agreed to conform to a given criterion of quality. As noted earlier, lead firm involvement in the arbitration of standards that reflect and refine broad social norms concerning quality has become an important element of GVC governance. But although these standards may be shaped by lead firms, the broad social norms that stand behind them are, like trade rules, to some extent removed from their influence.

To understand and incorporate this dimension of external regulation, and to develop an account of the cognitive and normative dimensions of GVC governance we use some of the tools that were developed in the convention theory literature. Convention theory suggests that all action is justified in relation to common sets of principles that coalesce in historically based "worlds of legitimate common welfare" (Boltanski and Thévenot 1991; see details in Chapter 6). Each of these worlds is organized around different types of qualification (both for people and objects) and forms of justification and challenge. In relation to economic activity, this means that, over time, different markets come to embody a succession of different criteria under which goods become qualified for trade, and in relation to which trade is subsequently managed.

Convention theory suggests that different forms of coordination and of enterprise emerge in relation to which quality conventions regulate specific markets, sectors, or value chains. When different criteria (or standards) come to characterize the process of qualification of products for trade, a change in the dominant form (or combination of forms) of co-ordination is likely to occur. Convention theory provides an innovative way of looking at issues of coordination of activities and mechanisms of enforcing governance through its cognitive and normative preoccu-pations. These can be used to understand why value chains are more or less coherent or articulated (and articulated in different ways) and how lead firms achieve and maintain their dominant position not only through economic means, but also through legitimation and justification processes. If GVC governance is the subject of a dynamic based on inter-linkages between trade rules and quality conventions on the one hand, and processes internal to value chains on the other, then recasting the analysis of GVC governance to reflect this represents a major challenge.

A first step in this direction is to distinguish between immediate forms of coordination and the overall form of governance. When overall forms of governance are examined, the producer-driven and, especially, buyer-driven chain categories remain valuable, both for describing historical processes and as a typological device. Obviously, one descriptor can-not capture the complexity of real-world value chains. However, in the same vein, one would not discard the concept of capitalism just because socialism is dead. Rather, one attempts a fine-tuning of the concept by adding underlying components to its description and makes predictions about the future based on historical dynamics, in line with the tradition of historical political economy.

It would be tempting to argue, against this background, that trade rules and quality conventions can be seen as bearing specifically on immediate forms of coordination, whereas endogenous and chain-specific economic developments bear on issues of long-term chain leadership. However, no such neat correspondence between internal and external factors on the one hand, and between forms of coordination and chain driving on the other, emerge from our empirical material. As will be seen in Chapter 4, several examples exist of situations where changes in trade rules have directly influenced whether producers or buyers drive a given chain. The two sets of distinctions, for the time being at least, must be considered analytically unrelated.

In Chapter 6, we will develop this approach in terms of linking (quality) standards to buyer-driven governance in two ways: on the one hand, more demanding standards may force lead firms to help and directly support their network of suppliers in the process of obtaining compliance, thus increasing the need for a hands-on approach to interfirm relationships; on the other hand, lead firms may be able to achieve a more hands-off approach if and when they can codify these standards so that they can be monitored (and certified) externally—and these auditing/certification procedures are (eventually) considered legitimate or widely recognized by other actors.

Firms that are able to codify information and fine-tune the measurement and specification of standards in ways that can be verified externally will then be able to externalize the function of matching standards in the same way they externalize other functions that are not considered core. As we will see in Chapter 6, the process of formation and application of standards not only links to the issue of immediate forms of coordination, but also touches on the possibility of a specific group of buyers to achieve and maintain leadership status over others and over a value chain as a whole.

## UPGRADING

The concept of upgrading in the GVC literature has been used, in broad terms, to highlight the possibility for (developing country) producers to move up the value chain, either by shifting to more rewarding functional positions or by making products that have more value added invested in them and that can provide better returns to producers. The appearance of this concept can be historically linked to the rise, in the early 1980s, of a new paradigm in political economy and industrial economics. Theoretically, this paradigm was based on the notion that capitalist economic systems were in the process of shifting from a "Fordist" to a "post-Fordist" basis. Fordism designated a system of mass production of undifferentiated commodity-type products for mass consumption. It was associated with large-scale and technologically relatively inflexible factories, with firms with high degrees of functional specialization, and with large concentrations of semiskilled labor. By contrast, post-Fordism designated a system of batch production of differentiated higher-value products for niche markets, smaller but more technologically versatile factories, and firms with competence in design and marketing (including branding in some cases) and with more highly skilled and more multiskilled labor. Correspondingly, firm-level upgrading was held to involve a transition from forms of enterprise organization of a Fordist type (assembly or own equipment manufacture, OEM) to ones of a post-Fordist type (own design manufacture, ODM; and own brand manufacture, OBM; Gereffi 1999).

A secondary element of the new paradigm involved a narrative concerning how upgrading comes about. Under Fordism, upgrading is said to have occurred on the basis of accretions of physical capital and technological innovation, leading to greater economies of scale as well as improvements in products and/or in manufacturing processes – often as a result of state intervention.[6] Under post-Fordism, upgrading is said to be occurring mainly on the basis of attaining higher levels of flexibility and adding new human skills/capacities, particularly design and marketing ones, often through interfirm networking and related organizational learning. Finally, the new paradigm presents post-Fordism and its associated upgrading model as an industrial high road of technological flexibility, high-value production, new levels of service provision (including branding), and enriched employee work experience. Fordism in contrast is identified as a low road of technological rigidity, commodity production, minimal service provision, and worker deskilling. This paradigm has been subsequently applied, directly or indirectly, in various literatures, from industrial districts and cluster studies, to work on innovation systems (Lundvall 1992), to the value chain approach of Porter (1990).

In the GVC literature, the upgrading process is examined through the lenses of how knowledge and information flow within value chains from lead firms to their suppliers or buyers (Gereffi 1999). Upgrading is then about acquiring capabilities and accessing new market segments through participating in particular chains (Humphrey 2003a). The argument is that upgrading in various forms can be effectively stimulated through learning from lead firms rather than through interactions between firms in the same functional position (horizontal transfer in clusters) or within the frameworks of common business systems or national systems of innovation. Some of the literature has distinguished types of upgrading and linked them to specific forms of chain governance. Humphrey and Schmitz (2002a), for example, have developed a typology of upgrading based on four categories:

1. *process* upgrading: achieving a more efficient transformation of inputs into outputs through the reorganization of productive activities;
2. *product* upgrading: moving into more sophisticated products with increased unit value;
3. *functional* upgrading: acquiring new functions (or abandoning old ones) that increase the skill content of activities;
4. *intersectoral* upgrading: applying competences acquired in one function of a chain and using them in a different sector/chain.

Although helpful as a starting point, there are difficulties with this classification. For example, it is sometimes difficult to distinguish product and process upgrading in the case of agricultural products (for example, the introduction of organic processes generates a new category of product). Also, the status of interchain upgrading is unclear, as it relates to a trajectory of upgrading rather than describing what aspect of a given business is being upgraded.

A further problem is that, although all four upgrading types are accorded a formally equivalent status, overwhelming attention in practice is paid to functional upgrading. In an early contribution to the discussion of upgrading in GVCs, Gereffi (1999) focused almost exclusively on functional upgrading in the clothing sector, where firms can turn onto a high road toward own-brand manufacturing. This implied the normative suggestion that such a change was more optimal than other possible upgrading options. However, as Gibbon (forthcoming) points out, although product differentiation and own-brand manufacturing do correspond to greater firm-level internalization of higher-value functions, they may also embody competency traps represented by design and branding in highly product-specific forms that cannot be generalized. This is particularly likely where distance to major end markets is great. At least for new or subordinate players such as suppliers in developing countries, there are equally or more profitable positions available within value chains and other available forms of upgrading.

Sturgeon (2002), for example, suggested that in the computer sector there are both easier conditions of entry (lower risk) and, sometimes, higher levels of profits to be found in the role of contract manufacture than in that of branding/marketing. By defining themselves as specialized manufacturers, and on this basis improving product quality and rationalizing their own sourcing, contract manufacturers can develop a highly profitable core competence that can be used across a diversified customer base within its subsector of origin and also extended across subsectors. Manufacturers of one kind of electronic equipment, for example, have developed competencies that can be used to manufacture related ones (see also Chapter 1).

Although functional upgrading continues to be regarded by GVC analysts as the optimal form of upgrading that developing country farms and firms can achieve, more attention has been paid recently to the practical difficulties lying in its path. Schmitz and Knorriga (1999) made the point quite early in the GVC upgrading discussion that lead firms in GVCs other than clothing often sought explicitly to block their suppliers from undertaking functional upgrading. At the same time, lead firms encouraged suppliers to undertake process and usually also product upgrading. Later, this argument came to form part of a more general theory seeking to link possibilities of upgrading to variations in the way that GVCs are governed (Humphrey and Schmitz 2003). In this theory, for example, upgrading in chains whose governance type falls into the captive category can take place only on the basis of suppliers breaking away from these chains— by using the knowledge they acquired in supplying lead firms to supply other (usually smaller) markets and/or participate in separate chains (intersectoral upgrading).

Another break-away path to upgrading noted in Humphrey and Schmitz (ibid.) is represented by a movement by suppliers from captive to modular value chains, although it is less clear what the determinants of this transition are. According to these authors, relational value chains seem to support a more open-ended path to upgrading, but they are unlikely to be present in developing countries (especially LDCs) due to the intense knowledge-based interactions they require. In chains characterized by market relations, developing country producers do not receive support for, but neither are they cut off from, upgrading (see also Humphrey and Schmitz 2002a).[7]

It is not clear how much this chain governance–based theory adds to an understanding of upgrading. The conclusions drawn go little further than repeating the reasons that we have provided elsewhere for why lead firms adopt one kind of governance form rather than another. For example, lead firms adopt hierarchical governance forms when they need to create from scratch a supplier base with specific competences. This argument is then implicitly restated in the proposition that such forms offer suppliers possibilities for rapid product and process upgrading.

Another way forward in unpacking the relations between governance and upgrading in GVCs may be through detailed empirical analyses (on a chain-by-chain basis) that identify concrete roles that offer suppliers higher and more stable returns, as well as the routes that they typically use for arriving at them. One example of such an approach is found in Gibbon's (forthcoming) study of restructuring in the Mauritian clothing sector in the second half of the 1990s. An aim of this study was to test the broader applicability of Gereffi's account of upgrading forms and paths in clothing, beyond their original but narrow Hong Kong–based point of reference. The study identified two distinct strategies followed by Mauritian-owned firms to remain competitive in a context of rising local labor costs and falling margins. The main features of the first strategy closely resembled Gereffi's Hong Kong story—companies upgraded functionally into own-design (own collections) and in some cases own-brand manufacturing. The main feature of the second was to concentrate on manufacture alone while opening satellite plants in neighboring (and much lower cost) Madagascar. Firms' objectives here were to produce a more basic range of products in very high volumes while retaining capacity in Mauritius for shorter lead time and higher-value work.

Interviews with company directors and analysis of (publicly deposited) company accounts revealed that, in Mauritius at least, Gereffi's Hong Kong route was both costly and unsuccessful. Mauritian companies were simply too far from end markets to set, or even closely follow, fashion trends. They were also too narrow in their range of managerial skills to wholesale or retail on their own account. Companies migrating to Madagascar also faced new costs, but until the involuntary contraction of production coinciding with the serious civil disorder of 2002, many appeared to have succeeded both in raising their margins and consolidating their customer base. In the normative terms of the existing GVC vocabulary, this was on the basis of *downgrading* rather than upgrading part of their product range and part of their production process (as well as the skill base of part of their workforces). Such a route nonetheless enabled the enterprises concerned to offer a broader mix of products with a wider range of price points and lead times to a wider range of customers, including some who, on this basis, offered them better contractual conditions (i.e., greater stability of demand) than they had enjoyed previously. With some justification this was even presented by the companies themselves as a type of functional upgrading, in the sense that it enabled them to offer customers an improved service.

Migration to Madagascar was initiated primarily for cost reasons, not only in terms of access to lower-waged workers, but also to the longer production runs associated with more basic products, and thereby to greater economies of scale. Fortunately for the companies concerned, it did not entail losing the advantages of cheaper costs by having to shift entirely into an unambiguously lower end-market segment. This was because its adoption occurred in a context where some of the E.U. high-street chains and French mail order companies that were the two main customer bases of the Mauritian industry had started to establish new, lower price range formats *alongside* their traditional midmarket ones to cope with a rising wave of competition from discount stores.[8]

This example, like Sturgeon's (2002), shows the importance of detailed study of the dynamics of specific value chains for understanding real-world patterns of upgrading. In the particular case described, this implies understanding changing patterns of Northern consumption, corporate restructuring, and corporate strategy—patterns that are captured at best only imperfectly by the notion of post-Fordism. Understanding the nature of the clothing chain, including its governance structure(s), is also necessary, but by no means sufficient. Moreover, Gereffi's initial characterization of this governance structure as buyer driven is actually much better at drawing attention to its operational outcomes (use of market power to demand from suppliers new services and ever-lower real unit prices) than are categories such as modular, relational, or captive.

For the theorization of upgrading within a GVC framework, this points in the direction of giving greater recognition to the importance of achieving greater economies of scale as a means of securing a stable and profitable supplier position in buyer-driven contexts. Analysis along these lines is the theoretical direction that the concept buyer driven-ness logically points toward. Such an analysis, when completed, should generate a new vocabulary of upgrading terms. Until it does, rather than using terms such as *process, product,* and *functional,* it may be better to identify structures of rewards available to suppliers within specific chains on the one hand, and concrete roles releasing these rewards on the other (see Chapter 5).

## CONCLUSION

The GVC approach provides a view of international trade that differs radically from that found in economic trade theory. These differences concern both the focus of analysis and the understanding of the mechanisms of trade. Neoclassical economic trade theory considers trade alone, in isolation from investment, finance, or other relations between parties to trade. It also assumes that both participants and transactions are separate and independent from each other. These constraining assumptions generate trade patterns that are determined by each country's endowments of production factors (see Raikes, Jensen, and Ponte 2000). Exceptions can be found in relatively recent contributions within economic trade theory that acknowledge imperfect competition and that can handle increasing returns to scale, learning by doing, and information asymmetries. However, most of these still have relatively little to say about the organization of trade and markets, especially in relation to issues of industrial organization. In contrast, the GVC approach discusses questions about what products countries import and export and what rewards accrue to whom. The prime concern of GVC analysis is with how lead firms go about setting up and maintaining production and trade networks. Therefore, it sees trade not only as being embedded in, but to a considerable extent determined by, specific (but changing) institutional structures. It also sees these institutions as arising from specific historical processes rather than evolving from systemic functional needs.

GVC analysis thus directs its attention to the organizational aspects of international trade but within a context that goes well beyond trade alone— to the whole range of activities from primary production to final consumption and to the linkages binding them (Gereffi 1994, 96). This involves trying to understand how lead firms build, coordinate, and control the linkages and flow of produce between raw material suppliers, processors, primary traders, wholesalers, retailers, and consumers. It also implies understanding the roles played in this process by contractual forms, by the coordination of finance and business services, and by the wider regulatory framework and changes in it.

The debates outlined in this chapter suggest that a lot of progress has been made since the early 1990s in theorizing governance and upgrading in GVCs, but more remains to be achieved. GVC analysts have not yet formulated a coherent theoretical framework (or frameworks) with significant explanatory power. Further debate is needed on clarifying key concepts and the historical dynamics of GVCs. Efforts are also needed in terms of better integrating issues of regulation and standards in value chain studies. Finally, a better understanding is needed of the conditions under which certain forms of governance emerge, and what the consequences of these forms are (both in theoretical and policy-oriented terms). In the following chapters, we attempt to address some of these outstanding issues. First, we analyze the emergence of buyer-driven chains (Chapter 4). Second, we examine the consequences of recent restructuring of GVCs for entry barriers, marginalization/exclusion, and upgrading (Chapter 5). Third, we unpack the role of quality conventions and forms of legitimacy in the governance of GVCs (Chapter 6).

# 4    The Rise of Buyer-Driven Value Chains in Africa

THIS CHAPTER addresses in detail some of the conceptual issues arising in GVC analysis that were outlined in the last chapter. It does so through an examination of fieldwork material collected during the study of specific value chains by the authors and their colleagues in the Globalization and Economic Restructuring in Africa (GLAF) research group during 1999–2003.[1] Each of these studies was based on extensive fieldwork in Africa and (for all chains but one) also in Northern countries. The salient characteristics of the studies focusing on specific products are summarized in Table 4.1.[2]

In the next three chapters, we examine this empirical material to address the following questions:

1. What explains the observed trend toward increased buyer drivenness in GVCs? What are its historical dynamics?
2. Who are the main actors in (selected) GVCs? What functional roles do these actors have? What kind of activities do they perform?
3. What is the role of regulation (domestic and international) in facilitating particular forms of governance?
4. What are the internal dynamics of governance? Are lead firms in a value chain found in one functional position or more than one (in other words, is the value chain unipolar, bipolar, or multipolar)? How do particular groups of firms achieve leadership status? How do they maintain it?
5. How much leverage can lead firms exert on to their first-tier suppliers? What mechanisms do they use? How is this leverage translated in relations between first-tier suppliers and others further along the chain? In other words, what constitutes driving and how is this manifested at various points in a value chain?
6. How is lead firm status legitimized and maintained? How do lead firms respond to threats to their leadership?

**Table 4.1**   List of GLAF global value chain studies

| Product | Countries covered | References* |
|---|---|---|
| Citrus | South Africa, U.K. | Mather (2002a, 2002b, 2002c, 2002d, 2004); Mather and Greenberg (2003) |
| Clothing | Mauritius, South Africa, U.K., France, Denmark, Sweden | Gibbon (2000, 2002a, 2002b, 2003, forthcoming); Gibbon and Thomsen (2002); Palpacuer, Gibbon, and Thomsen (2005) |
| Cocoa | Ghana, Netherlands, Denmark | Fold (2000, 2001, 2002, 2004) |
| Coffee | Kenya, Ethiopia, Tanzania, Uganda, Italy, U.S. | Daviron and Ponte (2005); Ponte (2001a, 2001b, 2001c, 2002a, 2002b, 2002c, 2004a, 2004b); Giovannucci and Ponte (2004) |
| Cotton | Tanzania, Zimbabwe, U.K. | Larsen (2002, 2003a, 2003b); Poulton et al. (2004) |
| Fresh vegetables | Kenya, Tanzania | Jensen, B. N. (2002), Jensen, M. F. (2000) |

Note:   * See also individual chapters in Fold and Larsen (forthcoming).

7. What are the entry barriers to different functions along a value chain? How are they changing? How are they related to processes of marginalization and upgrading and exclusion or inclusion?

The discussion is organized as follows. First, a historical analysis of the rise of buyer driving in the chains considered is carried out in relation to the broader elements of global capitalism as discussed in Chapter 1. This is followed by descriptions of the main actors at the Northern ends of these chains and of the general configurations of the chains concerned. The core of the chapter then examines two aspects of governance in these chains: first, the role of specific regulatory structures (international and national) in influencing changes in governance, and second, the types of action taken in relation to other chain actors by specific lead firms once they have assumed governing status. The discussion concludes by returning to the nature of chain driving and its manifestations, in terms of common and divergent features within and between value chains.

## THE RISE OF BUYER-DRIVEN CHAINS

In common with other literature on GVC, the studies in the GLAF program confirm the increased importance of buyer-driven chains in the global economy. Chapter 1 provided some discussion of the factors that have made this happen: the emergence of high levels of retail concentration; the rise of management prescriptions favoring the separation of higher from lower returns on capital employed (ROCE) activities—coupled with the outsourcing of lower ROCE activities; rising levels of market saturation; and increased competition around product differentiation and branding (together with the rising costs this entails).

In addition, it should be noted that structural adjustment and market liberalization in developing countries has meant that importers and international traders have been obliged to engage with developing country markets at more upstream stages than before to guarantee the volumes and/or qualities they were interested in. The abolition of export marketing monopolies also entailed a radical shift in bargaining power, for importers and international traders are no longer negotiating with a handful of exporters with large volumes and the resources to hold part of them back from the world market, but rather, with a multitude of small- and medium-sized, resource-poor local private players.

The developing country parties to international commodity agreements were national single-channel export marketing authorities. The commodity agreement system assumed the existence of such authorities, for otherwise national export quotas or retention schemes could not be used to stabilize markets. Even for crops for which there were no international agreements, single-channel authorities prevailed in most developing countries, for a variety of reasons. These included development-inspired crop diffusion on the basis of pan-territorial pricing and input credit schemes; establishing and maintaining national reputations on the basis of a single, mandatory system of quality control; seasonal and interseasonal price stabilization; earning commercial premiums through tender and forward sales; and—not least—cheap and effective export tax gathering. Each of these objectives is markedly more difficult to pursue in contexts of open market competition.

Yet, crop authorities tended to be inefficient, costly to run and susceptible to corruption. As donors began demanding in the 1980s that developing country governments use market liberalization to promote greater economic efficiency and to reduce the burden of marketing authorities on the government budget, single-channel systems were abandoned in most anglophone African countries. Although the resulting reform process in francophone Africa was generally much slower and often less radical, even in anglophone Africa there were considerable variations from country to country and from crop to crop. The most far-reaching liberalizations seem to have occurred in Tanzania and Uganda. Cotton marketing liberalization in Zimbabwe and Zambia was undertaken with greater caution (formal or informal restrictions on types and numbers of market participants), whereas coffee marketing in Kenya and cocoa marketing in Ghana were liberalized only to a very limited degree even as late as the end of the 1990s. On the other hand, South Africa after the end of apartheid liberalized most of its own export agriculture sectors on a comprehensive basis, without external pressure.

The rise of buyer-driven chains has been facilitated further by increased currency convertibility, transport market liberalization, and the reduced costs arising from technological developments in international communications and transport. Recent developments in telecommunications and the so-called information technology revolution are well documented (cf. OECD 1995). Yet, as far as international trade for primary commodities is concerned, containerization and shipping market liberalization have also been extremely important sources of reduced costs, not only with respect to transport itself but also to value chain coordination. Containerization promotes a more continuous flow of goods and also simplifies the process of transhipment between different transport modes, thus allowing for multimode door-to-door transport. This in turn has allowed the emergence of large transnational freight forwarding companies and of faster and more direct sourcing. Furthermore, as the result of shipping liberalization following 1992, the traditional route-based conference line system of shipping has been replaced by a hub-and-spoke system. The result has been the emergence of new round the world routes served by much larger ships (typically carrying 6,000 or more containers), into which all other routes feed through regional hubs, and reduction in sea transport costs by more than a third in real terms (Pedersen 2001).[3]

Driving in most of the value chains examined here is by buyers, in the sense that their lead firms are specialized retailers, branders, or traders, or have retailing, branding, and/or trading as one of their two main roles. As we will see later, different kinds of buyers have different significance for how the value chains are driven. Also, different end markets, and the same end markets in different historical periods, are characterized by different degrees of drivenness. The trend toward driving, although uneven, has become increasingly evident over the last ten years. Fresh vegetable and citrus chains ending in mainland Europe today are much less clearly driven than those ending in the United

Kingdom (see later). But the chain for fresh vegetables into the United Kingdom is now clearly buyer-driven, whereas as recently as the 1980s it used to pass mostly through importers and wholesale markets to what was then a relatively fragmented retailer segment. Even at the end of the 1980s, the citrus chain into the European Union was, if anything, producer driven. Supply and prices were managed by a few well-organized producer associations (Outspan in South Africa, Jaffa in Israel, the Moroccan Fruit Board, etc.). At the same time, only parts of the clothing chain into the European Union were buyer-driven, and this had been a comparatively recent development. Even in the United Kingdom, there was a concentrated clothing manufacturing sector with which retailers sought exclusivity contracts as late as the mid-1970s.[4] Meanwhile, the chains for coffee and cocoa were until the early 1980s not clearly driven at all. On the basis of international commodity agreements, producer associations represented a clear counterbalance to what were then relatively large populations of traders and roasters/grinders. The only chain among those examined here where there has been no clear emergence of a group of lead firms is cotton.

## MAIN ACTORS IN, AND CONFIGURATIONS OF, SELECTED GLOBAL VALUE CHAINS

The analysis of selected GVCs in this chapter is centered mainly around the relationships between so-called lead firms and their first-tier suppliers. Relations between first-tier suppliers and their own suppliers (so-called second-tier suppliers) and beyond are described in the next chapter. The term *lead firms* does not refer mainly to the market share of such firms, in comparison to other firms in the same functional position, but to the fact that they (as a group) control certain functions that allow them to dictate the terms of participation by other actors in different functional positions in the value chain. This capacity rests on factors that can be distinguished from those that are associated with one or more *particular firms* (rather than others in the same functional position) dominating a given link of a chain. In the case of particular retailers or branders, these factors may include: development of a strategic end-market share on the basis of economies of scale, or some other successful form of marketing strategy, or successful product differentiation; political connections allowing a firm's influence on the framing of favorable regulatory legislation; or "lucking in" on new locational advantages arising from geopolitical changes.

## Lead Firms

Table 4.2 identifies a selection of lead firms in each of the chains considered. It also shows that some of the value chains here share common lead firms. Nestlé appears as a lead firm in coffee and cocoa/chocolate,

**Table 4.2**   Lead firms in selected value chains

| Value Chain | Functional role(s) of lead firms | Name of firm | Market share (%) | Year |
|---|---|---|---|---|
| Coffee | Roasters-branders | Philip Morris (now Altria)/Kraft Nestlé Sara Lee Procter & Gamble Tchibo | 69 | 1998 |
| Cocoa | Chocolate manufacturers-branders | Nestlé Mars Philip Morris (now Altria)/Kraft Hershey Cadbury Ferrero | 60–70 | 1999 |
| Fresh fruit and vegetables | Large retailers (U.K.) | Tesco Asda (Wal-Mart) Sainsbury Safeway Somerfield | 55–60 | 2000 |
| Clothing | Large retailers (U.K.) | Marks & Spencer Arcadia Next Debenhams | 31 | 2001 |
| | Large retailers (France) | Carrefour Auchan Decathlon Galeries Lafayette La Redoute | 30 | 2000 |
| | Large retailers (U.S.) | Wal-Mart Gap | 17 | 2000 |

Sources:
Coffee: van Djik et al. (1998);
Cocoa/chocolate: Heijbroek and Konjin (1995), Losch (2002);
Fresh Fruit and Vegetables: UK Competition Commission (2000);
Clothing (U.K. and France): Palpacuer, Gibbon, and Thomsen (2004);
Clothing (U.S.): Retail Forward (2002), Gap Inc. Annual Report (2001).

whereas Wal-Mart is one for both clothing into the United States and fresh vegetables into the United Kingdom (via its subsidiary Asda, which is also in the U.K. top ten for clothing sales). The recent histories of four lead firms will be described here (Wal-Mart, Carrefour, Tesco, and Nestlé) to highlight some of the key features of firms of this kind. These happen to be the biggest or among the biggest in their category in the world. The reason for choosing them is not primarily to highlight the causes behind their dominance, but rather to illuminate the kinds of characteristics that other firms in the same category feel obliged to copy to be competitive with them. Wal-Mart is the largest retailer in the world (as well as the largest listed company of any kind by sales and profit and the largest private employer); Carrefour is the world's second largest and Europe's largest retailer and largest private employer. Tesco is the United Kingdom's largest retailer and largest private employer, and Nestlé is the world's largest food manufacturer.[5]

*Wal-Mart* was founded only in 1962 and has been the U.S. retail market leader since the mid-1990s. Since this time, it has dramatically extended its lead over competitors, on the basis of very high sales growth. This averaged 15.5 percent between 1999 and 2003 alone. Wal-Mart internationalized first in 1991 and is now present in nine countries (ten if joint ventures are included). These international operations generated almost 17 percent of total sales in 2003. Wal-Mart's power is remarkable in relation to its suppliers, between 200 and 500 of whom are said to have established permanent representation at or immediately around its headquarters in Bentonville, Arkansas, a town known in the trade as "vendorville."

Wal-Mart achieved its current position on the basis of implementing a broad combination of retail innovations. Although only one of these was entirely original, no competitors succeeded in implementing them as a group prior to Wal-Mart. The first, introduced almost simultaneously with Carrefour, was the hypermarket format: selling a very broad range of products (up to 15,000). The purpose of this format was twofold: to maximize margins by selling as many high-margin products as possible and to maximize volumes by optimizing customer footfall (amount of customer visits and time spent in store). The second innovation was to add a series of other shopping formats (hard discount, cash and carry, and neighborhood markets) to the hypermarket core, again to maximize volumes. The very high volumes that Wal-Mart turns over provide in turn one of the two main preconditions for what has become its unique price stance—"always low prices." The other

precondition of always low prices, which is indeed its only truly original innovation, was that of replenishment programs (see Chapter 1).
Wal-Mart pioneered the use of in-store information technology (electronic cash registers, bar scanners, back-end computers in stores) that
allowed it to establish just-in-time type inventory and logistics management arrangements with leading suppliers. These added to profitability both by taking out working capital costs and by minimizing
stock-outs[6] and large volumes of unsold stock that would have to be
marked down. As a result of having mastered the art of replenishment,
Wal-Mart now boasts an ability to generate significantly more annual
stock turns than its rivals.[7] A final innovation has been in achieving new
efficiencies/lower costs in handling on the basis of the use of delivery
centers. Delivery centers were originally designed to achieve economies
of scale in handling and shipping by centralization/elimination of as
much in-store handling as possible and by rationalizing distribution.
Later they were adapted to maximize the benefits of replenishment programs via cross-docking[8] and through the transfer of picking, packing,
and shipping responsibilities to suppliers.

*Carrefour*'s sales growth has been less spectacular than Wal-Mart's,
although it has accelerated sharply since 1999 (when it swallowed
Promodés) to average almost 29 percent annually in 1999–2002. Carrefour adopted the hypermarket format at the same time as Wal-Mart,
but with an anchorage in food products, which Wal-Mart adopted
later. Carrefour internationalized earlier (in 1969 by acquiring a Bel-
gian chain), entered emerging markets quicker (Brazil, in 1975) and is
today far more internationalized than any of its rivals (with roughly
half of all its sales outside France), except the troubled Royal Ahold
group. In all, it has a presence in thirty countries. The thinking behind
this emphasis is that, in the context of flat markets in Northern countries, long-term growth for its grocery anchor product lines is likely to
come only in developing countries where there are still major discrepancies between population and consumption levels (see also Reardon and
Berdegué 2002; Reardon, Berdegué, and Farrington 2002; Weatherspoon
and Reardon 2003).

Carrefour's strategy in Northern countries has come increasingly to
resemble Wal-Mart's. It has pushed its nonfood sales up to 20 percent of total sales,[9] promoted growth in Northern country markets
mainly through establishing new formats (supermarket, hard discount,
and convenience stores) and placed increasing emphasis on price and

promotions (see Carrefour 2003, 14). On the other hand, it lags long behind Wal-Mart in replenishment, in sourcing—which is still decentralized to fifty main centers (some of which are further decentralized)[10]—and in logistics.

*Tesco*'s sales overtook those of its closest rival Sainsbury in 1996, and the company has subsequently opened a 2 to 3 percent lead in U.K. grocery market share, on the basis of a growth in sales averaging around 8 percent since 1999. Strategically, it has trodden a path more similar to Wal-Mart's than Carrefour's. In common with both, it has diversified in Northern countries into multiple formats (with an increasing emphasis on convenience stores), increased its share of nonfood sales (although at 5 percent of all sales, this still falls well below Wal-Mart and Carrefour) and focused strongly on volume and price.[11] In 2001, the company's chairman claimed to have reduced the store's prices by 11 percent in real terms since 1997 (*Guardian* April 11, 2001). Meanwhile, its internationalization has been more cautious than Carrefour's, focusing only on those markets where it is certain to occupy a leading or a strong No. 2 status. Yet, the comprehensiveness with which it has adopted replenishment programs and the ruthlessness with which it has engaged in supply chain rationalization differs little from Wal-Mart.

*Nestlé* is in certain senses a perfect fit with firms of this kind, although its history and development take a very different form. Founded as a dairy products company in the 1860s, its current character dates from 1945–1975. In this period, its instant coffee product Nescafé, invented in 1938, attained its present status as the world's most popular coffee brand. Nescafé sales increased by 300 percent during the 1950s and by 400 percent between 1960 and 1979. Nestlé used the profits this generated to diversify from dairy, chocolate, and cocoa/coffee into a wide variety of foods (soups, seasonings, preserves, canned foods, frozen foods), cosmetics (with the purchase of L'Oreal), pharmaceutical, and ophthalmic products. Since this period, beverages have remained its core business, in 2002 contributing 26 percent of its total sales (which stood at US\$66 billion) and 33 percent of its profits (Nestlé SA 2002). But its food range has been thinned (with, e.g., the divestment of Findus frozen foods, acquired in 1963) and three largely new foci—on bottled water, ice cream, and pet foods—have emerged. In fact, pet food has become the company's major growth product in the last few years, rising to around 12 percent of all sales. The company is now in a market leadership position, in either the European Union or the United

States, if not globally, across a range of seven or eight broad product categories.

In contrast to the overwhelming majority of food manufacturers, this position allows Nestlé to deal with most retailers on its own terms. Its 2002 *Management Report* (Nestlé SA 2002, 11) states "increasing customer and channel contribution" among its three "long-standing strategies."[12] The report goes on: "the objective is to benchmark our performance (between) comparable retail customers and then work on improving the less performing ones... in terms of sales and... margins." Foer (2001) has described Nestlé as one of the food manufacturing companies that has best managed the transition from a world in which manufacturers' brands dominated retail to the world in which retail, via category management, has come to dominate branded food manufacture.[13] Its achievement of category captain status (see Chapter 1 ) for a spread of product groups across a range of leading retailers has given it a good understanding of the businesses both of its clients and its rivals, raising the latter's costs. It has simultaneously given it the resources to create market development funds with which to leverage its clout with single retailers from one or two categories to a much wider range, through additional discounts/rebates/payments to those retailers who support its full range of brands.

## First-tier Suppliers

Other than the fact that lead firms have retail/branding/trading as one or two of their core functions, another striking similarity in all cases is that immediately upstream of these are found other powerful agents who do most, or at least some, of the day-to-day work of chain coordination.[14] We define these as first-tier suppliers.[15] These partly play the traditional first-tier supplier role of sourcing from a range of smaller suppliers to provide a specific component/product category to their customers. But in addition, the most successful have taken on more of a broader system integration role, as global trade (and especially trade in outsourced inputs) has increased dramatically. The resources necessary to manage this new role include specialized communications, sector-specific technical knowledge, command of multiple languages and knowledge of supplying country markets, and knowledge of trade regulations and trade administration systems. Most lead firms would have to invest considerable resources to manage such a role directly— while, as noted, pressures in retail are in fact to get rid of as many back-of-house functions (and associated direct overhead costs) as possible.

If this provides demand-side reasons for the existence of first-tier suppliers, a series of supply-side reasons can also be detected. One of them is the existence of a large number of former Northern manufacturers and wholesalers that are seeking to reinvent their supplier status in new guises. Another is a process of rapid concentration and redefinition of roles among international traders in some sectors. Following international commodity market deregulation, falling prices and higher price volatility have entailed lower margins and more casualties among international traders. At the same time, concentration in the international transport sector and the emergence of globalized door-to-door transport providers have reduced the importance of the traditional activity of holding stock on own account for sale on the open market. They have also forced greater specialization by first-tier suppliers in providing unique services to lead firms. Finally, there has been a process of upward mobility on the part of some former producer-exporters based in developing countries who have internationalized and acquired new functions as a means of responding to pressure on their own margins from new Northern intermediaries. As will be explained later, the latter tends to be a much more common phenomenon in respect to (former) producer-exporters based in southern Europe, former white-settler colonies, and larger developing countries than in developing countries more generally.

In the case of coffee, the role of first-tier supplier is played by international traders, a very concentrated group of European companies (Such as Neumann and Volcafé). For cocoa, it is played by integrated international trading/grinding companies. Control over this link in the chain is so concentrated (ADM, Cargill, and Barry-Callebaut control over 70 percent of the world grinding capacity) that this chain may be interpreted as being bipolar (with two groups of lead firms in different functional positions competing for dominance, rather than just one group; see Fold 2001). Although two of the international trader/grinders are U.S.-owned, they have substantial operations also in Europe.

Five multinational fruit trading companies (Chiquita, Dole, Del Monte, Noboa, and Fyffes), all integrated backward into transport and (in most cases) production, control 39 to 40 percent of all globally traded fruit. However, these companies owe their position mainly to their overwhelming domination of the banana trade, where in 2000 they controlled 84 percent of all exports (Rabobank 2001). Market concentration both in citrus and fresh vegetables is considerably lower than for fruit generally, and more actors are involved. Nonetheless, as a result of diversification out of bananas, Fyffes—through its alliance with the South African company Capespan—also plays a leading role in citrus, as did Dole until its divestment of businesses in this subsector in 2000. Del Monte also plays a leading role in fresh vegetables. However, in deciduous fruit and citrus, now fully commercialized producer associations are still very important alongside a range of smaller-scale Northern importers; in fresh vegetables, it is the latter that play the main role. As noted in Chapter 1, in the United Kingdom these smaller importers tend to have some growing capacity of their own in producing countries. Although small in relation to the likes of Chiquita and Dole, their market share of direct supply to U.K. supermarkets is high. One of the largest U.K. supermarkets (Asda/Wal-Mart) uses only one citrus supplier (Thames Fruit).

Fresh fruit and vegetable chains into continental Europe also pass initially through importers, but the latter act predominantly as brokers in national and regional wholesale markets. Despite levels of grocery end-market concentration in mainland Europe on a par with those in the United Kingdom, the role of wholesale markets has been preserved, and a majority of large players still source through them. In France and Italy, the importance of wholesale markets has been preserved by law (in France, by "Le statut des marchés d'intérêt national" of 1953).[16] Also of significance is that a number of the largest mainland European supermarket groups are federations of independent owners for whom not all buying/sourcing is controlled centrally. However, it is commonly acknowledged in the industry that changes are under way, with a number of the largest mainland E.U. supermarket chains (notably Carrefour) shifting to the use of dedicated importing intermediaries only.

The configuration of the clothing value chain upstream of retailers is more complex than in the other chains described so far. In the first place, there are several groups of powerful intermediaries. Probably the most important are global trading houses, companies that finance and organize production in developing countries on behalf of retailers. The largest of these are overseas-Chinese-owned (Li & Fung, Linmark Westman), but other big ones are United States-owned (Mast Industries, SaraMax) or U.K.-owned (Dewhirst). Besides trading houses, one finds specialized importers playing an important role in many markets. Second, there are global contract manufacturers working on a nonintermediated basis for some of the large U.S. retailers, including ones that source a majority of their intake through intermediaries. Examples include the Hong Kong–owned Esquel (shirts) and Novel (denim and jeans), the Indian-owned Arvind Mills (denim and jeans) and the

Malaysian-owned Ramatex Berhad (knitwear). These contract manufacturers typically have production bases in several countries spread across at least two continents. As noted in Chapter 1, most of these first-tier suppliers are owned and based in end markets, close to end customers, although a few are based (and owned by actors in) developing countries or at least in NICs.

Individual exceptions can be found in each chain, where lead firms avoid the use of powerful intermediaries (traders or processors/manufacturers). In clothing, for example, Gap and Hennes & Mauritz source directly from manufacturers. In both cases, direct sourcing is seen by these enterprises as a leading competitive advantage, enabling them to capture margins that would be otherwise appropriated by intermediaries, and to exercise a more concentrated use of buying power in relation to the size of suppliers. Furthermore, even lead firms with considerable dependence on first-tier suppliers maintain some direct buying relations with second-tier suppliers. But generally, just as there is a material foundation for buyer drivenness, so are there also good economic reasons for lead firms to develop a high degree of coordination with smaller groups of first-tier suppliers.

The major exception to the kinds of configurations described so far is the cotton chain, which lacks both clear lead firms and a category of first-tier suppliers. Both cotton production and textile manufacturing are highly fragmented, and most spinners are based in developing countries—where they source a majority of their raw material requirements on their own domestic markets. Although most internationally traded cotton passes through the hands of international trading companies, it is also common for spinners to bypass international traders by sourcing directly from ginners (those processing raw cotton into cotton lint) in exporting countries. International traders generally seek to maximize both volumes and varieties, but perform few services for the spinners other than supplying to order. Traders do not blend cotton nor normally even measure any but its most traditional quality dimensions. Offering measurement of more modern, industrial properties via so-called high–volume instrument machines is more frequently undertaken by independent ginners trying to sell directly to spinners. Although international traders frequently use local agents (whom they finance in advance) to procure cotton on their behalf, they also invariably buy and gin on their own account in the most important supplying countries. In this sense, they cannot be properly regarded as lead firms or first-tier suppliers, or as themselves users of first-tier suppliers.

## FORMAL REGULATORY FRAMEWORKS AND HISTORICAL CHANGES IN GVC GOVERNANCE

The rise of buyer-driven chains, and of specific groups of lead firms within them, did not take place in an institutional and regulative vacuum. In its earlier guises, GVC analysis tended to link the emergence and implementation of particular forms of governance mostly to interfirm interactions and business strategies, as if governance mechanisms played out purely in a private corporate realm. Later work has gone beyond this limitation, but mostly on a case-by-case basis. In this section, we carry out a comparative analysis of historically changing regulative structures and how they have facilitated (or hindered) the rise of buyer-driven value chains.[17]

In the *clothing* GVC, changes in regulatory frameworks have impacted continuously on coordination, but not on the overall form of governance, which has remained buyer-driven for the last two decades. The main regulative change has been the development of a multiplicity of preferential trade arrangements alongside the framework of the Multifibre Arrangement, and a subsequent diversification in the nature of rules of origin applying to exports to the main end markets, particularly the United States. Under the Multifibre Arrangement, the most common rule of origin applied by the United States was based on that of its General System of Preferences, which in effect conferred origin in terms of the performance of cutting and assembly operations in the country of export. This was associated with value chains being coordinated, on retailers' behalf, by a mixture of sourcing agencies and developing country-based contract manufacturers. These financed and distributed orders and textiles for making up across plants in countries whose composition shifted according to quota availability and costs.

The period 1980–1995 then saw the superimposition on this template of production-sharing-based arrangements between the United States or the European Union on the one hand and countries in their immediate periphery on the other. These arrangements conferred origin on, and granted significant preferences to, clothing that was simply made up locally from components cut in the United States or the European Union. These arrangements, which were designed to preserve the competitiveness of U.S. and E.U. clothing manufacturers, led to the latter themselves taking up the role of international coordination. Since 1995, a third wave of trade agreements and rules of origin have emerged, which either reinstate the comparative advantage of Multifibre Arrangement–type

forms of coordination (in the case of AGOA's lesser developed beneficiary country rule—see later) or, more commonly, create opportunities
for new forms of coordination (in the case of the yarn-forward rule
of NAFTA; see also Chapter 2). Agreements of the latter type provide
advantages to first-tier suppliers who are vertically integrated manufacturers based in the country of export, as well as for those international
sourcing agencies that have specialized in matchmaking between locally
based textile manufacturers and clothing manufacturers in emerging areas such as Mexico or selected countries in Africa.

Among the value chains examined in the GLAF research program,
the most evident effect of regulatory changes in facilitating a shift in the
form of governance has been in *coffee*. Between 1962 and 1989, the GVC
for coffee was regulated by a series of International Coffee Agreements
(ICAs) negotiated between most producing *and* consuming countries.
The ICA regulatory system set a target price (or a price band) for coffee
and export quotas for each producer. When the indicator price calculated by the International Coffee Organization (ICO) rose over the set
price, quotas were relaxed; when it fell below the set price, quotas were
tightened. If an extremely large rise in coffee prices took place (as in
1975–1977), quotas were abandoned until prices fell back within the
band. Although there were problems with this system, most analysts
agree that it was successful in raising and stabilizing coffee prices. This
has been attributed to various factors: (1) the participation of consuming
countries in the working of the quota system; (2) the existence of producing countries as market units, where governments were in control
of decisions concerning exports (therefore, the possibility for producing
countries to achieve a lead firm–like status in GVC parlance); (3) Brazil's
acceptance of the shrinking market share that resulted from successive
ICAs; and (4) a common strategy of import substitution in producing
countries, which required maximum mobilization of export earnings—
and therefore high commodity prices (Daviron 1996, 86–89).

Under this regulatory regime, the GVC for coffee was not clearly
driven by any actor, nor was it possible to state clearly that producers or buyers controlled it. Entry barriers in farming and in domestic
trade were often mediated by governments. Governments also managed quality control systems and to some extent decided which quality
standards to apply at the export level. In the consuming country segment
of the value chain, roasters were increasing their leading role through
branding (and the accompanying process of embedding unique quality
attributes), advertising, and mergers and acquisitions. Yet, their control

of the GVC was limited by the quota system and by government control in producing country markets.

However, the ICA system was undermined by free-riding and squabbling over quotas. Other problems were the increasing volume of coffee traded with (or through) nonmember importing countries (at lower prices) and the continuing fragmentation of the geography of production (Daviron 1993, 1996). Furthermore, quotas were relatively stable because they were costly to negotiate. As a result, the mix of coffee supplied by producers tended to remain stable, although in the 1980s consumers in the United States progressively switched from soluble coffees (that employ a high proportion of Robusta) to ground coffees (that use a higher proportion of Arabicas).[18] The rigidity on the supply side worried roasters, who feared that competitors could get access to cheaper coffee from nonmember countries. This undermined their cooperation within the ICA system. In this context, the United States contributed to the collapsing of the ICA in 1989. Finally, the Cold War politics of the United States in relation to Latin America changed in the 1980s. The United States did not perceive the left in Brazil as a real threat anymore, and the rigidity of quotas meant that the U.S. administration could not punish its "enemies" in Central America (Bates 1997). The combined result of these changes led to failure to renew the ICA in 1989.

In contrast, the post-ICA regime exhibits many of the characteristics of an explicitly buyer-driven chain. From a fairly balanced contest between producing countries and buyers (importers, roasters, and their lobbyists in consuming countries) within the politics of the commodity agreement, the coffee value chain became dominated by consuming country-based agents (including their representatives based in producing countries), especially roasters/instant coffee manufacturers (hereafter roasters). The institutional framework moved away from a formal and relatively stable system where producers and producing countries had an established voice toward one that is more informal and buyer dominated—also because domestic market liberalization in producing countries entails that states as such cannot be considered market units (or lead firm–like) any longer.

Another chain where changes in regulation have been highly influential in facilitating an overall restructuring is *fresh vegetables*. These changes relate to food safety regulations and have taken place mostly in consuming countries, as most African horticultural sectors have never been subject to much regulation. The U.K. Food Safety Act of 1990 was a forerunner of current E.U. food safety regulation in allocating responsibility for the safety of food and ingredients at all stages of the chain to food retailers. This responsibility follows from the due diligence requirement for food producers, traders, and retailers, which refers to a legal duty to take all reasonable steps to ensure that the food they sell is safe (Dolan and Humphrey 2000; M.F. Jensen 2000; Marsden and Wrigley 1995). In the event that a company faced a food safety problem, it would have to prove that it had made an active effort to avoid the problem not only when the product was in its possession, but also further upstream in the value chain. This meant in practice that supermarket chains need to monitor their suppliers and keep records of the origin of the food they buy and also the conditions under which it has been produced and traded.

The initial expectation was that retailers would have to integrate vertically upstream to do so. As we shall see in Chapter 6, this did not happen because lead agents were able to codify their quality requirements through precise standards (both for products and for processing and production methods) that went even beyond what was required by the law. In this context, retailers also outsourced a number of other functions that they had performed in-house. Whereas previously most horticultural products were sold in bulk and anonymously to wholesale markets in the United Kingdom, currently retailer chains source prepackaged products from a small number of importers. These importers have also pushed some functions upstream (including washing, grading, packing, and even bar coding), mainly to large commercial farms rather than groups of smaller farms. In this case, the chain moved toward buyer drivenness, with retail chains as lead firms. This trend may be reinforced even outside the United Kingdom as the European Union determines how to implement its decision to require traceability for all food imports.

The same observation applies for the *citrus* value chain, but with some qualifications. In the case of citrus from South Africa, perhaps the most important regulatory change took place in the producing country. South African citrus production represented over half of Southern Hemisphere production in the 1970s and 1980s, and the local industry was highly regulated. Between 1940 and 1997, all exports were channeled through a "single desk," which exerted noticeable influence in the U.K. market. The chain could perhaps be characterized as a producer-driven one. As a result of the liberalization of South Africa's exports in the late 1990s, the chain now operates in a similar manner to other fresh fruit and vegetable GVCs, where retailers dominate (Mather and Greenberg 2003).

To some extent, the shift observed in coffee (see earlier) has been replicated in the *cocoa* chain. However, key differences exist between the two. First, the producing country cocoa cartel was never as effective as the coffee cartel, and it operated mostly on the basis of managing stocks. It did not attempt to fix quotas or to set price bands. Stock management started shortly after the establishment of the International Cocoa and Chocolate Organization (ICCO) and became the dominant regulatory mechanism. Stocks were finally liquidated through regular monthly sales between 1993 and early 1998. According to Losch (2002), increasing levels of industrial concentration at the industrial processing stage of production during the 1980s were associated with a major shift in market power that undermined the ICCO system. Even though production of cocoa beans was geopolitically highly concentrated, a handful of cocoa processors emerged with market shares for cocoa grindings even higher than those possessed by Côte d'Ivoire and Ghana for cocoa beans. Côte d'Ivoire, having re-entered the International Cocoa Agreement (ICCA) in 1986, tried to force the world price up by completely withdrawing its cocoa from the world market for a period of twenty-seven months (the so-called cocoa war of 1987–1989). Its failure in raising prices meant that producing countries did not continue enjoying the same influence as before.

Second, other forms of regulatory change outside of producing countries affected the cocoa value chain, particularly the outcome of the so-called chocolate war in the European Union, which related to debates among E.U. members over the appropriate definition of chocolate, that is, the maximum content of cocoa butter substitutes to be allowed (see Fold 2000). The issue was settled only recently, allowing some chocolates to contain a maximum of 5 percent cocoa butter substitutes, under the condition that this is clearly stated on the wrapping. This allows chocolate manufacturers to obtain more flexibility in their sourcing options than a more purist definition, but still places limits on what they can substitute cocoa butter with.

In general, the ruling has been interpreted as a defeat for cocoa-producing countries, albeit not a catastrophic one. Yet, following cocoa market liberalization in producing countries, as in the case of coffee, producers had already lost their bargaining power as market units. This has been particularly problematic for Côte d'Ivoire, which supplied 40 to 45 percent of the world's cocoa market in the mid-1990s. The current political instability in the country is affecting perceptions of supply and therefore pushing prices higher, but this can hardly be considered a form of strategic policy. The changes described have helped establish a buyer-driven dynamic in the global cocoa chain, but with different outcomes than in the case of coffee. As mentioned earlier, this chain can be seen as a bipolar one, where chocolate manufacturers and grinders are fairly dependent on each other, but where both have a high degree of leverage on other actors upstream and downstream.

Finally, in the case of *cotton*, the dynamics of change in the form of governance have been less clear in relation to changing regulation. This value chain is less driven than the others examined here, as both suppliers (cotton producers) and end users (spinners) are many and dispersed. International traders perform a key function in between these two, but do not dictate the functional division of labor along the chain as a whole; they uphold rather than arbitrate conventions governing cotton quality (see also Chapter 6; Larsen 2003b). The cotton value chain thus operates to a large extent on market principles. Yet, the power equilibrium between producers (at least developing country-based ones) and international traders has tilted to the benefit of the latter as producing country market liberalization has had similar effects as in coffee and cocoa. These countries have seen their export base fragmented. Most smaller producers lost key public services such as seed and other input supplies, credit, and extension. Producers in Northern countries like the United States, on the other hand, continue to benefit from public support and subsidies. Increases in buyer drivenness apply only in relation to developing countries.

## STRATEGIES OF LEAD FIRMS

This section examines some of the concrete actions taken by lead firms in the chains considered, in the wake of their acquisition of lead firm status. This discussion will provide material for a reconsideration of how chain driving occurs, with which this chapter concludes.

The *clothing* chain is currently characterized by two somewhat contradictory tendencies. On the one hand, the two decades in which this chain has been unambiguously buyer-driven have seen an increasing proliferation of types of intermediary and intermediating functions, immediately serving retailers and branders. Intermediaries include not only trading houses, global contract manufacturers, and Northern importers offering various constellations of services, but also agents in producing countries and various hybrids between these forms. For example, the overseas-Chinese-owned trading house Li & Fung has recently opened its own manufacturing capacity for the first time, which will be dedicated to producing Levi's jeans for a specific U.S. retailer's in-house brand. Not surprisingly, for risk-spreading and cross-costing reasons— and to encourage further competition between suppliers—most Northern retailers and branded marketers have some degree of involvement in a wide range of different sourcing channels.

According to which kind of sourcing channel is chosen, the range of functions devolved to first-tier suppliers will vary, as will the division of labor between first- and second-tier ones. However, a second general trend is for clothing retailers to emphasize supply-base rationalization and in particular chain shortening. This entails the (partial) adoption of so-called direct sourcing, in the sense of dealing directly with manufacturers in producing countries that are able to offer a large number of add-on services. The main reasons for doing so are generally given as higher margins (by virtue of cutting out intermediaries), increased control, and shorter lead times.

Expectations concerning which combination of services suppliers must offer differ between end markets and between buyers in these markets. But in virtually all cases, there has been a move toward demanding that suppliers finance and organize fabric procurement on their own account, even where control is retained by retailers over exactly which fabrics a manufacturer should use. Second, there is a very widespread move toward expecting that suppliers should hold fabric on their own account on a *long-term* basis (e.g., for the length of a season), either on the basis of replenishment-program commitments or even without a commitment having been made. In all cases, buyers (or those buying on their behalf) set fixed prices that have to be matched by their suppliers, with little or no room for negotiation. A clear tendency exists for unit prices to be forced down over time and for an increasing share of production to be contracted on lead times shorter than three months.

As seen earlier, in the *coffee* value chain, roasters now occupy lead firm status, as a result of the changing regulatory context, the growing saturation of the international coffee market that has followed this, and the increased flexibility they have achieved in relation to blending. Roasters have used this status mainly to redefine their relations with international traders. The main, but not the only, way in which this has occurred is through the implementation of supplier-managed inventory (SMI), that is, the externalization of a major function that was previously carried out in-house.

Supplier-managed inventory was first implemented by those roasting companies quoted in stock markets—and therefore more under pressure to maximize shareholder value (see Chapter 1). One of the reasons for doing so was the need to contain the size of inventories and of working capital within optimal parameters set by financial analysts—large inventories and a high ratio of working capital being normally interpreted as indicators of inefficiency. As a result of their absorption of the inventory management function—and in combination with market liberalization in producing countries—international traders had to strengthen their supply network. This has taken place through tighter coordination (financing or even vertical integration) with local exporters. In some countries, international traders have moved upstream all the way to domestic trade and sometimes even beyond this to estate production.

Holding inventory is not new for international traders. They did so even before roasters trimmed down their inventory management. The key difference is that, in the past, international traders held stock (often in consuming countries) on their own account and could dispose of it by selling on the open market to the highest bidder. Currently, they still hold stock on their own account—and are therefore liable to inventory costs— but increasingly they cannot dispose of it freely, as the stock of a particular kind of coffee is on hold for a particular roaster at a specified price differential. Traders are able to sell it to other clients only if they can replenish that particular quality and quantity quickly from other sources.

Roasters seem to have little interest themselves in vertical integration upstream (toward producers). They consider they are better off concentrating on roasting, blending, and branding, while leaving supply management to a network of independent traders. Some roasters (such as Nestlé) are said to source not only from a variety of international traders, but also directly from some local exporters. Others have their own trading companies, although they rely on these only for a fraction of their needs. The aim is, at least in strategic locations, to allow exporters and in-house buyers to compete with international traders. Such functional leap-frogging over networks of immediate suppliers aims at avoiding being outmaneuvered by international traders, who are themselves increasingly becoming fewer and bigger. Roasters have sought further to guard against dependence upon their immediate suppliers by acquiring more flexibility in blending formulas, which makes them less vulnerable to shortages of particular types of coffee.

At the same time, roasters require international traders to absorb the other major recent technical change in the industry, that of steam cleaning Robusta coffee. This allows roasters to acquire Robusta coffee with improved quality (and therefore to substitute poorer Arabica with premium-grade Robusta). The reasoning why roasters want to outsource steam cleaning while retaining control over blending is that steam cleaning is a publicly available technology, whereas blends are proprietal. Control over (and knowledge of) the latter is an important condition of control over the chain (Ponte 2002b).

The form of coordination that roasters carry out with their immediate suppliers is fairly hands-off. They buy from international traders after they have examined a sample, either on a spot basis or in relation to schedules. Coordination with retailers, with whom delivery schedules are also set (and special promotions and discounts negotiated), is likewise fairly arm's length in character. On both sides, levels of monitoring and formal contractual links are fairly low. The clearest indicators of the dominance of roasters even vis-à-vis retailers are that, first, coffee private labels (owned by supermarket chains) have not gained much market share, and second, that in some national markets branded coffee is sold by these chains even at a loss, in the expectation that consumers buying coffee will then buy other items at a higher profit margin.

In the wake of retailer acquisition of lead firm position in the chains for *fresh vegetables* and *citrus* in most European markets and in the United States, the former have cascaded an increasing number of functions to importers. As we saw earlier, they now stipulate specific dimensions of product quality and production as well as processing methods. In doing so, they have reshaped not only the functional division of labor along the chain, but have propelled the growth of a handful of preferred suppliers who can be relied on to match a set of increasingly complex and demanding standards (Dolan and Humphrey 2000; M.F. Jensen 2000). Initially, these suppliers transferred as many as possible of these demands farther upstream, to the few commercial farmers and packers/exporters that were able to match them.

Retailers maintain a higher level of monitoring of the overall chain than coffee roasters or chocolate manufacturers, with regular visits in origin countries. However, they have chosen not to become directly involved in operations at the source. This apparent absence of leap-frogging in the supply chain may come to create some problems for retailers, especially if specialist importers consolidate. However, more recently there are signs that producer country–based exporters are integrating downstream by establishing their own importing companies in the North. This may reduce retailers' potential dependence on a handful of suppliers and make the need to source at origin less important. Some observers actually argue that the industry is moving toward a governance structure based on modular networks, in a similar fashion to the cocoa one (Gereffi, Humphrey, and Sturgeon, 2004).

The broad direction of developments in the *cocoa* chain is more ambiguous, because although the chain is clearly driven, this is in the context of the presence of two competing but also cooperating groups of lead firms: chocolate manufacturers and grinders. Chocolate producers, including large branded manufacturers, have generally reduced their previous involvement in in-house grinding activities and outsourced some liquor, cocoa butter, and even standard (intermediate) chocolate manufacturing to grinding companies. Where they have not done so, this has been because they wish to preserve commercial secrecy about specific recipes for cocoa liquor (although there is generally less sensitivity here than there is in relation to coffee roasters' blends). But in this case, outsourcing appears to have occurred very much on the basis of consent. We should note that the functions that chocolate manufacturers are outsourcing are actually profitable for grinders—especially where they can achieve economies of scale by serving a number of large clients. In relation to this, the main reason for chocolate manufacturers to encourage a higher degree of outsourcing has been the fierce competition that has arisen from consolidation within this segment itself, which means that greater investments are now seen as being needed in product development and in marketing, especially in targeting specific groups of consumers (Fold 2001, 2002).

Manufacture of intermediate products has also become more profitable for grinders, thanks to technical developments. These allow them to deliver a broader range of cocoa products to chocolate manufacturers than previously, from the same raw material base. Subsequently, grinders have acquired a role resembling that of the global contract manufacturers that are emerging in the electronics and auto-component industries. The key in this kind of functional business is the ability to switch production between customers at low cost and short notice. This is made possible by increasing codification and standardization of a wide range of product qualities, which diminishes the costs of shifting between product types and the level of explicit coordination required. Both buyers and suppliers engage in volume spreading so that dependence is limited and firms do not become locked into bilateral trading relationships. This has contributed to a relatively stable balance in the cocoa chain where the power of contract manufacturers (grinders) is contained by the commercial and tactical strategies of lead brand-name chocolate manufacturers, and vice versa (Fold 2002). Yet, the cocoa chain remains fundamentally buyer driven (even if dominant buyers are in more than one functional position), whereas producers and local traders are price takers and have no influence on how the value chain is organized, even in their own countries.

Finally, the *cotton* value chain, as observed earlier, is subject to low levels of drivenness. International traders still perform classic intermediary functions. To the extent that they have increased their influence in any meaningful way, this would be through direct involvement upstream in developing countries where markets have been liberalized. But their direct involvement here has been only in a few cases extended to promoting production (normally through some kind of input-supply scheme). More often it has involved building ginneries and financing agents to buy on their behalf from direct producers. Furthermore, traders themselves construe such developments as reactive rather than proactive or bringing them benefits that were not realizable when they were dealing with export monopolies in earlier periods.

This section concludes with a couple of cross-cutting observations in relation to new threats that lead firms are sometimes cited as facing. Most obviously in relation to coffee, but increasingly also in regard to most of the other products discussed here, rising demand for social and environmental content is sometimes construed as affecting the way that buyer-driven governance may be practiced—in terms of making buyers more accountable. But rather than actually undermining buyer drivenness, lead firms' responses to these demands may end up escalating further their expectations of what services their suppliers should provide (Daviron and Ponte forthcoming; Ponte 2004a). This is likely to lead to further consolidation and to a reduction in the number of suppliers. Furthermore, it is clear that buyers may also appropriate whatever rent arises from meeting such demands. There are increasing fears among suppliers that instead of getting a premium for new quality traits embedded in the products they sell, they simply have to meet higher entry barriers (and costs) with no clear financial gain. Finally, the implications of greater buyer accountability for more direct buyer involvement in monitoring production conditions has probably been exaggerated. Although social and/or environmental demands initially led lead firms to get more directly involved in monitoring suppliers, this may have subsided as third-party certification has taken hold.

Another predicted source of threat to buyer drivenness comes from increased concentration of supply bases and the reverse dependency that may arise from this. In the coffee, fresh vegetables, and citrus chains—as well as to some extent in clothing—this has been avoided through encouraging new entrants among suppliers and playing off suppliers against each other. In coffee and clothing, countermeasures have also included sourcing directly in producing countries. So far, however, the only chain where supplier concentration is a serious issue (at both first- and second-tier supplier levels) is cocoa. Volume spreading has become relatively difficult for chocolate manufacturers, not least because grinders have internalized bean purchasing in West Africa and invested in origin-based grinding. Therefore, it has become more difficult for chocolate manufacturers to buy directly at origin. On the other hand, manufacturers have tried to compensate for this problem through side sourcing from the remaining medium-size grinders and from the (very) few remaining independent international traders.

## CHAIN DRIVING?

The notion of driving (and the related substantive drivenness) is the main conceptual entry point to examining power relations within GVCs. In Gereffi's (1994) original formulation, driving in buyer-driven chains was defined in terms of two effects: first, the transfer of so-called low-profit functions from lead firms to firms in other functional positions along the chain, and second, lead firms' attainment of enhanced organizational flexibility. Organizational flexibility appears to have two dimensions. Internal flexibility is achieved for organizations that outsource, because the resources tied up by in-house production are freed for other uses. External flexibility is achieved in the sense that outsourcing may be undertaken by a range of possible contractors. Within various GVC schools of thought, discussion around this subject has tended to be displaced by the related—but not identical—debate on forms of governance (Chapter 3). The main import of the new discussion has been to introduce the idea of different degrees and forms of coordination, ranging between vertical integration (hierarchy) and arm's length open market transactions. This approach is in turn related to a typology of lead firm characteristics, deriving partly from the transaction costs literature (Gereffi, Humphrey, and Sturgeon, 2004). As argued in Chapter 3, it is not yet fully clear where buyer-driven chains as originally defined by Gereffi are situated in relation to this typology.

Although it is necessary to acknowledge that some agrocommodity chains (e.g., cotton as well as fresh fruit and vegetables into mainland Europe) are of a predominantly open market kind, our own work suggests that forms of governance within chains that are more clearly driven seem to be quite similar and subject to increasing levels of convergence. At the same time, reaffirming the importance of buyer-driven chain governance as one of only two basic types of governance does not necessarily also entail reaffirming Gereffi's original definition of buyer-driven governance—in terms of externalization of low-profit functions and achievement of organizational flexibility. This definition, although reflecting important realities, suffers from normative and even teleological connotations. That is, modalities of driving are defined only in terms of the actions required to realize a set of outcomes from which lead firms will necessarily benefit (although others may benefit from them too).

Starting from a different, more empirical departure point, an initial conclusion from our own research program is that the overall process of driving rests on two separate sets of mechanisms. One set concerns relations between lead firms and first-tier suppliers (only touched on in this chapter), whereas the other characterizes relations between first-and second-tier suppliers.

In the GVCs discussed here, the mechanisms of driving *between lead firms and first-tier suppliers* consist of the following:

1. the definition (and occasional redefinition) of a functional division of labor between them;
2. the definition (and regular redefinition) of prices, commissions, payment terms, and other contractual matters;
3. the definition and redefinition of the performance criteria corresponding to the functions that first-tier suppliers are expected to play;
4. the definition of the quality of a product or service that is purchased, and in some cases of the process of arriving at the final product or service, plus the setting of technical specifications and possibly the identification of a given social and environmental content (in relation to conforming to codes of conduct and various kinds of certifications);
5. a combination of dependency and provision of new opportunities; this secures a degree of (nontransparent) competition within the supply base and simultaneously hardens and softens lead firms' use of power.

The practical content of these driving structures and processes differ systematically between chains, particularly with respect to specific functional capacities and performance criteria. Expected capacities and performance requirements also differ even more within single chains, according to end market, market segment (income group served) and market channel (type of intermediary involved). To take only one of these variables, there are significant differences in the scope and codification of performance criteria used in clothing chains between those chain segments or filaments ending in the United States and those ending in (especially) mainland E.U. markets.

In many cases, these differences in the parts of the chain ending in the United States and European Union respectively go beyond differences in performance criteria to include differences in expectations concerning functional capacities as well as in *modalities* of driving. U.S. lead firms expect their first-tier suppliers to impose on second-tier suppliers exact and non-negotiable product construction methods and measurement specifications; they also insist on process-based quality assurance backed up by their own outstationed quality controllers. Finally, they require frequent and detailed progress reporting and resort to bureaucratic and legalistic means to resolve disputes. E.U. lead firms want their first-tier suppliers to drive chains in ways that place higher value on suppliers' versatility and innovation, as well as on their capacity to follow instructions. Some of these differences reflect differences in sourcing history (many U.S. buyers started out with outsourcing only assembly, where suppliers were typically less capable and required greater supervision). But U.S.-European cultural differences/expectations also seem to play a role both in styles of driving and the respective values attached to specific performance criteria. Thus, market characteristics translate into different power dynamics and opportunity structures in chains.

Similar differences can be detected in the citrus chain, but in this case between the filaments ending with U.K. supermarkets and those ending in Japan (Mather 2002b). On the one hand, U.K. lead firms expect their first-tier suppliers to continuously seek new opportunities to fill product gaps (e.g., time windows when particular varieties are unavailable). They also rigorously enforce a wide range of quality standards (food safety parameters and conformity with so-called good agricultural practices).[19] On the other hand, first-tier suppliers in the Japanese citrus chain are typically independent agents working on commission for giant multiproduct trading houses (IPM, Royal, Union), who in turn sell into *all* end-market channels in Japan—wholesale, supermarkets, and smaller multiples. Since the mid-1990s, the chief tasks of these agents have been to enforce a rather narrow range of quality parameters, albeit to extremely demanding specifications and often on the basis of supplier investment in special equipment[20] and thorough intensive sampling at the packing stage. The quality parameters in question are very high sugar levels, conformity to one or another of three (larger) size groups, conformity with a specific shape (perfect roundness) and with a specific skin description. Second, agents have to ensure the conformity of the producing country part of the chain with Japanese public sanitary and phytosanitary standards. These entail passing a screening examination by Japanese government agents at the point of export and, immediately after, cold sterilization at minus 0.5°C for twenty days. First-tier suppliers are not expected to fill product gaps, and their own second-tier suppliers are not expected to follow any specific catalogue of agricultural or social practices that go beyond those strictly necessary to produce fruit specific to Japanese quality parameters.

Together with differences within and among chains, at least two new common tendencies can be detected in driving structures and processes in various chains. The first is for first-tier suppliers to be expected to have the capacity to manage inventory on behalf of lead firms. For example, when international traders and importing wholesalers played the main intermediation roles in cocoa and coffee, they held stock on the account of second-tier suppliers (exporters from developing countries) for resale over short periods (so-called consignment sales). They also held stock on their own account for speculative reasons. Finally, they held stock for immediate delivery against the order of a specific end customer, on the latter's account. Currently, these same actors—in their new guises—are expected (as a core function) to procure and hold stock, sometimes over a prolonged period, entirely on their own account. In other words, they are expected to themselves sell to lead firms on a consignment basis. Thus, trade finance is now among the functions that first-tier suppliers are expected to carry out for lead firms.[21] A second common tendency is that first-tier suppliers are expected to compete not only on cost, but also on volume and variety of service provision.

## CONCLUSION

The last twenty years, and especially the last ten, have seen an uneven but significant rise of buyer drivenness in GVCs. There are exceptions to this process, just as there are different starting points for it and different types of buyer involved, but the movement is widespread and in a single broad direction. Furthermore, common to a wide variety of buyer drivers, there are common stories about business strategy. These stories come in different languages—that of multiformatting, including a hard discount format, in the case of retail, and that of leadership across a variety of product groups in the case of branded manufacturing—but in all cases there is a common grammar of high volumes and low prices. Besides the factors discussed in Chapter 1, the strengthening of buyer drivenness has been facilitated by changes in international and national regulatory frameworks—such as trade and import liberalization, financial and currency liberalization, increasingly stringent food safety regulation, and the collapse of commodity agreements. In most but not all cases, the buyers occupying lead firm status in a specific chain appear to come from a single functional background, whether it is retail or branded manufacturing. In the cocoa chain, buyers from two separate functional backgrounds (cocoa grinding and chocolate manufacture) share chain leadership in an uneasy alliance. The groups of buyers identified rely in turn on a range of first-tier suppliers who play system integrating roles. These come from a wider range of backgrounds than buyers themselves, even within the same specific chains. Here are found manufacturers and ex-manufacturers, international traders and ex-international traders, Southern producers who have become globalized, and many others.

The empirical material presented in this chapter suggests that the most important element of power relations between lead firms and first-tier suppliers is control over the definition of the functions that first-tier suppliers should play, rather than the externalization of low profit functions as argued in earlier literature. As Sturgeon (2002) has noted (see Chapter 1), these externalized functions may be actually more profitable than some of those that are not discarded by lead firms. They are simply functions that lead firms do not want to carry out, either because of their medium-term overhead cost implications or, over the longer term, because of the redefinition of what firms count as their core competence. Decisions of this kind are never based on economic rationalities alone, but also on changes in organizations' internal balances of power and on fashions in the business consultancy sector.

Another observation emerging in this chapter is that, although lead firms' power is used to control the definition of functions performed by other actors in the value chain, dramatic redistributions of functions within chains are not especially frequent events. After leadership status has been captured, lead firms mostly use power to leverage changes in prices and contractual conditions (see Chapter 1), as well as to tighten performance requirements (including those related to quality; see Chapter 6), within a functional division of labor that is subject mainly to incremental change.

Finally, in the process of narrowing their range of activities and of concentrating more resources on those they deem to be germane, lead firms do not become more flexible. Actually, their need for flexibility from first-tier suppliers is amplified. A good part of these requirements have a temporary or cyclical character and can be met only if first-tier suppliers carry excess capacity and stock. This means that first-tier suppliers have to carry more risk, but also that lead firms may become dependent on specific first-tier suppliers. In this process, the flexibility of lead firms also declines. Effective countermeasures by lead firms include promoting new entrants to first-tier supplier status, resorting to the remaining small- and medium-scale suppliers for some nonservice requirements, and sourcing directly in producing countries (or skipping one functional position when buying). In the long run, though, dependence mostly runs in the other direction. First-tier suppliers are vulnerable in various ways, including as a result of the range of functions that they must carry and the chances of their second guesses being wrong. However, they are mainly at risk on the basis of a lead firm suffering business difficulties and pulling out of a particular market.

# 5   Entry Barriers, Marginalization, and Upgrading

IN THIS CHAPTER, we continue the empirical investigation of the GVCs for coffee, cocoa, fresh vegetables, citrus, clothing, and cotton through an analysis of how the restructuring of relations between lead firms and first-tier suppliers (described in the last chapter) affects second-tier suppliers. Because of the general absence of African enterprises from first-tier status, turning our attention to second-tier suppliers enables a clearer focus on Africa. In other words, the structural differentiation of roles within these GVCs is broadly (though not uniformly) paralleled by a geographical differentiation.

Particular attention will be paid to two aspects of second-tier suppliers' changing conditions of existence in these chains. The first aspect to be examined will be changes in entry barriers to these positions. The concept of entry barriers has a long history in the economic literature. A classic exposition, from the structure-conduct-performance school, is that of Bain (1956). In Bain's approach—and in most subsequent expositions including Gereffi's (1994)—entry barriers are treated from the viewpoint of competitive advantage, that is, mainly in terms of the benefits that they present to incumbents or firms that have already surmounted these barriers. In this spirit, three types of entry barrier are typically identified: economies of scale, cost advantages (themselves deriving either from first mover advantage or intrinsic cost efficiency), and product differentiation advantage (due to intrinsically better products or more successful branding strategies). All three are seen as essentially temporary in nature, since each is subject to modification either by market forces or by technological or marketing innovations carried out by competitors of incumbents. The only entry barriers that are not purely temporary in character are those created by monopoly cartels (although these tend to break down over time, as a result of their implicit inefficiencies) or by government action in the form of exclusive licensing, subsidies, tariffs, or regulations.

What is missing from this picture is the perspective of markets that are differentiated in tiers of enterprises performing different functions and with radically different resource bases—in other words, markets where there are a restricted number of lead firms and a large number of subordinate suppliers. Incorporating this perspective allows *innovation in supply chain organization* to be recognized as an additional form of competitive advantage and therefore as an entry barrier. Innovations of this kind have different outcomes for lead firms and for firms supplying them. Lead firms may have the resources to react to an innovation introduced by one of them; this reaction may cancel out the new entry barriers they may face. But their suppliers will, as a result of this process, face new entry barriers to their *own* positions. These entry barriers rise as competing lead firms mimic or improve on each others' supply chain innovations. Taking this perspective implies reversing the traditional entry barrier paradigm from one based on assumptions about cycles of innovation and resulting competitive advantage on a level playing field to one acknowledging differences between actors' structural positions, and therefore in patterns, magnitudes, and durations of change to entry barriers.

Acknowledgement of these arguments does not invalidate the point that government actions may also create entry barriers. In relation to the GVCs studied here, this is most obvious in the case of rules of origin in the global clothing trade. The highly demanding rules of the Lomé Convention and the Cotonou Agreement, for example, have led to inclusion of (firm- or cluster-based) vertical integration as a required functional capacity for ACP suppliers of clothing into the European Union.[1] More commonly, market and public regulatory-based entry barriers are often intertwined. This is clear in the case of the fresh vegetable trade, where a combination of E.U. food safety regulations and private standards have led to demands on suppliers for conformity with more exacting and costly production processes and internal monitoring mechanisms. In this case, E.U. maximum pesticide residue (MRL) regulations now require development of an approved spraying program (based on the evolving regulations but adjusted to local conditions), registration of total pesticide purchases, recording of all pesticide use, and ensuring the burning of used canisters. Meanwhile, via the EUREP-GAP project,[2] E.U. and especially U.K. supermarkets have collectively formulated a list of approved good agricultural and good manufacturing practices that refer to packinghouse infrastructure and organization (e.g., Plexiglas windows and light covers; provision of separate rooms for unpacked and packed vegetables; specific types of toilet, changing area, and washing-up facilities; chilled and chlorinated water supply), labor organization (e.g., assurance of clean overalls) and labor process (e.g., registration system for knives and adhesive bandages), pointing in a common direction toward audit-based traceability.[3]

Besides looking at entry barriers, this chapter also aims to treat their successful negotiation by some African second-tier suppliers. This will be examined in terms of the notion of supplier upgrading. However, this issue will not be approached on the basis of the typology of upgrading forms/opportunities that earlier GVC thinking has referred to, and which was criticized in Chapter 3. Earlier GVC thinking makes similar assumptions to those found in the classical discussion of entry barriers. It even identifies some types of upgrading that directly correspond to the dimensions of competitive advantage found in the classical discussion. Rather, the approach used here will focus on the evolving *reward structure* for suppliers implicit in the escalation of entry barriers and on the empirical roles available to trigger these rewards.

## Entry Barriers for First- and Second-Tier Suppliers

In the GVCs examined in this book, by far the most demanding entry barrier increases have been for first-tier suppliers. As described in the last chapter, such suppliers have in most cases faced pressure to add new functional capacities—particularly, but not only, that of inventory management—to their pre-existing ones. To a limited extent, first-tier suppliers have endeavored to pass on the provision (and associated costs and risks) of these capacities further upstream to second-tier suppliers. But in most cases this is impractical, because second-tier suppliers have no access to the resources necessary to absorb such functions. Thus, what first-tier suppliers mostly seek to modify in respect to second-tier ones are volumes, prices, payment terms, specializations, and geographical location—all within existing capacities. In other words, although lead firms re-engineer their supply chains largely in terms of outsourcing functions, first-tier suppliers do so mainly with the objective of establishing an optimally competitive portfolio of subcontractors.

As a result, two of the main ways in which driving between first-tier and second-tier suppliers differs from driving between lead firms and first-tier suppliers are, first, there is more emphasis on promoting internal competition within the supply base, and second, there are more actions by first-tier suppliers having the aim of improving the competitive position of specific second-tier suppliers. The latter is necessary to improve the competitiveness of the first-tier supplier itself vis-à-vis lead firms.

The emphasis on promotion of internal competition takes the form of active cross-costing[4] as well as active recruitment of more or less specialized new suppliers by price point, product type, technical capability, lead-time status, and trade regime status. Actions to actively develop suppliers tend to be confined to new supply markets or to the introduction of new product types that potential second-tier suppliers are able to handle. Part of the competitive advantage of first-tier suppliers depends on their ability to nurse some less-established second-tier suppliers. This entails providing them with resources—mostly technical, but occasionally also financial.[5]

Another type of supplier development takes the form of matchmaking new combinations of second-tier suppliers. This is done by first-tier suppliers to fulfill lead firms' expectations regarding product development. It takes place through securing links between previously unrelated competences among second-tier suppliers. It is a relatively expensive activity and its gestation time may be long, which makes this type of second-tier supplier development relatively rare.[6]

Against the background of these considerations, a central argument made in this chapter is that lead firms require more *functional capacities* from first-tier suppliers in all cases, as well as (in some cases) from second-tier suppliers and beyond. This development has taken place since the mid-1980s at least in some segments of the chains examined here (except for cotton). At the same time, lead firms require higher *performance* levels from second-tier suppliers in most cases. *Capacities* refer to ranges of activities that suppliers are required to carry out and the conditions necessary to fulfill them. *Performances* refer to standards for carrying out such activities. Capacities may be demanded explicitly by lead firms or first-tier suppliers, or may have become necessary to stay in the game without having been demanded explicitly.

What needs to be highlighted at this point is that second-tier suppliers do not face higher performance requirements in *all* chains. In certain agrofood value chains, there have been technological advances by first-tier suppliers that render second-tier suppliers' traditional performance levels irrelevant. In other chains, the disintegration of the institutional conditions that supported suppliers' abilities to meet traditional performance levels has meant that those still able to meet them have become preferred suppliers without any improvement in performance.

Certain agrofood value chains exhibit both of these developments. In the remainder of this section, we document these claims in more detail through two stories about change in entry barriers. The two stories point toward different sources and types—rather than to different degrees—of marginalization and exclusion.

## Story 1: Raised Entry Barriers for Both First-Tier and Second-Tier Suppliers

This story applies to *clothing, coffee, fresh vegetables,* and *citrus* (into the U.K. market). Space does not permit an extension of earlier discussion of raised entry barriers for first-tier suppliers in these cases. Yet, one common feature is that first-tier suppliers are now required to provide several varieties of a product (or products) throughout .the year and the same product from more than one country or developing region (where this was not already required earlier). A second common feature is that first-tier suppliers finance and hold inventory on behalf of lead firms and/or deliver it on a quick-response basis. For fresh produce, where inventory is perishable, quick response is secured through first-tier suppliers keeping reserve capacity on tap rather than holding inventory as such. A third common feature is that first-tier suppliers actively engage in identifying and providing additional services.

Table 5.1 provides an indication of changing functional capacities and performance requirements expected of developing country second-tier suppliers in the clothing and coffee chains—that is, developing country–based manufacturers and independent exporters respectively. The coverage is global for clothing and for liberalized domestic market systems for coffee. These two chains have been chosen because the products concerned have been traded globally for a long time (unlike, for example, fresh vegetables). Thus, escalations in demands in relation to them are easier to document.

As implied in the earlier identification of differences in driving related to the nature of end markets and business cultures, functional requirements in the clothing sector vary according to whether chains end in the United States, United Kingdom, or elsewhere. The U.S. market generally insists on minimum physical capacity measured in terms of number of employees, client-dedicated merchandizing,[7] (increasingly) fabric sourcing capacity, and (at least from larger suppliers) design input. Fabric sourcing capacity is sought more in respect to the financial capacity to carry it out, rather than the capacity to identify suitable textile suppliers. This is because there is a tendency for U.S.-based lead agents

**Table 5.1**  Functional capacities and performance requirements for second-tier suppliers (clothing and coffee chains)

| Functional capacities | Performance requirements |
|---|---|
| *Clothing* | |
| Minimum capacity (*N* employees; § volumes per style); | Meeting price points |
| | Manufacture to specified tolerances |
| Fabric sourcing (and related working capital requirements) § | Upward volume flexibility * |
| Client-dedicated merchandising * (numbers of merchandisers) | Machine inspection and maintenance routine *§ |
| Own laboratory for chemical tests * | Lead times—fielding inquiry *§ |
| Provision of design service/input | Lead times—sampling *§ |
| Product development capacity (in-house textile and clothing technologists) *§ | Lead times—piece good production (tightened) |
| | Comprehensive internal record-keeping system*§ |
| | Conformity to agreed critical path * |
| | Assurance of systematic separation of client's raw materials, components, and piece goods *§ |
| | Multistage in-line quality control (QC) system *§ |
| | Monitoring of client's specific QC needs *§ |
| | Conformity to client's storage norms *§ |
| | Reject levels (tightened) |
| | Delivery accuracy (not tightened but made more complex) and reliability |
| | Code of conduct *§ |
| | Needle policy * |
| *Coffee* | |
| Capacity to produce a sample for approval, in relation to a given taste/aroma profile (use of cupper; not new but has become more generalized) # | Access to a wider range of qualities * |
| | Monitoring for contamination / size/defects and for humidity |
| | Timely delivery to port |

**Table 5.1** *Continued*

| Functional capacities | Performance requirements |
|---|---|
| | *Coffee* |
| Ability to search for, procure, and deliver a minimum quantity matched to sample and related working capital requirements (search element new, procurement element modified) # | Certification of conformity with organic/environmental criteria *§ |
| Ownership of curing plant and access to pre-export storage and transport * | |
| Ability to use futures market * | |

Key: * new since the mid-1980s
§ required in some end markets/segments only
# applicable especially to Arabica coffee, less to Robusta coffee

or their first-tier suppliers to nominate textile suppliers. The E.U. (including the U.K.) market generally looks for physical capacity in terms of minimum volume/style, fabric sourcing in the full sense of the term,[8] client-dedicated merchandising, and design and product development (from virtually all suppliers). There are similar differences in respect to performance requirements, although in this case it is the U.S. market that demands more performance attributes and generally higher performance levels.

In clothing, a majority of required functional capacities and performances have originated since around 1985, with the onset of more systematically globalized sourcing. In addition, some traditional requirements have been tightened, such as lead times for piece goods. Transformations have also occurred in the complexity of how such requirements need to be met, as in the case of delivery requirements.[9] In the coffee chain, some functional capacities required of independent exporters are also either new or have been extended from a few end markets to a more general level. However, performance requirements for activities that existed already have not escalated in the same way as for clothing.

Buyer-driven factors in raising entry barriers are most evident in the case of clothing, especially in relation to lead times/upward volume flexibility, quality, and add-on services. Lead times for at least a part of all orders have fallen from traditional standards of five to six months to anything between one and three months, partly as a result of the shift from a four- to a six-season fashion year and partly as a result of orders being placed only at a stage within seasons when demand patterns for specific styles have been established. Linked demands for upward volume flexibility, which are completely new, reflect a particularly stark form of buyer drivenness. The lead-time changes just mentioned are linked with buyers' efforts to reduce risk by placing only very low initial orders. First-tier suppliers are expected to leave capacity open, which can be filled rapidly as and when required. This expectation is often passed onto second-tier suppliers.

A number of new functional capacities and performance require-ments in the clothing sector are also related to the escalation of norms for basic quality (now comprising a wider range of product attributes, such as maximization of color fastness, minimization of shrinkage, crinkling, etc). These capacities, such as in-house laboratories, are a reflection of retailers' desire to eliminate in-house product inspection. The new func-tional requirement for product development capacity reflects a parallel clothing retailer goal, particularly in Europe, to outsource previously back-of-house functions (as occurred in many cases with design at an earlier stage). In the United States, product development and design are typically demanded more from first-tier suppliers than ones in lower tiers, underlining U.S. agents' more differentiated sets of expectations.

Although exogenous factors such as pressures for code of conduct conformity and developments in information technology have played a part in reshaping buyers' expectations, buyer drivenness has played a role in the rapidity with which they have been integrated into the man-agement of supply chains. As noted in Chapter 1, the dependency of product differentiation on branding has been associated with an increase in the intangible content of brands and of in-house private labels. Al-though insistence on code of conduct conformity results from the in-creased vulnerability of brands to corporate social responsibility pres-sures, moral considerations now play a prominent role in brand equity and to this extent can be construed also as fashion statements.

Buyer-driven factors in raising entry barriers are also present in the case of coffee, but to a lesser extent. A majority of the new entry barriers in this trade derive from the demise of international and national regu-latory systems. When domestic markets were still regulated (as was the case in some East African countries until the early- to mid-1990s), inde-pendent exporters needed to cover the range of functions and related working capital costs from national coffee auctions downstream, rather than from the farm gate as is now the case. In markets where there was only a single buyer, exporters purchased coffee that was already cured at plants owned by cooperative unions or parastatal companies.[10] Curing now has to take place in-house by exporters if they are to meet lead-time constraints (toll curing at cooperatives can imply holdups in favor of coffee that cooperatives want to export themselves). Traditionally, ICA quotas also made export prices relatively predictable. Currently, if independent traders want to stay in the game under conditions of higher price volatility, they have to understand—and have the resources to operate in—futures markets.

The main buyer-driven change that has occurred in coffee (especially for the Arabica variety) is a shift in much of the trade from sale on description to sale against approved samples. This change partly reflects the consequences of deregulation, in the sense that the traditional varietal and quality characteristics of national crops can no longer be taken on trust. Partly, it is the consequence of increased product differentiation in end markets (with the emergence of specialty coffees). This is associated with heightened demand for specific properties and/or assurance of consistency in their supply. Hence, there is increased specification of profiles and ordering, and a checking off of deliveries against samples.[11] For second-tier suppliers to stay in the game, they need to have access not only to a range of qualities, but increasingly also to coffees that match certain social and/or environmental criteria (fair trade, organic, shade-grown, or "sustainable coffees").

Although escalations in demands are harder to trace for products that have not been traded globally for such a long time as clothing and coffee, it is still worth briefly considering the U.K.-destined chains for *fresh vegetables* and *citrus*. In the case of the fresh vegetable chain from East Africa to the United Kingdom, there has been little or no escalation in the demands applied to so-called Asian vegetables, which represented the largest single product group of all fresh fruit and vegetables exported from Kenya in 1984–1986 (38.9 percent by volume; M.F. Jensen 2000). Asian vegetables have a relatively low level of perishability and some can be exported without a cold chain. This group of products is still sold into U.K. wholesale markets, where apparently there is not only no concern that suppliers observe good farming practices, but also a lack of implementation of the due diligence provisions of the U.K. Food Safety Act (M.F. Jensen 2000).

The aggregate increase in demands concerning Kenyan suppliers' capacities and performance has two sources. The first is the increasing share in the country's total fresh exports represented by the supermarket-dedicated crops of green beans, snow and snap peas (rising from 20.8 percent by volume in 1984–1986 to 40.4 percent in 1997–1999; M.F. Jensen 2000). The second concerns supermarkets' ever-rising private standards concerning food safety, the environment, and labor conditions. Implied by this development is an extension of suppliers' functional capacities to include the performance and monitoring of certain new processes and tightened performance requirements across the board.

In the case of the citrus chain from South Africa into the United Kingdom, a significant escalation of buyers' demands became possible only following the liberalization of South African export marketing in 1997. Prior to this time, the producer association Outspan—by virtue of its export monopoly and its alliance with the corresponding deciduous fruit export monopoly Unifruco—commanded a sufficient global market share to be susceptible only to the most basic buyer demands. For example, Outspan was in a position to ignore U.K. supermarkets' emerging demands for product grading. The period since South African market liberalization has seen a consensual escalation of demands. Their content has become practically identical to that just described for fresh vegetables. But in this case, supermarkets are making them to a self-selected group of large private South African growers. The latter have sought to use the adoption of these demands to successfully replace Outspan (now Capespan) as the supply base of U.K. supermarkets. This has entailed massive changes for private growers in terms of the required functional capacities (their own packinghouse and cool chains) and in terms of enhanced performance requirements (among others, conforming to so-called good agricultural practices).

## Story 2: Raised Entry Barriers for First-Tier Suppliers and Unchanged or Even Reduced Ones for Second-Tier Suppliers

This story applies to *cocoa* and *cotton*—if in the latter case international traders are considered as first-tier suppliers. As noted earlier, the latter chain lacks a clear group of lead firms and, given the nature of its up- and downstream industrial structures, it is unclear whether it will ever be highly driven. There is nonetheless a kind of hierarchy within the chain, with a few large spinners, a small group of international traders, and a small group of developing country producer associations sharing influence. All of these trade on their own accounts and sometimes on those of others. Against the familiar background of market saturation, international traders seem to be the ones under most pressure to restructure their operations.

As in Story 1, space does not permit an extended discussion of raised barriers for first-tier suppliers in the cocoa chain. But the functions that are now carried out by lead international trader-grinders (Cargill, ADM, and Barry-Callebaut) revolve around the customized production of cocoa liquors, melted butters and intermediate chocolate products for chocolate manufacturers/branders. Trader-grinders also hold inventory on chocolate manufacturers' behalf, deliver to them on a just-in-time basis, and participate in product development. What trader-grinders do not need to do anymore (or not to the same extent) is to source multiple varieties of beans and to source beans from different regions, although they may still wish to do this for price reasons (there is still some residual price discrimination by national origin). They have partly freed themselves from these functional activities by introducing technical innovations enabling them to generate variety/quality in the liquoring process itself, essentially by prolonging this process beyond its traditional duration. It appears that the additional processing costs entailed are more than compensated for by the economies of scale that can be obtained as a result of shipping and storing beans in bulk (in a manner where they are not segregated along the lines of traditional quality dimensions).

The cotton chain appears to have moved toward a heightened degree of segmentation. Traditionally, large producer associations—especially those in the United States and Australia—tried to improve their margins by selling at least part of their cotton directly (or via agents) to larger spinners. However, a majority of the internationally traded crop was always sold through international trading companies such as Dunavant, Paul Reinhardt, Cargill, Louis Dreyfus, and Baumann Hinde. Over the last two decades, large producer associations in the United States, Australia, Brazil, and Israel have sought to upgrade their level of service provision to customers by providing more exact descriptions of the industrial properties of their crops. Traditional quality measures used in the international trade were originally based on visual properties that had industrial implications, but more directly reflected crop husbandry and postharvest practices. In some cases, the industrial relevance of certain traditional properties declined over time in the light of changes in spinning technology. As a result of the emergence of a new measurement technology (high-volume instrument machines) propagated by the U.S. Department of Agriculture, batches of cotton can now be separated according to more relevant industrial properties and sold to spinners on this basis, although customization in the full sense is not possible, since spinners always carry out further blending prior to spinning. At the same time, it seems unlikely that this practice will become a global norm. Many cottons can not at present be subject to measurement with high-volume instrument machines. For other cottons, there are doubts of various kinds about the accuracy of high-volume instrument readings. As a result, although these machines have now been installed in many tropical producing countries, it is only for the countries just listed that high-volume instrument readings are taken as definitive in the international trade.

Against this background, the division of labor between international traders and spinners remains largely unchanged. Thus, a fundamental difference exists between the cocoa and cotton chains. Whereas international trader-grinders have captured from cocoa growers the generation of underlying product quality, international cotton traders continue to sell cotton under descriptions in which national origin (and its associated complex of traditional quality and variety parameters) is the key indicator. On the side of common features, there have been some increases in entry barriers for first-tier suppliers in both cases. For cocoa, these relate to the combination of the technological demands necessary to capture the generation of underlying quality parameters and the scale levels necessary to make the corresponding investments profitable. For cotton, entry barriers relate to the changing conditions for obtaining a variety of national origins in interesting volumes and with traditional quality characteristics. As in the case of coffee, export market liberalization in developing country producers has undermined historical mechanisms of crop diffusion, input supply, and quality control. To ensure interesting volumes of a national origin with traditional quality parameters, international cotton traders have to go to the source, sometimes to the extent of initiating outgrower schemes.

There are virtually no corresponding new functional capacity or performance requirements for second-tier suppliers in these chains (Table 5.2). Indeed, at least in cocoa, the main tendency has been for a buyer-driven reduction in demands for both capacities and basic performance requirements. Because of the capture of the generation of quality farther downstream, it is no longer strictly necessary to grade by quality at any stage of the cocoa chain prior to export. The only cocoa beans still consistently separated by national origin for grinding purposes are those from Ghana. Although beans sorted by size still command a premium (in Ghana and elsewhere), it is no longer a functional requirement even for this type of screening to occur because grinders can compensate for

**Table 5.2**   Functional capacities and performance requirements for second-tier suppliers (cocoa and cotton chains)

| Functional capacities | Performance requirements |
|---|---|
| *Cocoa* | |
| Ability to search for, procure, and deliver a minimum volume | Certification in conformity with organic/environmental criteria *§ |
| Access to pre-export storage, transport, and packaging materials * | |
| *Cotton* | |
| Ability to search for, procure, and deliver a minimum volume of a given variety | Timely delivery to port |
| Access to pre-export storage, transport, and packaging material | |
| Ownership of ginnery | |

Key: * new since the mid-1980s
§ required in some end markets/segments only

the mixing of large and small beans by reversing the traditional order of roasting and grinding, so that the latter takes place first. In cotton, there is an implicit rather than explicit reduction in entry requirements for the open bulk market, following the fact that first-tier suppliers have partly internalized the role of providing crops that correspond to traditional quality parameters. Countries where quality control has broken down or where traders have not set up outgrower schemes are now incorporated in the chain from the outset for procurement of additional volumes or on the basis of discounts. Cotton from these countries is bought ungraded from second-tier suppliers.

In theory, the reduction of functional capacities and performance requirements for participation in the cotton and cocoa value chains should have led in the medium term to increases in the populations of second-tier suppliers (independent exporters), whereas reductions in their numbers might have been expected in clothing and coffee. In reality, at least in the countries covered by the GLAF research program (and in parallel work undertaken on cocoa in Côte d'Ivoire; see Losch 2002), populations of independent exporters first rose temporarily, then fell, except for clothing generally and cotton in Tanzania. In clothing, the population of third-tier suppliers (subcontractors to second-tier suppliers) has fallen instead. The reasons for these outcomes, and their consequences further upstream, are discussed in the next section.

## MARGINALIZATION AND EXCLUSION

The changes in entry barriers described in the previous section have direct implications for marginalization and exclusion. *Marginalization* is used here to refer to downgrading within given global chains—relegation to less remunerative and/or secure end-market segments or channels. *Exclusion* is used to refer to inability to enter, as well as to expulsion from, global chains. The analysis is based on a continuation of the two stories outlined in the previous section.

### *Marginalization and Exclusion Implications of Story 1*

The GLAF research program examined the *clothing* sectors of Mauritius and South Africa. Mauritius was already an established exporter to the E.U. and U.S. markets when the changes in functional capacities and performance outlined previously were introduced. South Africa's export trade to both markets was restricted or virtually nonexistent until the mid-1990s, when the apartheid era ended and trade liberalization started.[12] Yet, the South African clothing industry was actually larger than Mauritius' in terms of employment and output. These different trajectories mean that Mauritius has faced new entry barriers as adjustment challenges, whereas South Africa has faced them as obstacles to market entry.

For clothing manufacturers all over the world, price has been an ongoing constraint as a result of growing retail concentration and the continuous opening up of new sources of supply with lower labor costs. In a way that mirrors the economics of natural resource extraction in its consequences, as producing countries become more established, they tend to be less internationally competitive due to higher employment levels and therefore higher labor costs.[13] Mauritius has suffered from severe price pressures of this kind for ten to fifteen years, since near full employment was reached. Lomé-based trade preferences into the European Union and the island's possession of Multifibre Arrangement quotas into the U.S. market mitigated this price pressure,[14] but more in respect to delaying its impact than providing long-term relief. Among other entry barriers, new quality expectations were experienced mainly during the first half of the 1990s, whereas lead times have become a growing challenge over the past five to six years.

The Mauritian industry responded fairly successfully to new quality demands. It even exceeded them, since the main initial form of response to price pressures was to move toward higher market segments in both the European Union and the United States. But this movement has had exclusionary effects. Until 1992–1995, many of the orders received by larger Mauritian companies were outsourced to smaller owner-operated assemblers. Because increased quality requirements entailed ensuring greater consistency and control, meeting them meant that subcontractors had to be either integrated into larger plants or dropped. In most cases, the subcontractors were also the most price sensitive, since labor represented a very high proportion of their costs. An average of 15 percent of enterprises closed *per year* during 1992–1995, although sector employment dropped by only 13 percent over the whole period.

Larger Mauritian enterprises began to feel the full effect of price competition in the second half of the 1990s. Although some tried to avert this by seeking to upgrade functionally into own-brand manufacture (see Chapter 3), a more common and sustained response was to restructure costs by delocalizing some existing (and all new) business to Madagascar, where wages were only around 25 percent or less of those in Mauritius. A second response, in Mauritius itself, was to replace local labor with foreign contract labor. Wages for foreign labor were not lower than those of Mauritian workers, but foreign workers were perceived as having significantly higher productivity levels (figures of up to 30 percent were commonly cited in interviews) and could provide greater flexibility by being prepared to work twenty-five to thirty hours per week overtime. Mauritian enterprises created around 50,000 new jobs in Madagascar during the period 1996–2001, while replacing 20 percent of the domestic labor force with migrant labor. At the same time, a second round of corporate consolidation took place. This mainly affected larger companies that had failed to delocalize or that had delocalized late. It also affected smaller specialized companies providing services like washing, printing, and embroidery—services that larger companies felt compelled to internalize for lead-time reasons. The raising of entry barriers thus translated into exclusion of smaller enterprises (and that part of their workforce that was not absorbed into larger companies) and of a significant proportion of local workers in larger enterprises.

In the context of a heightened interest in Africa on the part of U.S. buyers arising from the ratification of the Africa Growth and Opportunity Act (2000), South African exports to the United States rose to $232 million in 2003. However, all but a handful of the exporting enterprises were owned by overseas Chinese and were situated in rural areas with low labor costs. They operated on the basis of the same business model of long runs of basic clothing found in Madagascar. The main differences between (mostly Chinese-owned) South African companies and Mauritian-owned Madagascan ones were that the former were exporting into even lower market segments than the latter and were mainly using fabrics from outside of the region.

The larger domestically-owned segment of the South African clothing industry was for the most part either not exporting at all or was doing so only marginally. These were enterprises located in urban areas with wage levels similar to those in Mauritius. Traditionally, they had developed overhead structures geared mostly to the demands of local retailers. These retailers had used the opportunities presented by South Africa's trade liberalization in 1994 to source their own long-run (high-volume) production offshore from Asia, leaving local manufacturers with short runs that were also design and service intensive. In contrast, global buyers were interested in long runs in South Africa, were not greatly interested in local service offering, and viewed the local textile industry as expensive and slow. In other words, locally owned companies were unable to enter the global chain without starting from scratch, that is, moving to rural areas and adopting a different business model.

The coffee sectors of Kenya, Ethiopia, Tanzania, and Uganda present interesting contrasts. In Kenya, a traditional regulatory system remains in place, with the role of foreign exporters limited to purchase from mandatory auctions. Coffee is supplied directly to the auction by cooperative societies and private estates. Before reaching the auction, it is cured in cooperative-owned or private processing plants. In this sense, there is no legal domestic trade, although the approval of a recent liberalization act may change the situation in the future. In Ethiopia, foreign exporters are not even allowed to participate in the auction (except for a few companies that have been operating there from before the onset of the Derg regime). The domestic market in Ethiopia is also in the hands of local traders. In both countries, there is a clean break in the coffee chain, with buyer drivenness impinging directly only in terms of the exercise of buying power at the auctions in relation to certain favored quality profiles. Although there is still strong buyer interest in continuing to engage with the Kenyan and Ethiopian systems on this basis, it remains conditional on the ability of these countries to reproduce their traditional varietal and quality profiles.

In Tanzania, exporters and other categories of trader were allowed to participate at all levels of the trade between 1994 and 2002. A compulsory auction still existed in this period, but only as a formality where exporters went through the ritual of repurchasing coffee that they had procured already upstream. As noted earlier, free competition for the crop inside Tanzania entailed that exporters had to finance crop purchase and storage from the farm gate onward, plus invest in curing plants. Competition led to an end of quality checks and grading at the first point of sale, on the grounds that the introduction of such checks by any single buyer would simply divert trade to competitors. Thus exporters were confronted with having to meet roasters' demands for more specific taste/aroma profiles from coffee beans that were of highly uneven quality. Exporters responded to this situation in a number of ways, including adjusting downward at least some of the taste/aroma profiles traditionally associated with Tanzania, taking discounts on consignments not meeting agreed profiles, and engaging in their own production to allow quality and volume to be ensured from source. The latter has occurred mainly for specialty coffee customers, where high premiums can be earned for estate-specific properties.

Marginalization in this case is manifested through the downgrading of the quality reputation of Tanzanian coffee (and premiums attached to it). In other words, Tanzanian coffee has shifted to a lower market segment. It is also being sold on less favorable terms than previously, in the sense that forward sales have fallen as a proportion of all sales and that, where they have been maintained, the length of forward sale periods has fallen. Exclusion has taken place in relation to local exporters and traders, many of whom have been pushed out of the market by international trading companies. Local companies cannot match the buying power of international traders, cannot buy in the quantities now necessary to obtain marketable volumes of higher profile coffees, and lack the knowledge/resources to hedge risk in the futures market. As a consequence, in 2000, international trading houses commanded much higher export market shares in Tanzania (55.5 percent) than in Kenya (28.4 percent; see Ponte 2001b, 2002c). This situation may change as a result of the passage of the 2001 Tanzania Coffee Act. The Act, which was first applied in the 2002–2003 marketing season, bans export companies from concurrently holding a license for the domestic coffee trade. In this way, it seeks to re-empower local companies in the domestic trade sector (Ponte 2004b). The results of this strategy remain to be seen.

The experience of Uganda with market liberalization in relation to marginalization and exclusion is a somewhat different one. Uganda liberalized its market fairly rapidly and consistently in the early 1990s. By the mid-1990s, a number of large international traders were trying to achieve control of the export market and were also attempting to integrate vertically into local primary procurement and processing. Vertical integration to a large extent failed. The local Ugandan market for coffee procurement and processing fell in the hands of a myriad of local actors, who faced few regulatory hurdles and had access to credit through social and family ties. The deterioration of coffee quality that often accompanied liberalization in other countries appeared in Uganda as well. But because Robusta coffee is less sensitive to handling-related quality deterioration, and because quality traits are less essential than in Arabica coffee, the reputation of Uganda coffee did not suffer dramatically. Also, as international traders gave up vertical integration, they devised cheap quality control measures for bulk deliveries in Kampala. These checks acted as an incentive for better quality management upstream. As a result, coffee quality recovered in the latter part of the 1990s. At the export level, international traders maintained a fairly large share of exports in the late 1990s (around 45 percent) when compared to Kenya and Ethiopia (Ponte 2002c).

In relation to the U.K.-destined *fresh vegetable* chain, buyer demands for extended shelf life and "good agricultural and handling practices" entail that exporters make substantial capital investments in a central packinghouse (costing about $500,000). In addition, growers need cool stores at field level to store the crop between picking and packing. Modern cool stores are also expensive, although some Kenyan growers apparently make do with charcoal-fueled stores that cost only $1,600. Where modern cool stores have been constructed, a Tanzanian grower reported that their minimum scale requirement for economic operation was equivalent to production from twelve hectares (almost thirty acres; B.N. Jensen 2002). There are obvious exclusionary implications in relation to each of these investments and other requirements. Not only are charcoal-fueled cool stores still beyond the reach of the great majority of Kenyan smallholders, but even Kenyan small-scale commercial farmers are unlikely to have access to the twelve hectares of contiguous or near-contiguous suitable land necessary to support a modern cool store. Furthermore, meeting demands for extended shelf life implies a need for increased coordination within a short time frame, creating advantages for vertical integration. Similar advantages arise in relation to implementing traceability requirements, which involve increased measurement costs.

Dolan and Humphrey (2000) recorded a major recent decline in smallholders' shares of total Kenyan horticultural exports. These findings were confirmed in more detail by work carried out in Kenya and Tanzania during the GLAF research program (see B.N. Jensen 2002; M.F. Jensen 2000). Smallholder producers, who had an approximate 40 percent export share for Kenyan green beans, snow and snap peas into the UK supermarket trade in the mid-1980s, had by 2001 been virtually eliminated from these chains both in Kenya and Tanzania. In a first phase of change, they were displaced largely by small-scale commercial farmer outgrowers. By 2001, the position of even this group had been seriously eroded – to the benefit of about 15 vertically-integrated exporter-growers.[15] The latter, in addition to providing volume, quick response, due diligence and reliability of delivery, also supply product development services. Small-scale producers meanwhile still account for a high proportion of production of fresh vegetable exports not destined for UK supermarkets, particularly for "Asian vegetables," where buyer demands are far lower. They are also prominent in Kenyan fresh fruit exports, which are destined mainly to the Middle East in the cases of mango and pineapple, and predominantly to France and Holland in the case of the only other significant crop, avocado. These markets are characterized not only by lower demands, but also by uncertain sales (on a consignment basis).[16]

Previous to *citrus* export market liberalization in South Africa, large and small commercial growers sold their crops through cooperatives. Through the producer association Outspan, commercial farmers had access to plant breeding services, research and development, extension services and credit, as well as packinghouses, a domestic cool chain, and specialized sea transport. Following liberalization, commercial farmers who wished to export to the United Kingdom outside the cooperative framework were obliged to build their own packinghouses, operate on a quick response principle, provide traceability, and conform to good agricultural practices. Those who wished to export on their own behalf rather than through agents were also expected to offer additional services. Only the largest and most creditworthy growers had the resources to operate outside the cooperative framework. This group was distinctive in other ways too, including having the capacity to provide a specific mix of cultivars (normally, several varieties of easy peelers) and having accumulated expertise in the sector for over four to five generations.

The withdrawal of an upper stratum of growers from the cooperatives created a series of ripple effects both in these organizations and in the export market. With the most high-value part of the crop bypassing their packinghouses, the unit costs of cooperatives rose. At the same time, unit returns fell even faster as the crop that remained theirs was of less interest to U.K. buyers and instead had to be sold on a consignment basis in mainland European markets. Meanwhile, cooperatives also began experiencing financial problems from another source, namely that the membership that remained had significant levels of debt to the organization, whereas those who had left were either less indebted or free of debt. To survive, some cooperatives privatized themselves, expelling their weakest members in the process. The latter were then unable to find an export market of any kind.

Most black growers, who in general were the most indebted, suffered particularly in this process, as well as from the disintegration of technical support institutions on which they were dependent. Those cooperatives that did not privatize also seemed to be squeezed gradually out of the export market. Therefore, by 2002, a three-way differentiation process had occurred. Larger individual growers and privatized cooperatives were exporting outside the framework of Capespan. The former were exporting mainly to the United Kingdom, the latter to other E.U. countries. An élite among the larger growers were exporting on their own account, as opposed to through agents. Together, these groups accounted for 65 percent of total exports by volume. Only 35 percent of exports remained with the nonprivatized cooperatives. These exported generally less commercially interesting varieties (Valencias, for example) to less remunerative markets (Eastern Europe and the former Soviet Union) on the basis of consignment sales.

Accompanying this restructuring process has been a corresponding differentiation in the conditions of farm workers. In the context of heightened attention from U.K. supermarket chains, large independent private growers have improved conditions for permanently employed labor and introduced equity ownership schemes (i.e., reserved a specific orchard as the workforce's own property). Alongside this, there has been an accelerated process of switching employment from permanent to casual workers. Thus, only a core of workers benefit from improved labor provisions. In less successful farms (and in less successful cooperative packinghouses), the main development has simply been retrenchments (see also du Toit 2002).

## Marginalization and Exclusion Implications of Story 2

Côte d'Ivoire and Ghana play strategic roles in the global *cocoa* trade, since they account for respectively 44 percent and 12 percent of the internationally traded crop (1999 data in FAO 2002). The importance of Côte d'Ivoire lies primarily in its high production level (see later), whereas Ghana's lies in the quality properties of its cocoa beans (high fatty content). Despite the recent capture of the generation of quality downstream in this chain (by Northern-based trader-grinders), fattiness remains important because it allows a shorter liquoring time, making for cheaper and more effective processing. This normally ensures that a premium is commanded by Ghanaian cocoa. Ghana has retained many elements of a state marketing system, including mandatory quality controls, fixing of margins at all levels of the domestic trade, and a public export monopoly (now unofficial).[17] This means that there is a publicly regulated break in the global cocoa chain originating from Ghana, just as there is one in the coffee chains that originate from Kenya and Ethiopia.

In contrast, Côte d'Ivoire has experienced comprehensive liberalization. This has been associated with vertical integration by the large international grinder-traders, as well as by a few members of the dwindling group of specialized international traders. Both groups of companies compete to finance local-level traders. By 2001, around ten companies, including all the major global players, controlled 85 percent of exports. Their reasons for vertical integration were simply to ensure volume (no inputs were supplied). The strong presence of giant traders-grinders (such as ADM, Cargill, and Barry-Callebaut), or at least their interest in vertical integration, may seem paradoxical, for quality characteristics no longer play the same role in international cocoa trade as they did even a decade ago. Their presence is nonetheless explicable in terms of Côte d'Ivoire's national volume status. An important effect of the falling importance of bean quality considerations has been to concentrate the international trade on a few major supplying countries where high volumes can be guaranteed. Cargill in particular is tied to high-volume producing countries since it has introduced an in-house dedicated transport fleet (or transferred some of its grain carriers to this role), including ships with capacity to transport 3 to 10,000 tons of cocoa beans.

On the one hand, Côte d'Ivoire (and its producers) has thus suffered marginalization in the sense of losing the premium earlier attached to its national origin and the opportunity to benefit from forward sales that went with a state marketing system. On the other hand, it has gained in the sense that the interest of all the global players is focused on competing over its output—although things may be changing given the highly problematic political conditions that have developed there since late-1999. By the same token, the relative interest of global players in lower volume supply markets is falling. In this context, the three big West African players, Côte d'Ivoire, Nigeria,[18] and Ghana have seen their collective market shares rise from 83.9 percent of all African and 49.4 percent of all world exports in 1986–1989 to 91.4 percent of African and 63.5 percent of all world exports in 1996–1999 (FAO 1990, 2002).[19] Ivorian national exporters have been excluded in this process, especially as the domestic credit system has collapsed. The ten leading local players of the late 1980s had all been taken over or forced out of business a decade later. According to Losch (2002), the last survivors were eliminated as a result of the larger players block booking the capacity of the main supplier of internal transport and of bagging materials.

Research in the GLAF program covered the *cotton* sectors of Zimbabwe and Tanzania. Both sectors underwent liberalization during the mid-1990s, opening them in principle to the exercise of a greater degree of buyer power, although not (because of the structure of the cotton chain globally) to buyer drivenness. However, quite different stories of marginalization and exclusion followed. In Zimbabwe, liberalization led to the emergence of an effective local market duopoly in which the players were the privatized former marketing board (Cottco) and Cargill.[20] Cargill is a major player on a global scale in the sector, buying from enough producing countries to give it both large volumes and a wide varietal profile. Cottco took the decision to continue with a strategy established already in the period when it was a parastatal enjoying an export monopoly, namely to maintain and defend the quality reputation of the national origin (which has usually commanded a 10 percent premium above the international price index Cotlook A). It used this strategy as a lever to bypass international traders and to sell cotton directly to spinners, mostly based in Europe. It also acquired high-volume instrument machinery, but how much of its crop is sold on the basis of this description is not clear. This experience will be returned to in the next section of this chapter in the context of a discussion of upgrading.

Both players in the Zimbabwean sector had an interest in maintaining both high volumes and the practice of grading cotton purchases at the level of primary purchase to defend the national reputation and hence the premium. As a result, they competed internally mainly on market coverage and supply of inputs rather than on price. Cargill operated an input voucher scheme and subsidized input prices whereas Cottco operated input credit schemes that until very recently embraced around 28 percent of all cultivators (and eventually boasted a 98 percent repayment rate). These interventions resulted in record levels of production (despite the steady withdrawal of large-scale commercial farmers from the crop) and rising yields for those smallholder producers who were members of these schemes (Larsen 2002).

Up to around 2000, the Zimbabwean story was one of inclusion rather than marginalization. But marginalization has begun to emerge as a potential issue in recent seasons, as Cottco decided that it could obtain the volume security it required more economically by investing more input credit in fewer smallholders. Yield-related entry barriers to its schemes were raised. The overall effects remain to be determined, but may have been partly mitigated by Cargill's decision in 2003 to open a rival input credit scheme (replacing its own input voucher scheme) in Zimbabwe— apparently the first it has operated anywhere in the world.[21]

The Tanzanian cotton liberalization experience has been an almost completely contrasting one. Market liberalization was associated with the proliferation of mostly small-scale trader-ginners (twenty-seven were operating in 2001), fierce competition on price, and the elimination of grading at the first point of sale (similar to the Tanzanian coffee experience). Private ginners bought cotton across different subvarietal zones and irretrievably mixed the local seed stock. Inputs were supplied by only a few ginners, and then only episodically and on a cash basis. Insecticide availability declined by two-thirds between 1994 (the start of liberalization) and 1997. Once world prices began falling steeply after 1997, local prices and production also dropped.

A much smaller proportion of Tanzanian exports is now traded via Northern European ports,[22] and that part has seen a decline in the premium that it traditionally commanded. As a result of falling volume and quality, some leading international traders appear to have lost interest in the crop (Larsen 2003a, 2003b). Despite building two large ginneries, Cargill withdrew in 1998, returned in 2000, and withdrew again in 2001. Hence, producers and ginners risk marginalization because of low volumes. Tanzanian cotton still commands a premium on the world market, but mainly on the basis of its time window (appearing at the beginning of the world cotton new year) and near-unique traditional (roller) ginning method. The time to market has decreased rapidly with liberalization and the proportion of the crop sold through the time premium window has risen sharply. Whether this was enough to keep the country in the game was being questioned within the sector by 2001, when government agencies and leading ginners launched a new initiative to increase input availability and restore quality control.

In this section, we examined the consequences of the two entry barrier stories for developing country producers, processors, and traders. Several differences by story, value chain, and country of origin emerged in relation to processes of exclusion and marginalization. At the same time, some common features could also be traced. In the first story, where entry barriers are raised for both first-tier and second-tier suppliers, marginalization and exclusion are generated within and between suppliers on the lines of price competitiveness, consistency of supply, lead or response times, and ability to ensure one or more specific special attributes of interest to buyers. Yet, it should be noted that price competitiveness works in different ways for manufactured goods, traditional export crops, and fresh fruit and vegetables. For manufactured goods, a major component of price competitiveness is labor costs; for traditional export crops, it is marketing costs; for fresh fruit and vegetables, it is costs of monitoring quality. Also, special attributes tend to be entirely chain specific. In coffee, they are a specific taste/aroma profile and increasingly some form of environmental or social qualification. In clothing, they are often service attributes or superior ability to work with a particular fabric type. In citrus, they include easy peeling, sweetness and shape. In fresh vegetables and citrus, they include the ability to supply a specific varietal constellation and conformity to good agricultural practices.

In the second story, which is confined to traditional agrofood value chains, entry barriers are raised for first-tier suppliers (or in the case of cotton, for those occupying or aspiring to occupy an international trader role). However, entry barriers are mitigated in important respects for second-tier suppliers. Here, marginalization and exclusion are generated either by low volume alone—which translates into high marketing costs—or by a failure to combine volume with the preservation of the historical quality characteristics that confer a price premium.

Perhaps not too strong a contrast should be drawn between the details of these lists of sources of marginalization and exclusion. Volume and related economies of scale are important in both stories, although important on their own only in versions of the second one. There are also certain common threads. Wherever supply market liberalization has led to quality decline (coffee, cocoa, and cotton), first-tier suppliers have integrated vertically to different degrees into producing countries. Local traders, as a result, have found it difficult to compete and have mostly survived only by working for first-tier suppliers on an agency basis. The major contrast is in the broader consequences of the two stories. In the first story, entry barriers for second-tier suppliers (and beyond) are multiple, to some degree mutually reinforcing and generally higher. In the second story, they are less numerous and do not necessarily mutually reinforce each other. In relation to developing countries, it should be in principle easier to negotiate a single entry barrier like volume than multiple entry barriers, even though the subsequent rewards are correspondingly restricted. The fact that some countries have had great difficulty in doing so indicates quite fundamental problems of public coordination.

## *Living Under Contract?*

The two stories concerning entry barriers, marginalization, and exclusion in buyer-driven chains described here may serve as a useful rectification of earlier efforts (based on the analysis of contract farming) to understand the changing role of Africa in global agriculture (Glover and Kusterer 1990; Porter and Phillips-Howard 1997; Watts 1994). These contributions took issue with the conventional agricultural economics of contract farming (e.g., Binswanger and Rosenzweig 1986), which explained its incidence in tropical countries in essentially technical terms— length of crop maturation period, combined with levels of crop perishability and the dependence of processing technologies on economies of scale. According to Watts, the agricultural economics approach overlooked the broader global context, particularly the crucial link between the accelerated growth of contract farming in tropical countries and the spread of cultivation of high-value fresh produce from temperate countries to tropical ones. For Watts, the link in question reflected the emergence of a new international food regime, incorporating a combination of new affluent dietary trends in the North, a heightened (postadjustment) demand for export revenues in developing countries, and a growing transnationalization of so-called agrofood capital in search of cheaper and more flexible forms of labor supply. For highly labor-intensive crops subject to rising demand in the North, contract farming enabled agrofood capital to gain access to cheap Southern smallholder labor supply while meeting stringent quality standards—without incurring the risks of direct investment or the social costs associated with direct employment.

The broader context of contributions such as Watts' was the ambitious project of a group of critical academics (see, among others, Bonanno and Constance 1996; Friedmann 1993; Friedmann and McMichael 1989; most recently, see Pritchard and Burch 2003) to relate some of the concepts of regulation theory to agriculture, and more particularly the notions of Fordism and post-Fordism. The appeal of this project consists in its broad historical sweep (the elaboration of a succession of international food regimes); its linkage of developments spanning the consumption, production, and processing of food; and its concern with labor, on the basis of arguments that were critical of the more optimistic versions of post-Fordism. Subsequent criticism of the contribution of this school concerns the sketchy nature of many of its theoretical propositions and the empirically problematic nature of some of the generalizations that these appear to be founded on. This includes its generalizations concerning contract farming (see Raikes and Gibbon 2000).

Watts himself appears to acknowledge in places (1994, 42), even at the time he was writing, that the international trade for most types of fresh produce was increasingly managed at arm's length by large retailers, rather than being directly controlled by international agrofood companies. As they had done for most of the preceding century, the latter played a significant role only in relation to traditional, mainly processed, tropical agricultural products such as rubber, palm oil, sugar cane, and tea. Furthermore, even in these cases, the parameters of their production were being defined increasingly by end users. Contract farming played some role in the (indeed expanding) contemporary fresh produce export trade from tropical countries, but in most cases those issuing the contracts were not international companies but local exporters who were in the process of shifting toward own-account production (see Jaffee 1994). As noted previously, the early 1990s was a period of transition away from contract farming in Kenya. Initially, this was the result of growing problems of smallholder side selling, but later end-buyers' quality requirements escalated to levels where costs of conformity with them became prohibitive for smallholders and where costs of monitoring smallholder conformity became prohibitive for exporters.

On the contrary, for crops where buyers' demands concerning quality have remained broadly constant over an extended period (as in the case of cotton), contract farming re-emerged in some African contexts in the second half of the 1990s as a successor to parastatal-organized input credit and quality control schemes. Here, the main players have included international traders such as Dunavant and Cargill for cotton and Damon for tobacco. The context is a combination of ongoing interest in specific traditional crop varieties and quality dimensions on the one hand, and instances of market liberalization where it has been possible for private agents to exercise a degree of coordination on the other. Private coordination has mitigated the risks of smallholder side selling, which, together with monitoring conformity with more exacting quality requirements, remain the main obstacles to the success of such arrangements (see Poulton et al. 2004).

## Upgrading

As argued earlier, a first step in understanding the upgrading opportunities available to second-tier suppliers in specific GVCs, is to spell out the current reward structures of these chains and the nature of the second-tier roles that trigger special rewards. A second step is to examine the extent to which African producers have attempted to occupy these roles or to graduate to first-tier supplier status. The following discussion is largely confined to upgrading opportunities for second-tier suppliers and for African entrepreneurs. The discussion presented on clothing is abbreviated, as some of the cases concerned have been tackled already in Chapter 3.

### Reward Structures and Roles Attracting Rewards

Security of contract, and ability to compensate for secularly falling prices by obtaining orders for higher volumes, are the most common rewards available for second-tier suppliers in the global *clothing* chain. Since base prices are those found in the anonymous market where importers buy job lots speculatively on consignment,[23] premiums as such can be considered to apply to sales ordered in advance by trading houses and to direct sales to retailers. They may also apply temporarily to being a recognized producer of a product type that suddenly attracts buyer interest, or on a longer-term basis to meeting special delivery conditions such as delivery on a call-off basis. However, the latter entails taking on a function that also is normally expected only of first-tier suppliers. Theoretically, premia at a much higher level apply to one's own branding and retailing on one's own account, but for developing country suppliers the resources required for undertaking this step are generally prohibitive (see Chapter 3). In practice, the most common way for second-tier suppliers to maximize rewards is through a combination of direct sales to retailers and achieving security of contract/access to higher volumes across a range of clients.

Recent developments in the global *coffee* chain have seen significant changes in the rewards available for second-tier suppliers in the bulk or commercial market, mainly for Robusta coffees. According to Rabobank (2002b), a clear division has opened up between anonymous and nonanonymous sales. Nonanonymous sales emanate mainly (but not only) from large or very large grower-exporters, mostly in large producing countries in Latin America. These are able consistently to supply high volumes, meet specific quality requirements, guarantee proper handling, provide efficient logistics up to the loading of a ship, and engage in direct marketing. Besides achieving reference prices, this role commands medium- and longer-term purchasing commitments from traders. These growers typically operate high-input, irrigated, and mechanized farms in frost-free areas. By contrast, the anonymous market is supplied mainly by smaller individual producers and a cross-section of smallholder organizations, often through a series of intermediaries. Only relatively large smallholder organizations in the more strategic supplying countries appear able to export directly.

A second area where rewards have been redistributed between groups of producers has been within the Arabica market, toward producers of specialty coffees. In the United States, the specialty market has been growing annually by around 30 percent since 1999, and in 2001 accounted for roughly 17 percent of imports by value and for 40 percent of retail sales (Ponte 2002a). Specialty coffee refers to all coffees to which either top-end traditional quality parameters and/or new private parameters are applied. Because of growing demand in this segment, relative fragmentation on the specialty buyer side, and low availability, the premia accessible in this market are considerable. Sales into this market are often direct ones, and buyers often offer medium- or long-term purchase commitments and sometimes also multiseason prices. However, most second-tier suppliers into this market are estates or large farms (Daviron and Ponte forthcoming; Ponte 2004a). In the remainder of the Arabica market, as noted earlier, traditional rewards are conferred only in the case of favored origins (e.g., Kenya) or coffee from other origins that can demonstrate conformity to a specific taste/aroma profile and be delivered on a short lead time. Although accessing the accompanying rewards has become more demanding, it does not entail upgrading to better prices or contractual conditions than existed before.

Traditionally, opportunities in tropical countries for upgrading to first-tier supplier status on the basis of industrial processing/roasting have been restricted. First, this is a matter of coffee's physical properties.

Although green coffee (the usual form of export) can be stored for a couple of years under good conditions, roasted coffee becomes stale much more quickly. Second, most coffee roasters in the commercial market use blends of a variety of origins from around the world. This restricts the nature of the final product and therefore the market for Africa-based roasting.

Reward structures in *fresh vegetable* and *citrus* chains are broadly similar. Unlike in the coffee market, there is no clear price premium for quality, only for producing specific varieties (whose identity changes over time). Over and above this, the main reward for second-tier suppliers comprises security of contract and stability of prices over periods ranging from three to nine months. Such commitments (usually unwritten) seem to be available only to importers serving large supermarket chains, usually U.K. ones. Stability of contractual arrangements allows longer-term planning, including planning of additional volume. This in turn allows greater economies of scale and a greater possibility of cross-subsidizing new product development (which in turn allows better risk spreading). As in other chains, premia also attach to being able to make direct sales to end buyers, in this case supermarkets (e.g., by attaining a first-tier supply role). However, this implies having one's own cool chain and delivery center operations in the importing country.

In *cocoa*, as noted earlier, the classic reward structures for primary producers have largely disappeared, except in the cases of rewards for some fine and flavored Latin American cocoas and (to a lesser degree) for cocoa from Ghana. As a result, second-tier suppliers, in the form of local exporters or smallholder cooperatives, can upgrade only by taking on first-tier supplier roles—that is, by engaging in international trading and/or grinding. As in the case of coffee, serious obstacles (physical and financial) used to apply in relation to developing a local grinding industry. Origin grinding was traditionally profitable—and then merely marginally—only for beans classified as of subexport standard. The industry's marginal profitability was a reflection of the lower quality rating that origin-ground products commanded on international markets.

During the 1990s, however, the reshaping of the world cocoa bean market changed the economics of grinding in the country of origin. The combination of concentration in international trade and elimination of traditional quality standards meant that exporters were left in origin countries with much larger quantities of beans that were unprofitable to ship to the North for grinding. At the same time, techniques emerged that better enabled some origin-ground products to be used as intermediate inputs in the grinding industry in the North, thus some-what improving their reputation. This allowed entry by West African agents, mainly but not only parastatals, in the grinding sector (see later).

Because of the *cotton* value chain's much less buyer-driven character, reward systems still primarily reflect the global supply/demand bal-ance, adjusted for the balances for specific recognized cotton varieties—while subject to exogenous distortions such as producing country subsidies. Rather than evincing a tripartite division into anonymous bulk, nonanonymous bulk, and specialty markets as in the case of coffee, the international cotton trade is organized in a single nonanonymous market bifurcated between coarser and finer cottons. These are differen-tiated in relation to each other and according to globally recognized na-tional origins and quality descriptions. National origins are a summary of varietal characteristics, typical forms of harvesting (mechanical or by hand), and types of ginning (roller or saw), whereas quality still refers in large part to those physical properties of the crop that reflect husbandry practices, such as contamination levels. Global reference prices exist for finer cottons (the Cotlook A index) and for coarser ones (the B index). As noted previously, because of the limitations of high-volume instrument quality measurement technology, the main impact of demands for im-proved or new qualities on the part of more technologically advanced spinners has been to put a greater emphasis on the implicit *reputational* dimensions of national origins. Thus second-tier supplier upgrading is still a possibility, but entails an improvement in such reputational di-mensions.

Premia also still attach to form of sale (forward, tender) and timing of sale (early market window), as well as for making sales direct to spinners, whether high-volume instrument measured or not. Therefore, upgrading may also be said to occur where these are accessed for the first time and sustained over a period of time. The relative size of premia of all sorts, but especially national origin ones, has increased over the last decade as a result of market oversupply.[24]

## Upgrading Performance

Among the *clothing* producers of Mauritius, many companies achieved a diversification of market segment coverage and an increase in oper-ational scale on the basis of investment in Madagascar. One was par-ticularly successful in the scale with which it expanded and in its com-bination of this with an increase in the proportion of its direct sales. This firm, Compagnie Mauricienne de Textile, internationalized beyond

Madagascar also into Senegal. Interviews with Northern buyers and sourcing agencies indicated that it was almost universally regarded as the most capable, efficient, and reliable on the island, characteristics that played a major role in influencing sourcing decisions. The only notable upgrading experiences in the South African clothing sector were by overseas Chinese-owned companies. These, for the most part, took the form of backward integration into textile manufacturing—for reasons to do with a combination of trade regulation and lead time requirements.

Only a few upgrading instances have taken place among second-tier suppliers (exporters) and third-tier suppliers (local traders) in the *coffee*-producing countries studied. Investment in curing and export preparation plants has generally supplanted government- or cooperative-owned capacity, thus redistributing the same kind of function rather than creating a new function. On the other hand, there is now more export processing capacity in East Africa than a decade ago, which means that the coffee crop can be turned around more quickly. Newer machinery also allows better grading (but of a poorer quality crop in the Tanzanian instance). Instances of clearer (but limited in size and scope) processes of upgrading have been the following: (1) the participation by mainly private and foreign-owned estates in specialty coffee direct sales; (2) a limited number of smallholder cooperatives and groups have been able to sell new quality content through fair trade and organic channels; (3) in Tanzania, smallholder farmer groups are now allowed to sell their coffee directly at the auction; and (4) a few local traders have established wet processing plants, thus becoming able to offer coffees with intrinsically higher quality profiles. But, in general, locally owned export companies have gone through a process of downgrading, now carrying out local trading functions for MNC exporters. Also, more classic forms of upgrading have not materialized: local roasting has emerged only at a small scale for the tourist market; instant coffee manufacturing had already been established in Tanzania in the 1970s (with public investment). Currently, it serves almost exclusively the regional market and supplies a lower-quality product (powder instant coffee is less valued than its granule form).

A number of large Kenyan *fresh vegetable* exporters consolidated their position as premium-earning second-tier suppliers to U.K. supermarkets in the second half of the 1990s by expanding their scale (including by investment in Tanzania), improving quality assurance, and by product diversification into snow/snap peas and/or cut flowers.[25] A direct transition to first-tier supplier status was successfully undertaken by Kenya's largest fresh vegetable and cut flower producer/exporter, Homegrown. By 2003, Homegrown had 6,000 local employees and an approximate 15 percent export market share. It operated its own nightly freight flight to the United Kingdom. The previous year, the company, which had opened its own importing arm in the UK some time earlier, took over two British suppliers to form Flamingo Holdings Ltd. One of these suppliers was Flower Plus, a flower importer/bouquet trader that had recently become Marks & Spencer's category manager for cut flowers. The other was Flamingo U.K., an importer, packer, and distributor. Subsequently, Flamingo Holdings acquired Zwetsloots, a U.K. flower supplier specializing in imports from the Netherlands and Spain. In 2003, Flamingo Holdings became the U.K. distributor for the largest Zimbabwean fresh produce exporter, Hortico, and expanded Homegrown's production base in Kenya by taking over the Commonwealth Development Corporation's stake in Sulmac, formerly Kenya's leading cut flower exporter. After the absorption of Zwetloots, Flamingo Holdings' 2002 sales reached around £155 million. To raise funds for these acquisitions, Homegrown borrowed from venture capital funds, including Modern Africa Fund Managers. In this way, Homegrown mirrors the business history of leading U.K. first-tier suppliers in the fruit trade that originated from Spain (Thames Fruit and Muñoz-Mehadrin).

The South African *citrus* sector embodies a number of cases of successful upgrading by large growers to relatively secure second-tier supplier roles. Some of these involve instances of upgrading in respect to product quality, especially for grapefruit into the Japanese market. Others represent instances of upgrading in terms of social practices and, consequently, reputation—in this case from an earlier international pariah position. Both these types of upgrading are underwritten by investments in on-site packinghouses. In the process, the companies concerned have come to enjoy longer-term contractual relations. A small minority of the growers following this course of action have gained access also to price premia by becoming exporters in their own right.

Against the background of domestic market deregulation, the former monopoly exporter Capespan embarked on an extremely ambitious strategy to become a multinational fruit trader. Other temperate zone fruit producer associations, notably the New Zealand apple and pear growers' association ENZAFRUIT, had already pioneered this strategy. Capespan sought to emulate ENZAFRUIT through a combination of vertical integration, negotiating a major joint venture, and valorizing some of its intangible domestic assets. Cooling and handling facilities were built or purchased at a series of overseas ports to enable Capespan to supply non-South African fruit on a counterseasonal basis. A formal alliance was established with the multinational banana trader Fyffes in order to improve the scale economies of these investments. Finally, Capespan sought to valorize the results of its many years of research and development through systematic patenting. The extent to which this strategy would have been successful had domestic market conditions remained stable is unclear. In any event, the strategy was severely undermined by Capespan's loss of two-thirds of the South African citrus supply base over a period of only five years. This turned potential scale economies into nonperforming overhead costs. As a result, by 2002, Capespan was already selling off many of its recently acquired assets.

As indicated earlier, the only upgrading opportunity available today for second-tier suppliers in the *cocoa* value chain is to acquire first-tier supplier status by engaging in grinding. Even this status is on a lower rung than that occupied by Northern grinders, because of the lower international rating of origin products. Parastatals and public/private joint ventures in Ghana and especially Côte d'Ivoire indeed established origin grinding operations in the period 1985–1995. In one case, the Ivorian company SIFCA upgraded much more extensively by building a new plant in France to produce customized products for the European chocolate industry, as well as taking over a Spanish company that was making mixtures with cocoa cake from cheaper origins. This occurred with the participation of the U.S.-owned Grace Cocoa as a junior partner. Later, SIFCA upgraded its plant in Côte d'Ivoire to make a critical intermediate product normally produced only in the North (cocoa mass).

By 2003, all these ventures were in foreign hands. Mills in Côte d'Ivoire are today owned by Barry-Callebaut, ADM, and the French chocolate manufacturer Cantalou; Ghana's single mill is owned by the world number four grinder, Hamester. Meanwhile, Cargill has built a new mill in Côte d'Ivoire. Thus, although the country now accounts for 13 to 15 percent of global grinding capacity, it can no longer be regarded as having upgraded. SIFCA's mill is now owned by ADM. The sale of the controlling interest in it occurred in 2000, after SIFCA's parent company SIFCOM made a major trading miscalculation. However, SIFCOM was already severely overextended as a result of following a policy of trying to merge all the remaining Ivorian-owned cocoa businesses under its control, with the direct support of the country's president of the time.

While Tanzanian *cotton* was experiencing downgrading in the 1990s, the Zimbabwean company Cottco succeeded in consolidating its status as a minor first-tier supplier. Although its lint continued to trade at its historical premium, the company undertook vertical integration into spinning of cotton knitting yarn, on the basis of a joint venture with a local mill, and into agroinput supply via the takeover of a local core supplier that was in financial difficulties. It further established a status of regional player via its acquisition of a cotton concession in Mozambique, presumably to be able to give its parallel investments in ginning and agricultural services greater economies of scale.

The analysis carried out in this section suggests that there have been relatively few examples of clearly successful local upgrading. Indeed, even active attempts at any form of upgrading are few. At the same time, a number of the upgrading instances described here are very recent and their results still remain unclear, and thus it is difficult to generalize meaningfully. Yet, opportunities for upgrading of any kind by African participants seem to be limited in the value chains examined. Where they have arisen, they seem to have a common volume element, irrespective of whether they occur in value chains where quality is important or ones that, upstream at least, are heavily volume focused. Where other types of upgrading appear to have been successful, they have often been preceded, or at least accompanied, by scale upgrading. This is the case for overseas Chinese-owned clothing firms in South Africa, for Homegrown (the Kenyan fresh produce business), and for the Zimbabwean cotton exporter Cottco. Given the size of national supply markets in Africa (and intraregional differences in trade preferences), effective versions of such scale upgrading appear to entail regionalization. Furthermore, although some successful upgrading to first-tier supplier positions has proved possible, this has taken place in chains where competing first-tier suppliers are relatively small in scale (fresh vegetables) or where the market structure is highly fragmented (cotton). Finally, combining internationalization and functional upgrading in the form of moving into multiple downstream functions or processes is often extremely resource demanding and leads to dangers of overextension, particularly for actors with highly specialized and/or politically dependent resource bases (as in the cases of Capespan and SIFCA).

Instances of successful second-tier supplier development on the part of first-tier suppliers appear to be also largely absent from Africa. In certain chains, particularly clothing, this has not been for want of trying. But in other chains, there has been no evidence of it being attempted.

Evidently, African second-tier suppliers are considered less potential material for such efforts.

## CONCLUSION

In the previous chapter, we suggested that to remain competitive in GVCs, first-tier suppliers need to match an increasing number of functions and stricter performance requirements. This, in turn, means higher requirements for Africa-based second-tier suppliers, at least in some GVCs. In this chapter, we have seen that these combined processes have tended to marginalize or exclude many Africa-based second-tier suppliers (while also selectively marginalizing or excluding third-tier ones). Yet, marginalization and exclusion may also arise when demands on suppliers are reduced in number since those that remain nevertheless become more difficult to meet. This is the case in value chains such as cocoa, where first-tier suppliers captured control over the generation of quality, but where this was combined with a rationalization of supply bases, to concentrate on high-volume markets only. The emergence of new, more demanding first-tier supply roles can also be considered to have important implications for upgrading opportunities. On the one hand, for local suppliers to aspire to a lead firm position seems increasingly unrealistic. On the other hand, there may be new and highly profitable roles that can be occupied upstream from lead firms. In general, these entail less demanding upgrading trajectories. They may sometimes be extensions of more familiar commercial or industrial strategies such as aiming to achieve greater scale economies and/or earn higher margins.

In the six GVCs discussed in this book, there are no African lead firms and only a handful of first-tier suppliers. More depressingly, only in the case of the clothing chain emanating from Mauritius (and then not even for the whole of this)[26] and perhaps the cotton chain, are there even more than a handful of African-owned second-tier suppliers. At the same time, Africa's third-tier suppliers have been eliminated from clothing and their position is under pressure in coffee, as well as in low-volume supplying countries for cocoa and cotton. As regards historical contrasts, the relative power of African enterprises has not changed greatly in respect to clothing in the last twenty years. For coffee, it has deteriorated in the Tanzanian case. This is also true for Tanzanian cotton, South African citrus, and Kenyan fresh vegetables. On the other hand, there has been no substantial deterioration in their position in relation to Kenyan, Ethiopian, and Ugandan coffee, whereas for Zimbabwean cotton there has been an improvement. In comparison to other value chains, African cocoa producers have done better than others.

The overall pattern emerging here is consistent with two broader processes. One is the tendency for globalization, in the absence of appropriate interventions by developing country governments, to reproduce and extend pre-existing patterns of inequality. The other is the widening gap between the capacities of most African governments and those of other developing countries to design and implement appropriate interventions. Kenya, Ethiopia, and Ghana have remained in advantageous positions in the coffee and cocoa chains respectively as a result of inertia rather than action, whereas the success stories of Zimbabwe cotton, Mauritian clothing (up to the late 1990s), Kenyan fresh vegetables, and South African citrus owed more to private coordination than to public action. Successful private coordination in these cases in turn rested on high concentrations of private economic power. Such concentrations hardly exist outside a few countries in the region, and these countries tend to have non-African business élites. As a result, any meaningful improvement in Africa's position within GVCs is bound to rely on foreign direct investment in the short term and a resuscitation of the capacities of the African state in the longer one. This raises an issue that combines both methodology and policy. There is a need to weave together the analysis of sources, exercise, and consequences of private economic power within GVCs with discussion about new frameworks for public regulation. This is particularly the case for agricultural products, where regulation has a potentially decisive role in lowering entry barriers for local producers.

# 6   Quality Standards, Conventions, and the Governance of Global Value Chains

CONVENTION THEORY, like GVC analysis, provides key elements for understanding changes in the global economy and the role of Africa in it. In this chapter, we return to the discussion on governance in GVCs initiated in Chapter 3, through an analysis of standards as elements of governance. We focus in particular on quality standards and related quality conventions in relation to the GVCs described in Chapters 4 and 5. The aim is to use some of the insights of convention theory, especially its cognitive and normative aspects, to advance the broader theoretical discussion of (private and public) forms of governance in the global economy.

"Standards are agreed criteria ... by which a product or a service's performance, its technical and physical characteristics, and/or the process, and conditions, under which it has been produced or delivered, can be assessed" (Nadvi and Wältring 2002, 6). As highlighted in Giovannucci and Ponte (2004), Nadvi and Wältring (2002), and Wilson and Abiola (2003), standards are important for developing country farms and firms because they determine access to specific segments of markets (e.g., by defining forestry products that are sustainable), to specific countries (e.g., through regulations on food safety and technical requirements), as well as setting the terms of participation in GVCs (e.g., through specifying quality standards). On the one hand, standards set entry barriers to new participants to a value chain and raise new challenges to existing developing country suppliers. On the other hand, the challenge of rising standards provides the opportunity for selected suppliers to add value, assimilate new functions, improve their products, and even spur new or enhanced forms of cooperation among actors in a specific industry or country (Jaffee 2003).

*Quality* standards communicate information about the product's degree of excellence, as embodied in specific attributes. These attributes can be classified depending on the ease with which they can be measured. *Search* attributes are those that can be verified at the time of the transaction (the color of a coffee bean, for example). *Experience* attributes can be assessed only after the transaction has taken place (the taste of brewed coffee). *Credence* attributes cannot be objectively verified and are based on trust (whether coffee is organic; Tirole 1988). This classification, however, is not without problems. It assumes that the evaluators of attributes have identical capacity to assess them. In reality, these capacities vary dramatically among individuals and across time, countries, and cultures. As we shall see later, convention theory helps to illuminate the cognitive and normative dimensions of these variations. Whatever classification of attributes we adopt, it is useful to further point out that they can pertain to the product itself (coffee appearance, taste, cleanliness, absence of taints) or to production and process methods, which may include elements related to authenticity of origin (geographic indications), safety (pesticide residues, levels of toxins), and environmental and socioeconomic conditions (organic, fair trade, shade-grown coffees).[1]

The evolution of the role of quality standards in shaping access to GVCs (and thus international trade) should be understood in relation to the changing features of consumption in the North. Consumption is increasingly characterized by food and/or user safety awareness, globalization of consumer tastes, and social and environmental concerns. This, together with market saturation for goods with commodity traits, has stimulated product proliferation and differentiation. It has been also accompanied by an increased importance of issues of quality control and management, traceability, and certification. In the world of mass consumption of relatively homogeneous commodities, quality standards created economies of scale and facilitated the creation of futures markets (Busch and Tanaka 1996; Cronon 1991; Daviron 2002). In the current situation, quality standards are proliferating and becoming more specific. They also tend to focus increasingly (sometimes exclusively) on production and process methods rather than on the product itself (Giovannucci and Ponte 2004; Giovannucci and Reardon 2000; Reardon et al. 2001). In other words, the formation and use of standards is "undergoing a shift from being neutral market lubricants to also being tools of product differentiation. This implies a fundamental shift in the role of G&S [grades and standards] from just reducing transaction costs of commodity market participants, to serving as strategic tools for market penetration, system coordination, quality and safety assurance, brand complementing, and product niche definition" (Giovannucci and Reardon 2000, 1).

Contemporary consumers in high-income economies increasingly demand complete information on a product so that they can make individual choices in relation to personal beliefs (e.g., on food safety, labor rights, and environmental protection) and taste preferences. In this situation, consumer protection is not uniquely a matter of food or user safety, but also of supplying reliable information to facilitate consumer choices (Valceschini and Nicholas 1995, 18). Therefore, the management of quality may also be seen as a question of competition and/or cooperation between the actors in the same value chain, each one having only partial access to, and control of, information on the product and its related production and process methods. Key actors' choices relating to solving quality information problems will then help determine the form of coordination in a specific segment of a chain. As quality content becomes more complex (e.g., by pertaining to experience and/or credence attributes rather than search attributes, and/or referring to production and process methods rather than the product), one would expect that firms move toward hands-on forms of coordination (closer to vertical integration). Yet, this is not necessarily the case. If economic actors are able to embed complex information about quality in standards, labels, and certification procedures, they may still be able to operate with more hands-off forms of coordination (closer to arm's length relations).

As argued in Chapter 3, *forms of coordination* should be distinguished from the *overall form of governance* of a GVC. A GVC may be characterized by different forms of coordination in various segments, yet a relatively coherent form of overall governance. Governance in GVCs is the process of achieving a certain functional division of labor along the chain—resulting in specific allocations of resources and distributions of gains. It entails the power of defining the terms of chain membership and the capacity to incorporate other actors in the chain to perform value-added activities that lead firms do not wish to perform, or alternatively to exclude other actors. Rules and conditions of participation are the key operational mechanisms of governance. These may translate in different organizational setups (or forms of coordination) that vary not only between value chains, but also between different segments of the same chain. Marginalization/exclusion and upgrading/participation are the axes along which (re)distributional processes take place.

Governance in GVCs may be expressed in more or less elaborated requirements for functional capacities and specifications of performance along the chain. Increasingly though, lead firms are devising mechanisms of hands-off governance that are exercised on the basis of setting precise standards, modularization of production specifications, and/or codification of knowledge requirements that not only apply to immediate suppliers, but filter down the length of the value chain. These specifications are left to first-tier suppliers to implement further up-stream. This often results in more hands-on forms of coordination be-tween first-tier and second-tier suppliers and beyond. In this way, lead firms may drive the value chain without actually directly controlling it (or possessing the functional capabilities to do so) in its entirety, or even in large segments.

In this chapter, we further develop our argument, introduced in Chap-ter 3, that the original distinction made by Gereffi (1994) between buyer-driven and producer-driven forms of governance remains a key one for understanding current changes in the global economy. This classification is helpful even though producer-driven chains may be in the process of becoming less important. In previous chapters, we sought to specify the historical dynamics of the rise of the buyer-driven form of governance in the context of changing regulatory environments. In this chapter, we focus on how lead firms define and manage quality, and we argue that this process is critical to the shaping of the functional division of labor and entry barriers along the chain. Furthermore, we argue that lead firm status does not depend only on economic attributes (levels of concentra-tion, market share), but also on the diffusion of one (or more) normative paradigms that provide legitimacy for the mechanisms used to exert leadership. In other words, the legitimacy of the content of quality and the tools for managing quality will depend on the capacity of lead firms to gain consent for particular definitions and procedures for measur-ing the quality performance of other players—that is, for the quality convention (or combination of conventions) these refer to.

## QUALITY IN ECONOMIC ANALYSIS

Placing quality issues at the heart of an understanding of how GVCs work is a radical departure from established epistemologies in economic analysis of the global economy. Quality considerations entered the cos-mos of neoclassical economics only fairly recently. In its stricter inter-pretation, neoclassical economics does not consider quality at all in analyses of market equilibrium. The object of exchange is considered to be homogeneous; therefore, all economic agents (both firms and consumers) are fully informed about the quality properties of the good or service that is being exchanged. Quality considerations explicitly entered the neoclassical framework (albeit as an exogenous factor) in models in which the consumer estimates the generic characteristics of products and compares them to his or her ideals of those qualities. Key assumptions behind these models are that product characteristics, consumer tastes, and expectations about these characteristics are objective, known, and do not change in time, and that producers, traders, and retailers deliver full information on quality and do not cheat on product characteristics (see Lancaster 1966; cited in Levy 2002).

Real world observations of quality, however, suggest that in many cases product characteristics (not to speak of production and processing methods) are not directly observable. This has led to neoclassical reformulations of the problem of quality through the analysis of information asymmetry. Akerlof (1970), in his discussion of used cars, introduced the possibility of more than one level of quality (a used car can be good or defective). Since the seller knows more than the buyer about the characteristics of the car, the exchange becomes more difficult. The owner of a good car will not get the price he/she wants because the buyer fears that the car may be defective. As a result, the owner may not be motivated to sell it. This entails that the majority of used cars for sale may actually be defective, depressing prices even more. In the presence of a market inefficiency of this kind, sellers will try to signal that their cars are good (for example, through reputation or warranty).

The signaling literature considers various ways in which quality information is transmitted. One stream argues that the object of exchange embodies quality characteristics through its price: the higher the price, the better the quality (Wolinsky 1983). These models assume that the consumer knows both the production function of the firm and the price premium that delivers a certain level of quality. More realistic models use advertising or, more broadly, reputation as quality signals (Milgrom and Roberts 1986). Reputation, however, is supposed to be understood universally by all consumers irrespective of their geographical location. All these approaches consider quality as an exogenous problem, any solution which should allow the preservation of underlying assumptions such as perfect competition, general equilibrium, complete information, and perfect rationality (for a review, see Levy 2002, 258–59).

A related approach to solving the problem of quality is found in transaction cost economics. Although sharing many of the tenets of neoclassical economics, transaction cost economics moves one step forward in focusing on which institutional arrangements and contractual forms minimize costs of searching for information (see Williamson 1979; Williamson and Masten 1995). It is not our aim here to cover the evolution of this school of thought and the large debate that addresses its limitations. For the purpose of our argument, it will suffice to say that transaction cost economics does not adequately explain issues of opportunism in the handling of information and related issues of power and authority. Quality standard setting and enforcement is entangled in assymetrical relationships, and conformity to standards is not necessarily the result of transaction cost minimization, but also of lack of better choices for some actors (Busch and Tanaka 1996). As argued by Barzel (1997), the higher the asymmetry of information in a transaction, the more likely it is that a party will try to exploit the situation by appropriating some value from the product that is not measured accurately. Therefore, institutions will not necessarily arise with the purpose of minimizing transaction costs. As North (1990) suggested, inefficient institutions may be maintained for relatively long periods of time because they fit the interests of powerful groups. One could also add that there are no universal and self-evident reference parameters for what an efficient institution is, and that these parameters vary historically and geographically.

This brings us to the discussion of the most glaring limitation of these attempts at considering quality: the assumption that economic agents share a universal idea of quality, which entails predetermined preferences that do not change in relation to the behavior of others. If we accept that economic agents (especially consumers) make quality decisions also on the basis of imitation and/or the achievement of distinctiveness, then we need a more adequate conceptualization of quality that relates to cognitive, intersubjective, and normative aspects. This possibility is provided by convention theory.

## CONVENTION THEORY

### Main Tenets

In convention theory,[2] conventions are defined as a broad group of mutual expectations that include, but are not limited to, institutions (see also Lewis 1969). Although institutions are collective and intentional objects that are set up for the purpose of implementing an intention, conventions may also arise from a shared set of regularities that are unintentional. To use Salais' wording (2002, 1), "people do not (necessarily) need institutions to know how to act." For convention theory, rules are not decided prior to action, but emerge in the process of actions aimed at solving problems of coordination. Conventions are then mechanisms of clarification that are themselves open to challenge (Wilkinson 1997, 318; see also Raikes, Jensen, and Ponte 2000). They are both guides for action and collective systems to legitimize those actions—which can also be submitted to testing and discussion. Thus, we can see a convention as a system of reciprocal expectations about the behavior of others (Salais 1989). More precisely, "Conventions are shared templates for interpreting situations and planning courses of action in mutually comprehensive ways that involve social accountability, that is, they provide a basis for judging the appropriateness of action by self and others" (Biggart and Beamish 2003, 444).

According to Boltanski and Thévenot (1991), all action is justified in relation to common sets of principles. The authors develop six historically based worlds (also known as *cités* ) of legitimate common welfare that draw on particular paradigms of moral philosophy. Each of these worlds is organized around different types of qualification (both for people and objects) and forms of justification and challenge. Boltanski and Thévenot elaborate an account of how these worlds are embedded in the behavior of firms on the basis of organizing principles.

- The *inspirational world* rests on the principle of common humanity and nonexclusion (based on Augustine), and agreement about evaluation and action refers to grace and divine inspiration (in firm parlance, creativity).
- The *domestic world* is founded on the principle of dignity (Bossuet), and agreement is founded on the basis of tradition (firms draw on the concept of loyalty).
- The *opinion-based world* is structured around the principle of difference (Hobbes) and objects, and subjects are evaluated through the opinion of others (firms use the concept of reputation).
- The *civic world* is based on the notion of common welfare (Rousseau), and agreement is founded on the fact that individuals are sensitive to changes in common welfare (firms are organized around the concept of representation).
- The *market world* finds its justification in the notion that difference is justified by sacrifice, effort, or investment (Smith), and agreement is found on the basis of market principles such as price (firms organize themselves around the concept of competitiveness).

- Finally, the *industrial world* is based on the existence of orders of greatness (St. Simon), and agreement is based on objective (technical and measurable) data (firms evoke the concept of productivity).

In more recent work, convention theorists and other scholars have developed further types, such as the green world (Latour 1998; Thévenot, Moody, and Lafaye 2000), the information world (Thévenot 1997), and the network world (also known as project-oriented or connectionist; Boltanski and Chiapello 1999; see also Thévenot 2002).

The proliferation of categories in convention theory may be problematic. Yet, convention theory does not give a hierarchical value to these worlds, nor does it portray them as historical inevitabilities. "Worlds" are neither permanent nor are they linked directly to specific social groups. Furthermore, at any particular time and locality, there may be multiple justifications of action operating at the same time. Finally, although there is an internal coherence in each world, there are also qualifications that bridge different worlds. The consequences of such a heuristic framework for the concept of quality are far-reaching, suggesting that: (1) there is no universal understanding of quality, (2) quality is cognitively evaluated in different ways depending on what world is used to justify evaluation and action, and (3) there is a direct link between understandings of quality and the social organization of production and exchange.

Convention theory indicates that—over time—markets come to embody a succession of different criteria under which goods become qualified for trade and according to which trade is subsequently managed.[3] One of its main tenets is the observation that, until the early 1970s, quantification was the main criteria for arbitrating exchange of relatively homogeneous products, whereas the current economic dynamic is based on an obsession with quality. As we have seen in previous chapters, the obsession with quality does not necessarily mean that volume, economies of scale, and price are out of the picture. More likely, they still play a role, together with more refined aspects of quality in defining the parameters of competitiveness.

In convention theory, markets are said to function on the basis of principles of product qualification. At the same time, quality is a key organizational concept for understanding the basis of emerging competitive strategies (Allaire and Boyer 1995; Valceschini and Nicholas 1995). These lines of thinking have been developed further in two directions: (1) Salais and Storper (1992; see also Storper and Salais 1997) have developed a typology of worlds of production as a combination of technologies and markets, product qualities, and practices of resource use; and (2) Eymard-Duvernay (1989) has formulated a typology linking quality conventions to forms of coordination. Both contributions seek to formulate forms of coordination specific to the nature of the product that is exchanged and the means of justifying its quality claims.

In Salais and Storper (1992), four worlds of production are distinguished on the basis of two dimensions that can take two values: the first dimension is related to the available supply of technology, information, and skills at the production level, and whether these are restricted to a community of specialists or not (yielding specialized or standardized products respectively); the second dimension is related to whether demand is anonymous and uniform or not (yielding demand for generic or dedicated products respectively). The four possible combinations lead to a classification of worlds of production as follows: (1) industrial world (production of standardized-generic products); (2) network market world (standardized-dedicated); (3) Marshallian market world (specialized-dedicated); and (4) world of innovation (specialized-generic). Slightly different labels are used in Storper and Salais (1997).

Although each world has its specific characteristics, Salais and Storper (1992) also point out that there are frictions, failures, and compromises between worlds. They argue that each world of production involves coordination between agents that is affected by conventions. Two kinds of conventions are then explored: (1) *quality conventions* that "establish the boundaries of competition in a world by defining the relative economic values of qualitatively distinct factors of production" (ibid., 179–80); in this case, the authors base their discussion to a large extent on Eymard-Duvernay's (1989) typologies, which will be discussed later, noting that each world of production is characterized by a specific mode of evaluation of the quality of goods; and (2) *conventions of flexibility* that define practices of resource deployment, noting that these shape the difference between specialized and standardized products.

In our discussion in the rest of this chapter, we will draw inspiration from Salais and Storper's work in terms of separating the discussion of quality conventions from conventions on resource deployment (while also focusing on strategic aspects of the latter, thus on conventions of corporate organization and interfirm relations). However, we will not use their world of production categories, whose features are too product-centered[4] and predetermined by a series of given factors that are only loosely linked to historical and regulative processes (see similar criticism of Gereffi, Humphrey, and Sturgeon in Chapter 3). Also, we will argue that there is no automatic link between quality conventions and specific forms of coordination.

Eymard-Duvernay (1989; see also Sylvander 1995; Thévenot 1995) develops a typology of quality conventions and related forms of coordination. His main point of departure is that price is the main management form of a particular market only if there is no uncertainty about quality. If this is the case, differences in price are equated with quality. This characterizes what convention theory calls *market* coordination. When price alone cannot evaluate quality, economic actors adopt conventions that are linked to three other forms of coordination. In *domestic* coordination, uncertainty about quality is solved through trust (long-term relationships between actors or use of private brands that publicize the quality reputation of products). In this case, the definition of quality is resolved internally, and the identity of a product is guaranteed or institutionalized in the repetition of history by its region or country of origin or by a brand name. In *industrial* coordination, uncertainty about quality is solved through the actions of an external party that determines common norms or standards and enforces them via instrument-based testing, inspection, and certification. More recently, an additional category has been added, *civic* coordination, where there is collective commitment to welfare, and the identity of a product is related to its impact on society or the environment.

Each of these forms of coordination implies asymmetries of information that benefit certain groups of participants over others. Different forms may exist side by side at the same time, even for the same product. According to Allaire and Boyer (1995), these forms of coordination may exist in a state of tension where one is either resisting or encroaching on other modes. When different criteria come to characterize the process of qualification of products for trade, a change in the dominant form (or combination of forms) of coordination occurs. Thévenot (1995) highlights some of the major historical changes that have taken place in the twentieth century. He argues that the dominant form of economic organization in the postwar era was the result of a compromise between industrial and market coordination—with a tendential predominance of industrial notions of productivity, economies of scale, and technical progress. This configuration is said to have tilted to the side of market coordination and its underlying concept of competitiveness as a result of the processes of market liberalization and deregulation of the 1980s. Thévenot also claims that, at the same time, market coordination co-exists with domestic forms of coordination such as indication of origin and branding—as well as with the underlying civic content of environmental and socioeconomic standards and labels. Furthermore, industrial norms are seen as being increasingly applied to the management of quality control.

Another way of looking at changes in the combinations of dominant conventions in different historical periods is to refer to the underlying logic of the original Boltanski and Thévenot's list of worlds (1991), to which Boltanski and Chiapello (1999) added a new, emergent configuration—what they call the network world. According to these authors, the evolution of capitalism over the last century or so can be understood through the emergence of different, albeit overlapping, value systems. In this perspective, the end of the nineteenth century was characterized by the so-called first spirit of capitalism, which was something akin to a domestic world based on the entrepreneurial bourgeois.[5] The second spirit of capitalism, which is seen to have lasted from the 1940s to the 1970s, was based on an industrial and meritocratic logic, economies of scale (productivity), and the ideal of a large and integrated firm focusing on capturing market share. The third spirit, said to have emerged in the 1980s, is based on a network logic and a new type of ideal firm (flexible, organized by projects, lean). Under this spirit, competitive firms are smaller, innovative, and generally better able to plug into several different networks.

Although some of the ideas incorporated in the formulation of the network logic are not new (see Castells 1996), Boltanski and Chiapello (1999) do underline the ideological underpinnings of its emergence. Furthermore, they point out that the idealization of the firm as flexible and lean does not necessarily translate into "small is beautiful." Being big (if not in terms of employees, at least in terms of market share) is still important (Harrison 1994) and volume, economies of scale, and low prices are still key aspects of competitiveness. Also, as we argued in Chapter 3, by externalizing noncore functions, lead firms can be seen as losing some aspects of flexibility while gaining others. In a sense, the network world, rather than being another category of convention, may be better seen as a new way of achieving an industrial-market compromise in a corporate world increasingly influenced by financialist prescriptions (see later).

*Applications of Convention Theory in the Anglophone Literature*

In the previous section, we highlighted the main theoretical contributions of convention theory as emerging from French scholars and as reviewed in some anglophone contributions (Biggart and Beamish 2003; Raikes, Jensen, and Ponte 2000; Wilkinson 1997). However, convention theory has also been adopted by anglophone scholars, especially in the disciplines of geography and sociology and in relation to the broad field of agrofood studies. In this section, we cover two groups of contributions that use convention theory: (1) the literature on alternative agrofood networks (AAFN), and (2) the work of a multidisciplinary team at Michigan State University working on grades and standards.

The convention theory–inspired literature on AAFN includes two distinct strands: one emerging from the so-called quality turn literature (Marsden, Banks, and Bristow 2000; Murdoch, Marsden, and Banks 2000; Murdoch and Miele 1999); the other arising from the literature on fair trade, organic, and ethical trade networks (Barham 2002; Freidberg 2003b; Raynolds 2002, 2004; Renard 2003). The quality turn literature relies almost exclusively on case studies based in the North (and especially in Europe). It argues that (Northern) consumers have turned away from industrial agrofood products and toward high-quality products. These products include those characterized by organic or low external input practices, specific locations or regions, and those supplied through farmers' markets, short/local food supply chains, and agrotourism or other kinds of multifunctional agricultural enterprises. The quality turn is explained in part by consumers' heightened reflexivity (both in relation to intrinsic quality and to production and process methods) and in part by reactions to repeated food scares in the 1990s (bovine spongiform encephalopathy or BSE, E. coli, salmonella). The combined result is seen as having led to the increasing importance of transparency in agrofood networks—embedded in practices of quality assurance, traceability, geographic origin, sustainable agroecological practices, and direct marketing schemes (for a review, see Goodman 2004).

A convention theory reading of these changes has led Murdoch, Marsden, and Banks (2000; but see also Murdoch and Miele 1999) to claim that there has been a movement in agrofood networks from industrial conventions (and the logic of mass production) to domestic conventions based on trust, tradition, and place. Murdoch, Marsden, and Banks argue that quality is coming to be seen as inherent in more local and natural foods, thus that "quality food production systems are being reembedded in local ecologies" (2000, 103). Yet, a number of recent contributions in agrofood studies suggest that "local is not an innocent term" (Goodman 2003, 3; see other contributions in the same volume), and that the quality turn literature leads to a "reification of the local" that neglects "social processes and relations of power that produce, reproduce and restructure the scale of the local . . . [as if] local embeddedness of economic forms preclude[d] exploitation" (Goodman 2004, 5).

The case studies in the quality turn literature are instructive in the variety of trajectories that enterprises follow as they move from one set of overlapping conventions (or worlds of production as in Murdoch and Miele 1999—drawing on Storper and Salais 1997) to another. However, they often draw from small niche markets whose relative significance in terms of volume or value for individual sectors or products is rarely disclosed. Where the case studies cover more substantial sectors, evidence of trends that counter the portrayed movement from industrial-market to domestic-civic conventions are ignored or downplayed. For example, little is made in the quality turn literature of the emergence of the industrial-market logic in organic and/or fair trade markets (as shown in Allen and Kovach 2000; Guthman 2002, 2003; and Raynolds 2002, 2004). Finally, in the quality turn literature (as well as in much of the AAFN literature more generally), convention theory categories are applied as given to selected case studies without a critical and reflective reasoning on their applicability and on their underlying content.

Raynolds (2002, 2004), in her work on organics and fair trade, uses conventions to understand how quality contestations arise and are resolved in global commodity networks, and how "contestations over divergent qualifications and how collective enrolment in particular conventions permits forms of control at a distance" (Raynolds 2002, 409). She investigates how actors materially and ideologically engage with norms, rules, and quality constructions in production, distribution, and consumption areas. Her case study of coffee shows how fair trade networks have challenged quality norms based on market conventions. Drawing on Whatmore and Thorne (1997), Raynolds sees fair trade as enacting a "mode of ordering of connectivity," where discursive and material relations are based on renewed investment in trust (domestic convention). Furthermore, she points out that fair trade refers to civic norms and qualifications that are based on collective responsibility for (and evaluation of) societal benefits—thus extending domestic conventions to socially and spatially distant peoples and spaces. At the same time, she shows that fair trade is also rooted in commercial conventions as it deals with mainstream distributors and retailers. Finally, fair trade is engaged in industrial conventions rooted in formal standards, inspections, and certifications (on similar lines, see Renard 2003). A similar set of observations are made in Raynolds (2004) in relation to global organic networks.

Raynolds (2002) acknowledges that market and industrial conventions are important in fair trade (and organics), but argues that civic and domestic conventions are not vanquished. This is because standards in fair trade are not only referring to minimum levels, but also to process; inspections are not based on objective scientific assessments, but draw on local inspectors who know the local conditions (to what extent this is correct is debatable), while documentation and reporting obligations are of relatively minor importance. On this basis, she concludes that fair trade is better able to deliver progressive social change than voluntary initiatives and certifications that are based on industrial-type certifications.

Freidberg (2003b) provides a convention theory–inspired perspective that is critical of both trust as the basis of quality in agrofood networks and of the ability of alternative networks to promote meaningful socioeconomic change in developing countries. Her historical and comparative analysis of conventions in anglophone (Zambia to the U.K.) and francophone (Burkina Faso to France) horticultural trade, she finds that "relationships based on trust . . . are often just situations where one or all parties has no choice but to hope for luck or mercy. . . . Economies of quality . . . are not necessarily less exploitative than others" (ibid., 98). She also notes that, in North-South trade, "situations of exchange" are such that actors do not necessarily share ethical or behavioral norms. Rather, producers comply with retailers' demands because they have no choice (see also Busch and Tanaka 1996), even though ecological and sociocultural conditions of production are different from the ones predominant in the country of consumption.

In her analysis, the anglophone value chain for horticultural products is characterized by institutional conventions of quality assurance, whereas the francophone one draws on transactional conventions.[6] Freidberg argues that even in the anglophone context, the technologies of ethics (see du Toit 2002) that allow retailers to act at a distance are reinforced by personal communication and visits (direct contact). Trust is thus seen as being still important even as impersonal forms of quality assurance are imposed by retailers.

Freidberg's work (see also Freidberg 2003a) is also relevant to our discussion of the role of standards in the governance of value chains. Her contention is that current supermarket practices in relation to codes of conduct are not leading to more transparency along value chains, and thereby they are not defetishizing the commodity.[7] On the contrary, she argues that standards contribute to a process of double fetishization (standards become fetishized too). In her words, "The appearance of transparency ... has become the new *packaging* model" (Freidberg 2003a, 29; original emphasis) in the same way that traceability has become a standard part of supply chain risk management.[8]

A second group of work drawing on convention theory has been produced by researchers attached to the Institute for Food and Agricultural Standards at Michigan State University, led by Lawrence Busch (see, among others, Busch 2000, 2002; Busch and Tanaka 1996; Sterns and Busch 2002). In this literature, standards are seen as instruments that are used to subject people and nature to rites of passage to assess their goodness (Busch and Tanaka 1996, 5). This approach is explicitly linked to Boltanski and Thévenot's (1991) discussion of greatness. Four kinds of rites (and associated tests) are highlighted in Busch and Tanaka (1996): (1) Olympics, where the winner surpasses all others in a competition; (2) filters, where the good and bad are sorted out via a minimum standard; (3) ranks, where levels of goodness are arranged on a scale; and (4) divisions, where the scale does not necessary indicate goodness or badness (as in coffee taste profiles, for example). These tests have different consequences for behavior and different effects on how power and status are (re)distributed among actors (both human and nonhuman).

The importance of these observations is in that tests (and associated standards) "create, maintain, and change [commodities, while at the same time] monitor, control, and organize the behavior of each of the actors" (ibid., 23). In a similar vein, Busch (2000) argues that "grades and standards are ways of defining a moral economy, of defining what (who) is good and what is bad, of disciplining those people and things that do not conform to the accepted definitions of good and bad" (ibid.: 274). In short, standards "(1) are the means through which objectivity is produced in the market, (2) can never be fully specified and are always subject to renegotiation in light of future events; and (3) are always discussed *in practice* as subject to complete specification" (ibid., 276; original emphasis).

Our review of the anglophone literature suggests that convention theory can be usefully applied to a number of different settings and that its terminology can be used to illuminate previously unexplored dimensions of value chains and their governance. However, three limitations characterize this literature. First, convention theory tends to be drawn on only as a preliminary guide to promised new research, which to our knowledge has not yet appeared. Second, in much of the empirical work that is reported, the concepts of convention theory are used simply as redescriptions for empirical categories that could equally be formulated without using them. Third, the empirical material is rarely used to develop convention theory as such. In the next section, we highlight some of the limitations and potentialities of convention theory and some of the overlaps with other theoretical approaches that can be usefully applied to GVC analysis. In the rest of this chapter, we shall reflect on several empirical case studies both to critically engage with convention theory itself and to take further our understanding of governance in GVCs.

## Convention Theory and Beyond

Convention theory may be criticized for its speculative character, its multiplication of typologies, and its historical periodizations. Its classification of worlds is not dissimilar from the forms of public authority delineated by Weber (1978). Its contemporary focus on networks and flexibility obscures the fact that being big (if not in terms of employees, at least in terms of market share) is still important and that volume, economies of scale, and low prices are still key aspects of competitiveness. Convention theory has also been taken to task for its exclusive micro focus and lack of explicit discussion of power relations. Yet, at the same time, its worlds seem to operate as normative orders embodying implicit but powerful constraints on behavior (Durkheim 1950).[9]

While opening up for a treatment of collective constraints on action, convention theory also suggests that actors have a say in the formulation of conventions. A political economy reading of conventions indicates that some actors are more influential than others, and that many actors express preferences within limited parameters of choice. This issue is particularly relevant in relation to the role of consumers—whose power in the contemporary global economy is often romanticized in marketing and management manuals and sometimes in analyses of agrofood networks as well.[10] Although convention theory does refer to the role of consumers in the arbitration of quality, this is usually only in relation to niche markets and local/regional foods where the distance (geographic and virtual) between producers and consumers is short.

The role of consumers as actors shaping ideas of quality is perhaps better approached through the economy of qualities approach of Callon, Méadel, and Rabeharisoa (2002). According to this formulation, one of the main concerns of lead firms[11] (retailers, branded manufacturers) is to prompt consumers to question their preferences and, indirectly, their identities. Thus, they try to steer spontaneous and gradual processes of qualification and requalification of products to their advantage. They do so, inter alia, by setting up forms of organization promoting collaboration between suppliers and consumers in the qualification of products. In this way, competition can be thought of as turning around "the attachment of consumers to products whose qualities have progressively been defined with their active participation" (ibid., 212; see also DuPuis 2000). In other words, it is based on the "formatting of sociotechnical devices [such as advertising, shelf positioning, presentation of products, focus groups, evaluation forms, point of sale data] which, distributing and redistributing the material bases of cognition, format the bases of calculation and preferences" (ibid., 213). These processes of explicit and implicit collaboration between economic agents are said to apply to material products and service provision alike, but to be functioning more strongly in the services sector, where the mechanisms of singularization and (re)qualification can be operated on a more continuous basis.[12]

For the purposes of our discussion, the economy of qualities approach suggests that consumers are active agents, along with others, in formulating how the qualification of products should occur—and therefore in the governance of a value chain. At the same time, it suggests that consumer preferences (or at least inconsistencies within them) can be manipulated by other agents to the advantage of the latter. Wilkinson (2002, 340), for example, shows how functional foods[13] have been developed "in a climate of constant opposition from consumer associations, [which means that] leading agro-food players are committed to imposing strategies that fly in the face of a 'demand-oriented food system.'" The apparent paradox is the development and marketing of products that are unwanted by consumers but that are based on marketing strategies depending on consumer dialogue.

In sum, convention theory provides an innovative way of looking at issues of coordination of activities and mechanisms of enforcing governance through their cognitive/normative, and not only material, preoccupations. It can thus be used to reconceptualize governance in GVCs through the analysis of how, in buyer-driven chains, there is a shift from direct control and rule-setting to a mixture of hands-on and hands-off control that is built around the management of quality and performance requirements. These mechanisms combine specific networking norms and a heightened explicit role for quality within a general framework of control at a distance (Latour 1987; Lockie 2002; Murdoch, Marsden, and Banks 2000; Rose and Miller 1992) and the increased importance of auditing technologies and methods (Hughes 2001; Miller 1998; Power 1997; Shore and Wright 2000; Strathern 2000).

The main links between conventions and value chain governance are fivefold: (1) value chains can be considered more or less coherent or articulated (and articulated in different ways), depending on which quality convention—or combination of conventions—are present along their length; (2) lead firms compete with each other by qualifying differentiated products with more complex quality attributes within the broader context of conventions elaborating public norms concerning product quality; (3) lead firms seek to manage production and sale of products in ways consistent with a financialist logic and/or a related network convention of corporate organization; (4) the content of chain leadership seems to have shifted in the direction of the promulgation of standard sets of quality requirements for suppliers; supply chain standard setting enables coordination to take place in a relatively hands-off manner; and (5) chain leadership and subordination are to a large extent determined by which group of agents is deemed to be injecting the key ingredients of quality (as seen in Chapters 4 and 5).

## Quality, Entry Barriers, and Governance in GVCs: Empirical Evidence from Africa

Combining the insights of convention theory and GVC analysis allows us to return to the key issues of chain governance and entry barriers via a quality reading of the empirical material arising from Africa-originating value chains. The nature of quality conventions and the possibility of standardization play a critical role in shaping the governance structure of value chains in two ways: (1) through the possibilities they open and close for how value chains are coordinated (in relatively direct or indirect ways and in material or normative forms) at individual links in the chain; and (2) through providing lead firms with a legitimate vocabulary to define what makes a product fit for trade. However, the main issue at stake here is not only how broader social narratives and practices concerning quality may partly shape different forms of coordination and entry barriers at different nodes in a chain (and even in the same segment of it), but also how quality conventions (and related business cultures) shape the mechanisms of governance and their legitimacy.

These mechanisms are contested and open to change, redefinition, or renegotiation.[14]

In *clothing*, as well as other value chains for labor-intensive manufactures, capacity to reach what is considered a basic level of quality is an entry barrier in the strong sense for suppliers. That is, at any given time it is a nonadjustable requirement for participating in virtually any segment of the global chain for new clothing—regardless of end market and supply/demand balance. Although the content of some aspects of basic quality, such as faults in make, have not changed for half a century or more, there is a trend for quality to be defined in terms of an increasing range of physical parameters, such as color fastness, and for certain pre-existing parameters (such as shrinkage), to be defined in more exacting ways. However, a more profound change has occurred in quality management. Here clothing buyers are shifting emphasis from direct monitoring to "control of control," whereas suppliers are undertaking a parallel shift emphasizing prevention of defects, rather than post hoc identification and rejection or repair of defective products.

At the same time as basic quality becomes increasingly universal, clothing buyers are placing much more emphasis on suppliers' ability to internalize less tangible properties of quality such as "handle"[15] and compatibility of vision between suppliers and buyers. Buyers subsume compatibility of suppliers' products with their conventions for assembling collections, displaying products, and designing their stores. Buyers refer to their specific ways of carrying out these activities as their "handwriting." Achieving these dimensions of quality is considered the responsibility of suppliers alone. Suppliers are supposed to familiarize themselves with clients' preferred handle and handwriting in ways that are specified mainly in intuitive terms and that ideally include noncontractual interactions such as "hanging out in our stores" or "soaking in our way of doing things." Buyers' management of this aspect of quality is also largely intuitive. But at the same time, willingness to learn (such as active efforts on suppliers' part to visit buyers' stores at their own expense) is taken as an operational indicator. Thus buyers combine an increasingly hands-off approach over the more material aspects of product quality with demands for suppliers to internalize their culture in ways that are simultaneously more diffuse and more demanding (Gibbon 2000, 2002a, 2002b).

*Coffee*, like other agrofood products, is more prone to quality variance (due to the vagaries of the weather) than clothing. Although there are some minimal regulatory requirements for coffee to be fit for trade, the focus of economic agents is mainly on additional quality characteristics of a particular batch or delivery. In the mainstream coffee market, roasters have maintained a dominant position—among other things—through effective management of asymmetry of information on quality. Essentially, roasters buy coffee with complete quality information from international traders. Once coffee is blended and roasted, it is sold to consumers under a brand name. That means that roasters use brand reputation as a proxy for variance in quality. This does not mean that a higher price necessarily buys a better coffee. Packaging, shelf placing, and advertisement also play a large role in establishing consumers' ideas of quality. The important point here is that roasters have complete information on quality when they buy coffee, and they release next to no information to their customers.

The major threat to mainstream roasters' dominance of the coffee value chain comes from changing ideas (and conventions) of quality that are emerging in a fast-growing segment of the coffee value chain—the specialty industry. Not only do consumers require more information on (and higher levels of) intrinsic coffee quality (product attributes), they also include environmental and socioeconomic aspects in their consideration of quality (attributes of production and process methods). Roasters are then under pressure to "solve" the measurement of complex quality content that tends to entail more direct control of operations and more exacting and expensive quality checks. As certification and auditing systems are developed, however, roasters can take a more hands-off approach to quality management. As in clothing, we observe a shift in focus from direct control to "control of control."[16] Furthermore, as these certification systems gain wider acceptability, mainstream roasters can include them in their quality management system. In a sense, the distinction between the specialty and commercial coffee markets becomes more blurred (Daviron and Ponte 2004; Giovannucci and Ponte 2004; Ponte 2002a).

As explained in detail in Chapters 4 and 5, in *fresh vegetables* and *citrus*, quality is perhaps the main mechanism of value chain governance. Fresh vegetables used to be sold in Europe through wholesale markets, where quality demands were relatively basic. In citrus, the South African producer association even managed to disregard some of the quality demands placed by supermarkets, at least until market liberalization took place in the country. One interesting twist in this case is that (contrary to coffee, cocoa, and cotton) market liberalization has actually led to increasing levels of quality in supply markets—or at least in certain of their segments (Mather 2004; Mather and Greenberg 2003). The previously regulated environment operated on the basis of Fordist principles (focus on volume and homogeneity rather than quality), whereas the new configuration is driven by quality-conscious retailers. Currently, both fresh vegetables and citrus are sold predominantly by supermarket chains in European markets and in the United States. Supermarkets have been able to set stringent content for product quality specifications and dictate production and processing methods (Dolan and Humphrey 2000; M.F. Jensen 2000). In doing so, they determine the functional division of labor along the chain, including the emergence of preferred first-tier suppliers, who alone can match a set of increasingly complex and demanding standards. At least some of these demands are then passed on further upstream, where (increasingly) only the most resourceful commercial farmers and packers/exporters are able to match them. Hence quality demands have been both one of the main expressions and instruments of increased buyer drivenness.

What roasters achieved in the coffee chain can be said to apply to grinders in the *cocoa* chain. The main difference between the two value chains is that, whereas coffee is still segregated by identity of coffee type, origin, and sometimes region (so that roasters can achieve their blending objectives), cocoa grinders have promoted a vulgarization of quality. In other words, the characteristics of cocoa beans coming from specific origins has become unimportant, with the exception of fine and flavored Latin American cocoas, Ghanaian cocoa (for its higher fatty content) and some Cameroonian varieties (for their red color). This has led to the emergence of a global cocoa bean, which is loaded in ship holds (rather than in bags or containers) and transported cheaply to consuming markets (see Chapters 4 and 5). This process was facilitated by market liberalization in producing countries and the de facto abolition of quality controls in these markets. Quality deterioration does not matter too much to grinders because they are able to compensate for lower and more uneven quality through innovations in processing. By downgrading and simplifying the quality content of cocoa beans, grinders have been able to minimize quality risk. They have not been able to achieve lead firm status in the value chain because they do not supply branded products (contrary to coffee roasters) and have to match quality specifications that are set by chocolate manufacturers (Fold 2001, 2002).[17]

In relation to *cotton*, attention can be drawn to two points. First, quality deterioration in producing countries in Africa has not occurred where institutional setups (and oligopoly rather than competitive markets) facilitated coordination measures for the provision of inputs and services to farmers (Zimbabwe), or where public regulatory structures have been left in place (some countries in francophone West Africa). However, in other countries, buying in grades has been discontinued, services have broken down, and there are signs that lint quality is deteriorating (Tanzania). Second, the emergence of a very sophisticated quality evaluation instrument (high-volume instrument) developed in the United States has the potential to facilitate the creation of a two-tier supply system. Producers of upland varieties in temperate areas of Northern countries (the main high-volume instrument users) are able to define a larger number of characteristics, or measure much more precisely a single characteristic, of each bale of cotton. This only enhances lint properties to a certain extent, in the sense that spinners usually blend even high-volume instrument–measured cotton with other cottons that might not have been measured in this way or may even be nonmeasurable (e.g., West African cottons do not lend themselves to high-volume instrument readings; Larsen 2003b). In general, producers in developing countries are able to deliver only cotton with more traditional specifications, in relation to which there has been little change in prescribed quality norms. It is in the interest of international traders to maintain this situation because the wider the applicability of high-volume instrument becomes, the more likely it is that they will be bypassed (or subject to more claims for not fully meeting contract specifications).

## Conventions and the Governance of Global Value Chains

In this section, we reflect on the empirical material presented earlier to consider historical changes in the composition of quality conventions and to highlight some of the key elements of governance in GVCs today. First we critically use the four categories of quality conventions used in the literature to date: market, industrial, civic, and domestic (see Eymard-Duvernay 1989; Sylvander 1995; Thévenot 1995). We then go on to analyze conventions that relate to corporate organization and inter-firm relations. In this case, we do not use Boltanski and Thévenot's (1991) complex and (Boltanski and Chiapello 1999) proliferating list of worlds, but rather, examine some of their underlying dynamics. Finally, we use the discussion of quality conventions and related corporate strategies to return to the issue of governance.

## Changes and Overlaps in Quality Conventions

A cross-cutting theme arising from quality issues in the value chains examined earlier has been the emergence of new, divergent, and sometimes contested notions of quality as the quality of process and production methods has become as, and in many cases even more, important than product characteristics. This reflects increasing competition around product differentiation, preoccupation with product safety, attention to reducing the costs that follow from perceived poor quality, and the emergence of environmental and socioeconomic concerns. These processes have been associated with a proliferation of quality management and quality certification and monitoring systems (such as HACCP and ISO 9000 and 14000 certifications),[18] with environmental and social labels and certifications, and with codes of conduct.

As noted earlier, against the background of a claim that the current period is witnessing a return to the dominance of a market convention, Thévenot (1995) suggests that domestic and civic conventions can still be observed in certain sectors, and that industrial norms are now increasingly applied to the management of quality control rather than to product quality as such. Analysis of selected GVCs originating from Africa suggests that purely market-related quality conventions are actually far from dominant, and that industrial norms are being applied to the management of quality control as well as (still) to product quality itself. Furthermore, the purported resilience of domestic conventions is problematic in at least two respects: (1) domestic conventions, with their reference both to localistic and brand-based justifications, include remarkably different mechanisms of quality negotiation and arbitration; and (2) the nature of these mechanisms has shifted over time, and thus the category has little explanatory power.

Domestic conventions on quality (as presented in convention theory) embed very different systems of quality management and power dynamics—the identity of a product can be guaranteed or institutionalized in the repetition of history by its region or country of origin, or its brand name, or simply through repeated interactions between actors. Perhaps a better approach would be to differentiate strictly domestic conventions (which in the French literature mostly refer to regional geographic appellations or indications and repeated social interaction in localized markets) from proprietary conventions, where quality attributes are "owned" by brand manufacturers or processors.[19] If in the past many brands were based on household (sur)names, and thus on a familial kind of trust, most successful contemporary brands currently refer to different identities drawing on ideas of personal fulfillment, differentiation, connectedness, or sophistication.

The case of specialty coffee, for example, suggests that shifts within domestic forms may be as important as between these and other forms. Information on quality in the mainstream coffee market at the retail level is normally embedded in brands (thus, through proprietary mechanisms). In the specialty coffee sector, much more information on quality is passed on to the consumer, but largely in relation to coffee origin—thus on the basis of narratives of place (domestic trust). At the same time, there is a specific attempt to encode information about ambience of consumption in the language of quality (the quality of consumption environments/experiences and of individual consumers). These narratives may also be materialized in a standard manner for mass consumption (Starbucks), thus recalling industrial quality conventions.

Origin-based trust narratives also tend to be replaced by certified quality systems (the coffee standards on intrinsic quality being developed by the Specialty Coffee Association of America, for example; see Ponte 2002a) that partially delink quality from place. In any event, strictly domestic conventions are under threat in relation to the protection of geographic indications. The preservation of unique geographic indications has been part of high-level struggles at the WTO level, with "traditional" producers of wine and spirits (chiefly, France and Italy) pitched against "new world" producers (Australia, Chile, the U.S., Argentina, and South Africa). The latter argue that some geographic denominations, including those for some cheeses and meat preparations, have lost their relation with locality and have become simply generalized ways of producing a specific food or beverage.

Overlaps between conventions also arise *along* value chains. For example, in the mainstream coffee value chain, relational contracting between roasters and importers, and between importers and exporters, usually takes place in an environment of fairly accurate information on coffee quality (industrial convention). In producing countries, on the contrary, most transactions take place with only limited information on quality communicated. When differences in quality are not so important (Robusta coffee), a market convention dominates in the exchange between local producers, traders, and exporters. When quality differences are more important (Arabica coffee), lack of certainty on quality is resolved through repeated interactions (a strictly domestic convention).

At first sight, the value chains examined in the previous section also provide evidence that civic content is becoming more important in the negotiation of quality in GVCs (as is argued by Thévenot 1995, among others). In practice, though, this trend is often counteracted by others. As seen earlier, Raynolds (2002), for example, explains how fair trade coffee (and for that matter citrus, cocoa, cotton, or fresh vegetables) embodies not only civic norms (paying a fair price, helping small farmers' organizations), but also a more direct, but still virtual, contact between consumer and producer (invoking a domestic convention). At the same time, labeling and certification are organized in terms of an industrial convention, and relationships with some mainstream marketers who carry fair trade coffee are based on a market convention. A similar argument can be made in relation to organic products (see Allen and Kovach 2000; Guthman 2002, 2003; Raynolds 2004).

A parallel trend may be observed in the case of clothing, where ostensibly civic requirements on suppliers, such as absence of child labor in-house and among subcontractors, and absence of dangerous foreign objects (especially needles) from products, are incorporated in the form of multipurpose rules within industrially certified quality assurance systems. Workers' age documentation, excessive overtime, and correct payment of wages are controlled for partly via requirements on suppliers to maintain comprehensive payroll records and records of all transactions with subcontractors. These records, when coupled with other standard technologies, also can be used to allow precise attribution of product defects to specific employees and individual subcontractors. Checks for the presence of such multipurpose rules are part of supplier questionnaires used by buyers such as Tommy Hilfiger and Gap (Gibbon 2002b, 54; Gap 2004).

The setting of strict and objective quality standards in many initiatives that promise sustainability (Giovannucci and Ponte 2004; Ponte 2004a) can also be interpreted as an attempted incorporation of industrial conventions, which in the process subordinate engagement with domestic and civic norms to other ends. In other words, lead firms may attempt to fold the threats to leadership arising from the increasing importance of civic conventions into the operational environment of the market-industrial convention (codification of such parameters into broader systems of standards, certification, and labeling).

If a broad historical interpretation can be attempted at all using convention theory categories—considering the overlaps and complexity of quality conventions within and between value chains—we would argue that industrial conventions are indeed being applied to new quality arenas, notably the process of managing quality, but also that they are still applied to product quality itself. Industrial conventions are increasingly embedding traits that according to convention theory are domestic (branding), but that could be better viewed as proprietary (without implying that a new category or a new classification is essential). At the same time, civic conventions may tend to shorten the distance between geographically distant actors, allowing virtual repeated interactions, the building of trust, and the generation of new configurations of proximity. Thus, there is a blurring of the boundaries between domestic and civic conventions. But, contrary to the contention of Murdoch, Marsden, and Banks (2000), there is no necessary relation between the length of a chain/network and the degree of power exercised.

We would also argue that, as knowledge of quality becomes embedded in technical instruments such as standards, and codes of conduct, there is less need for repeated interactions and the building of the personalized relationships that are the third leg of domestic conventions (the other two being branding and geographical origin); in a sense, we can say that trust becomes institutionalized in the label or code of conduct, rather than by reference to a specific firm. When measurement and transmission of information is not possible (or too costly) on the basis of standardization, "osmotic" processes get prescribed for the transfer of information about quality—such as inviting clothing suppliers to understand retailers' ways of doing things by "coming back to see us (again)." Although this is another instance of repeated interaction, it does not embody trust as normally understood. Thus, it can be seen as another expression of the subsuming of quality (in this case through intuitive and indirect processes) within a market convention, rather than being an example of a domestic convention per se. Finally, we would argue that, as brands, standardization, and certifications become globally known and/or accepted, and as complex manufacturing processes become modularized and more widely understood (see Sturgeon 2001, 2002), the boundaries between market and industrial conventions become increasingly blurred.

In sum, what is taking place in the GVCs covered in this book is a reconsolidation of a compromise between industrial and market quality conventions—rather than an outright dominance of market conventions as argued by Thévenot (1995). This becomes clearer when one considers the underlying bifurcation of quality experiences in these value chains. On the one hand, increasingly complex quality content is codified in equally complex standards (e.g., certified specialty coffees or exclusive lingerie in entirely new fabrics). On the other hand, in some branches of the clothing, coffee, and cocoa sectors, quality content is vulgarized or becoming so.[20] This is happening against a weakening of domestic conventions based on trust and repeated social interactions. Domestic conventions based on geography of origin and civic conventions that cater to specialty and ethical markets could be considered forms of resistance against this trend (although there are ambiguities here too). In a sense, there may be more continuity in the market-industrial compromise than previously thought—as features of domestic and civic conventions are absorbed into industrial conventions, and as the differences between industrial and market conventions may be decreasing with improved prospects for standardization within a large number of differentiated product lines.

## Conventions on Legitimate Forms of Corporate Organization and Interfirm Relations

Thus far, we have drawn on empirical material on quality to reflect on the categories of quality conventions and historical changes in the constellations that they present. In this section, we move from product, production, and process quality conventions to conventions that relate to firm organization, legitimate corporate strategies, and interfirm coordination. In much of convention theory, there is no clear distinction between the two types. Contrary to Eymard-Duvernay (1989), we argue that there is no one-to-one link between quality conventions and specific forms of intra- and interfirm coordination. Rather, although forms of coordination are indeed subject to conventions, these may correspond to narratives and derive from norms that have arisen in contexts completely different from those relating to the quality of products and quality management processes.

The literature on shareholder value and corporate financialization also supports this understanding of the legitimacy of specific forms of corporate organization (and restructuring) and interfirm relations. As highlighted in Chapter 1, corporate financialization has emerged globally in the last two decades, but more forcefully in the United States and United Kingdom than in continental Europe and Japan. The term refers to the generalization of ownership of corporate equity in most

Northern countries but especially the United States and United Kingdom, the resulting increased power in national financial markets of investment funds applying performance-related investment criteria, and the increasing dependence of corporate creditworthiness on equity prices. These phenomena have been accompanied by the emergence of a doctrine of maximizing shareholder value. This entails restructuring operations, externalizing noncore activities, and reengineering supply chains to match a set of financial market indicators, most importantly a given ratio of post-tax return on capital employed. If these indicators are met, then share price performance is said to benefit and with it corporate credit ratings. This set of changes is said to have facilitated a shift at firm level from competitive strategies formed predominantly on the basis of maximizing market share to strategies (also) aimed at maximizing financial performance (see Chapter 1 for more details). We could describe this set of performance indicators as embodying a financialist convention for corporate performance.

These observations have direct relevance to the discussion of governance in the GVCs considered here. In both the coffee and clothing value chains, for example, lead firms that are financials (those that are quoted on stock exchanges) have been under pressure to externalize inventory management to reduce stock holding. This is done to contain the size of circulating capital, and the costs of administering it, within optimal parameters set by financial analysts. Large inventories and high ratios of circulating capital are normally interpreted by markets as indicators of inefficiency; in the clothing chain it is also generally accepted that they may lead to losses resulting from having to mark down a product that goes out of fashion. In both cases, however, outsourcing inventory may also be damaging for the firms undertaking it. For example, when the futures market for coffee is carrying (as it has been in recent years), positions further in the future are valued more than nearby contracts. In this situation, if the costs of stock holding (warehousing, finance, and insurance) are lower than the spread between positions, the holder of stocks can make a profit just by holding inventory. In clothing, outsourcing inventory management leaves retailers vulnerable to "stock outs," or sales opportunities that are lost by virtue of shortages of product that suddenly becomes "hot"—unless accompanied by special supply chain management techniques such as model stock replenishment programs. The fact that quoted roasters and clothing retailers keep outsourcing inventory management indicates their captivity to the (currently dominant) logic of financial markets, which prioritizes market capitalization over other indicators of performance.

Financialist logics are less dominant in public companies in non-Anglo-Saxon countries and in private companies in Anglo-Saxon countries. In these contexts, outsourcing-based network types of interfirm coordination are often also present but do not necessarily imply the same divisions of labor along the value chain as those described here. Palpacuer, Gibbon, and Thomsen (2005) identify different forms of coordination characteristic of clothing value chains led by large British, French, and Scandinavian retailers. Although the British chain largely follows the financialist logic described, outsourcing by French and Scandinavian retailers does not encompass inventory management. In the French case, this is associated with a more dispersed supply base as well as greater informality in supply chain management. In the Scandinavian case, it is associated with a relatively concentrated supply base, but one managed according to market principles.

It is clear that quite different kinds of conventions are relevant in relation to quality and its management on the one hand and to the management of interfirm relations on the other. However, conceptualizing the latter in terms of conventions rather than in terms of the intrinsic properties of transactions, information, or firms themselves allows a reintroduction of historical and cognitive/normative dynamics that otherwise appear in danger of disappearance from thinking about the global economy.

## Conventions and Governance

In relation to quality conventions, we have learned so far in this book that control over the qualification of specific products is a key source of power for lead firms. Sometimes, it may also be a terrain for counteractions by other actors that attempt to challenge the status quo. It is worth adding here that the tendency to outsource—which, as seen earlier, is greatest where financialist logics are most prevalent—may exist in tension not only with profit opportunities arising from holding inventory, but also with retention of control over product qualification. The outsourcing of the inventory management function in food retail chains, for example, is typically associated with outsourcing others, such as shelf placing and new product development, which entail secondary aspects of qualification. At the same time, third-party certification and influence on the content of standards are key tactics for lead firms to transfer the costs of quality control to suppliers and to achieve control at a distance.

In relation to conventions concerning corporate organization, we have highlighted how the degree to which lead firms in GVCs aim at, as well as actually achieve, the externalization of an increasing number of functions (in other words, how they define the functional division of labor along the chain) depends on, first, how sensitive these firms are to pressures arising from maximizing shareholder value and broader concepts of how a firm should be organized to deliver in financial markets; and second, broader cultural assumptions and regulative frameworks bearing on appropriate forms of interfirm relation. Also relevant is the degree of internal coherence of reference values within firms—for example, between financial and technical functions—and what set of strategies besides pure outsourcing ones may be available to meet a given set of (financialist) expectations. Only within this broad context will factors such as those considered primary by Gereffi, Humphrey, and Sturgeon (2004) come into play, namely how feasible it is for lead firms to externalize functions—both technically and organizationally—and whether there will be an internally competitive market of competent suppliers available to absorb them.

Returning to the relation between the basic concepts of convention theory and GVC analysis, we now draw a series of parallels between the two frameworks that can clarify the dynamics of GVC governance. In Table 6.1, parallels are drawn in relation to the four quality conventions highlighted earlier. Note that market and industrial conventions are put here in the same box, since the difference between the two is becoming less discernible, as discussed earlier. This framework does not entail blind acceptance of these labels, nor their watertight division. In both the convention theory and GVC columns there are considerable overlaps between categories, but also significant differences. The first column indicates types of quality convention. The second lists the organizing principles attached to such conventions. The third indicates quality-related mechanisms for driving. The fourth lists the type of lead firms that have been empirically observed (rather than predeterminately expected) to be linked to given quality convention in the last two decades. The fifth column attempts a link between conventions, specific forms of governance, and different degrees of chain drivenness. Finally, the sixth column lists examples of specific value chains that fall in each category of quality convention.

Two major differences exist between the approach taken by Gereffi, Humphrey, and Sturgeon (2004) and the one taken here. First, their analysis of power relations suggests that, as one moves from hierarchy to market forms of coordination, the degree of power exercised by the dominant actor in the value chain decreases. We argue that, as one moves from hands-on to hands-off coordination, the way power is exercised changes, not its magnitude or who exercises it. The fact that clothing retailers or coffee roasters exercise hands-off forms of coordination does not mean that they are less powerful in their value chains. Their degree of power corresponds to the level of drivenness of the value chain, rather than being the property of the incidence of one or two mechanisms of coordination found within it—as Gereffi, Humphrey, and Sturgeon would have it. Second, our focus on the mechanisms of transmission of information on quality (and related discussion on normative values of corporate organization) helps to go beyond immediate forms of coordination to understand how a GVC is governed *as a whole*. Our approach, rather than focusing on predefined sets of independent variables yielding a dependent outcome (one kind of coordination or another), is based on recognizing different degrees of power and the historical processes contributing to empirically observed increases in buyer drivenness.

Table 6.1 suggests that a high level of drivenness occurs in GVCs that are characterized by the dominance of industrial-market quality conventions. Lead firms in this box are branded manufacturers such as Nestlé (with a tendency toward the side of industrial conventions), retailers such as Gap or Tesco, and discounters such as Wal-Mart (with a tendency toward the side of market conventions).

The actual forms of coordination between lead firms and first-tier suppliers (and their hands-on or hands-off character) vary depending on the mechanisms for transmitting knowledge and information about quality and on the (conventionalized) strategic values guiding lead firms. Firms with a financialist-network set of values tend to: (1) be more hands-off with their immediate suppliers, (2) outsource more noncore functions, (3) nominate preferred suppliers, (4) have stricter supplier selection criteria, (5) focus on squeezing more out of less, and (6) fine-tune economies of scale and scope. Firms that are not exposed to the same extent to the dictates of financial markets may have more hands-on forms of coordination with their immediate suppliers, or alternatively, more market-based ones where there is no investment in deeper relations with suppliers (see earlier).

In GVCs that are characterized by civic conventions, marketers of ethical products and civil society groups play an important role in defining the division of labor along the chain—at least until mainstream buyers

**Table 6.1** Linkages between key categories of convention theory and GVC analysis

| Convention theory: quality convention | Convention theory: organizing principle | Global value chain analysis: quality-related mechanisms for driving | Type of lead firms | Mode of governance (and degree of drivenness) | Examples of specific value chains |
|---|---|---|---|---|---|
| Industrial Market | Productivity Competitivness | Influence on setting content of quality and standardization or codification; codification of production techniques and (branded) products into a few broad standards; alternatively, ability to convey mindset and operational culture; ability to capture rents through management of information asymmetry on quality; minimizing cost of matching civic quality content through external certification processes (or formulation of internal codes of conduct) and moving these costs upstream | Branded manufacturers Retailers Discounters | Buyer driven (high) | Mainstream coffee, cocoa, fresh vegetables and citrus, clothing |

| Civic | Welfare | Capacity to match civil society demands in terms of minimum socioeconomic and environmental standards; packaging these achievements in terms of differentiated product and service offering | Marketers of ethical products Civil society groups Certifiers, auditors | Moving toward buyer driven (medium) | Fair trade, organic and other sustainable coffee, cocoa, cotton, fresh vegetables and citrus |
|---|---|---|---|---|---|
| Domestic | Loyalty | Capacity to develop trust through repeated interactions and/or geographic appellations; extract rents from the uniqueness of products or production/trade relations | Producer groups under appellation systems International traders Niche/specialty marketers | Producer driven, but often not driven at all (low) | Specialty coffee, fine and flavored cocoa, cotton, haute couture clothing |

come into the picture and civic content becomes embedded in standards, certifications, and codes of conduct. Certifiers and auditors also play a key role in negotiating the demands of buyers in relation to the possibility of standardization on the production side. In this sense, they are also active (but indirect) participants in the formulation of the division of labor along the chain. However, as we have argued previously, the process of certification and codification itself facilitates the emergence of market-industrial conventions and of economies of scale. In this respect, these value chains have tended to become more buyer driven in the last decade. In GVCs where quality is embedded in domestic conventions, there is a low level of drivenness. In other words, only little or no effort is invested in engineering a detailed functional division of labor in relation to (or beyond) immediate suppliers. These value chains are local—or related to a narrative of place (local, regional, and gourmet foods and beverages; Paris, Milan, or London haute couture; products that have geographic indication or appellation systems); and/or they require repeated interaction and the building of personal trust (reputation).

Finally, we would like to return briefly to the role of consumers in the governance of GVCs. An economy of qualities (Callon, Méadel, and Rabeharisoa 2002) reading of the empirical material presented here suggests that lead firms are by no means in complete control of the governance of consumption. Broad quality conventions relate to fundamental social-structural trends, and even modifications in their mix and hierarchy are shaped largely independently of the wishes of lead firms. The latter may occur, for example, via the rise of new social movements (organic, fair trade; see Raynolds 2002, 2004) or through the institutionalization of new bodies of expertise concerning good taste, developed for example by lifestyle journalists and gurus, fashion scouts, property makeover consultants, and celebrity cooks.[21] In the GVCs analyzed here, lead firms attempt to take advantage of changes in consumption and its governance via the (re)qualification of fashionable products in proprietary forms (brands, patented products, and processes) rather than trying to govern consumption as such.

## CONCLUSION

This chapter has used some of the key concepts of convention theory to further our understanding of governance in GVCs. It has underlined a historical trend away from more hands-on and toward more hands-off forms of coordination between lead firms and their immediate suppliers (or buyers)—one that is linked to a strengthening of market-industrial conventions. In all the chains examined in this book, quality management is one of the key aspects of chain governance. Lead firms in many of these chains seem to have developed relatively hands-off forms of coordination with their immediate suppliers and have outsourced a number of previously in-house performed functions. Their suppliers, however, have often had to seek more hands-on forms of coordination with actors upstream, and sometimes even vertically integrate. This means that relatively hands-off forms of immediate coordination may coexist with high levels of drivenness. This occurs through the codification and standardization of quality and performance requirements, and through the adoption of third-party certification or monitoring to manage civic concerns. Where this is not possible, buyers seek to adopt other relatively hands-off forms through suggesting informal learning processes in which suppliers are invited to understand the mindsets and organizational cultures of buyers.

This discussion underlines that forms of coordination are different from forms of governance. A GVC may be characterized by different forms of coordination in various segments, yet a relatively systematic form of governance. A general observation is that, historically, GVCs are becoming increasingly buyer driven. Such chains are characterized by a dominance of market-industrial quality conventions. The distinction between buyer-driven and producer-driven chains then remains a useful device for the analysis of governance, both as a typological instrument and as historical categories, irrespectively of the nature of the forms of coordination that exist within and between individual segments of a value chain.

To understand how buyer-driven governance arises, what forms it takes, and how it changes, we need to clarify how lead firms achieve flexibility and externalize functions (to the extent that they need to) while, at the same time, keeping control and shaping (driving) the value chain. Their degree of success in doing so seems to depend on how well they have been able to transfer mindset information/assumptions to their suppliers, or to standardize, codify, and/or obtain credible external certification for increasingly complex quality content of goods and services. Control over the qualification of specific products is a key source of power in GVCs, and of countermeasures to defend threats against leadership. Yet, this yearning for control exists in a tension with a wish to outsource (for cost control purposes) some secondary aspects of qualification (e.g., shelf placing, new-product development). Finally, third party certification allows suppliers to transfer the cost of quality control to suppliers.

In this chapter, rather than attempting to resolve convention theory's inconsistencies and inadequacies, we have used some of its fruitful basic concepts to highlight the cognitive/normative aspects of governance in GVCs through a quality reading of the Africa empirical material. The analysis undertaken here does not provide all (or even most of) the answers to the key question of governance in GVCs. However, it underlines that quality issues (in addition to volume, economies of scale, and prices) are central in understanding the way lead firms shape the functional division of labor and entry barriers along a value chain. Furthermore, it suggests that the mechanisms of governance will depend on what set(s) of shared values and procedures for measuring quality performance are dominant. Against this background, further work is needed on clarifying the historical dynamics of GVCs in relation to mechanisms of legitimation and justification of leadership, ways of measuring success (of suppliers and buyers), and the (changing) composition of the quality conventions found within GVCs.

# 7    Trading Down?

## AFRICA, VALUE CHAINS, AND THE GLOBAL ECONOMY

HAS AFRICA become more peripheral in the global economy? The analysis carried out in this book suggests uneven trajectories within the continent—depending on which global value chain (GVC) is considered. The increased integration of some African industries in the global economy goes hand-in-hand with a greater marginalization of others. In some chains, new opportunities are materializing but have high costs and often come with benefits that are generally low, unpredictable, and nontransparent.

Africa participates in the global economy on the basis of specific investments, exchanges, and contracts that express the calculations (and miscalculations) of specific enterprises and individuals. These processes take place in the context of increased economic globalization, corporate financialization, the emergence of the doctrine of shareholder value—and the resulting corporate strategies that are adopted to meet financial targets (oligopolistic rent-seeking, brand culling and refocusing, and ever-extended forms of outsourcing). However, shifts in corporate strategies do not materialize in a regulatory vacuum. Markets in developed and developing countries have been moving toward deregulation. In international trade, new kinds of regulation are taking place, with the progressive emergence of a new regime from the early 1990s. This regime has significantly modified the conditions under which Africa trades with the rest of the world.

A central feature of the international trade regime associated with GATT (1947–1994) was that it tacitly acknowledged the structural problems faced by developing countries and, on this basis, provided some opportunities to mitigate them. GATT was a forum where political compromise prevailed over the enforcement of rules. Against the background of more balanced distribution of global economic power in the 1970s, it accepted developing countries' own definition of their problems in relation to the international trading system and legitimized nonreciprocal obligations in relation to them. Developing countries could opt out of multilateral agreements that were not to their advantage, could form cartels to sell commodities, and obtained some nonreciprocal preferences for their exports of manufactures. However, opt outs were often used to pursue unrealistic domestic policies, the commodity agreements rested on the fragile consent of consuming countries, and nonreciprocal preferences for manufactured goods were often undermined by restrictive rules of origin.

In principle, the new international trade regime that has emerged under WTO (1995 to present) creates conditions under which better trade opportunities for developing countries could be institutionalized. WTO differs from GATT in a series of fundamental ways. It covers a large proportion of world trade. It incorporates a much wider set of agreements than GATT, dealing with domestic as well as border issues. So far, all its member countries are obliged to be party to all its agreements (the single undertaking principle), and conformity with the resulting obligations is now subject to juridical rules and enforcement mechanisms. Reciprocity of trade preferences between developed and developing countries is now a requirement, with exceptions only for limited time periods and for unilateral offers in relation to all least developed countries (LDCs). Although there are still remnants of special and differentiated treatment for developing countries, the specific structural problems of developing countries are not taken as a starting point for determining this treatment. Rather, the WTO framework is guided by the perspective that developing countries are simply at a lower stage of development, which will be overcome by being allowed more time to catch up.

Having much more of a mandatory and rule-bound character than GATT, WTO should have led to improved market access. In practice, gains for developing countries (and especially LDCs) remain small. Many of the new WTO rules make the growth of trade and exports from Africa more rather than less difficult. Most of the traditional trade barriers that African countries have always faced remain, although sometimes in new guises that are less easy to recognize. In addition, the new agreements and mechanisms inaugurated in 1995 tend either to create new barriers to access or to remove the possibility of using key instruments to mitigate them. This is happening as Africa experiences slower export growth than other regions, a declining role as a trade partner with Northern countries, relatively slow growth in intraindustry trade (elsewhere one of the most dynamics areas of growth in global trade), and only a very limited degree of diversification away from primary commodities. This level of diversification is lowest (or nonexistent) for African LDCs.

Another feature of the new regime is that WTO has been accompanied by a proliferation of bilateral arrangements. After the failure of the Cancun Ministerial Meeting in September 2003, this process appeared to speed up. Where special and differentiated treatment for LDCs is written into these arrangements, it occurs on the basis of non–bound offers rather than agreements. These offers are used to extract concessions from weaker trading partners concerning domestic market deregulation— over and above those already achieved through the WTO. The result is an encirclement of multilateral agreements and institutions by an array of inconsistent and sometimes conflicting sets of preferences, exceptions, and conditionalities.

It is against this background that one can make sense of the apparently increasing differentiation in trade performance between African countries and the rest of the world. The new international trade regime, like public policy generally, redefines the pursuit of equality not in terms of modest degrees of distinct treatment for the disadvantaged as prior to 1995, but rather in terms of equality of opportunity. As with other such provisions, the outcome is to allow for much greater play for differences in endowments, from classic factor endowments to new ones like intellectual property holdings and access to lawyers. This is happening in a context where the economic bargaining power of African governments, farms, and firms has markedly decreased as a result of the disappearance of international commodity agreements and the twin processes of structural adjustment and market liberalization. In the 1980s, donors began demanding that African country governments use market liberalization to promote greater efficiency and reduce the budgetary cost of single-channel marketing systems, which tended to be resource intensive, inefficient and susceptible to corruption. Single-channel systems were abandoned in most anglophone and lusophone African countries. In francophone Africa, the process was generally much slower and often less radical. The abolition of export marketing monopolies in Africa entailed a radical shift in bargaining power. Importers and international traders are no longer negotiating with a handful of (state-controlled) exporters with large volumes and the resources to offer stock in advance or hold stock back from the world market, but mostly with a multitude of small- and medium-sized local private players with access to limited resources.

Africa faces daunting challenges not only from the new trade regime and domestic market liberalization, but also from the tightening demands associated with participation in GVCs. Governance of GVCs is defined in this book as the process of defining the functional division of labor along a chain. This is used to shape the terms of chain membership, oblige other actors to perform unwanted value-added activities, or alternatively to exclude them. Defining participation requirements, and by implication entry barriers, is the key operational mechanism of governance. This translates into organizational arrangements that may vary both along and between value chains. A GVC may thus embody different forms of coordination between various links or nodes, yet a relatively coherent form of overall governance. Marginalization/exclusion and inclusion/upgrading are the axes along which (re)distribution processes take place in GVCs.

All but one of the six GVCs examined in this book have become increasingly buyer driven in the last two decades. Different buyers drive these value chains—those with direct contact with consumers in citrus, clothing, and fresh vegetables; and branded processors/manufacturers in coffee and cocoa. An exception to this trend is cotton, where there is no clear group of lead firms. Immediately upstream of these lead firms, there are usually other powerful actors (first-tier suppliers) who do most of the day-to-day work of chain coordination for lead firms and who maintain relatively hands-on relationships with actors further upstream of them (second-tier suppliers and beyond). Unfortunately, there are no African lead firms in these value chains, and only a few first-tier suppliers. More than a handful of African second-tier suppliers are present only in the case of (parts of) the clothing chain emanating from Mauritius and in the cotton chain.

The changing pattern of Africa's participation in GVCs is consistent with two broader processes. One is the tendency for economic globalization, in the absence of appropriate interventions by developing country governments, to reproduce and extend pre-existing patterns of inequality. The other is the apparently widening gap between the capacities of most African governments and those in other developing regions to design and implement appropriate interventions. Kenya, Ethiopia, and Ghana have remained in (relatively) advantageous positions in the coffee and cocoa chains respectively as a result of inertia rather than action. The success stories of Zimbabwe cotton (up to ca. 2002), Mauritian/Madagascan clothing (up to 2001), Kenyan fresh vegetables, and South African citrus owed more to private initiative and/or private coordination than to public action. Both these conditions rested in turn mostly on high concentrations of private economic power. Such concentrations hardly exist outside a few countries in the continent, and these countries tend to have non-African business élites. As a result, it seems that any meaningful improvement in Africa's position within GVCs is bound to rely on foreign direct investment in the short term and a resuscitation of the capacities of the African state in the longer one.

Yet, African countries (and in particular LDCs) still have some opportunities under the current international trade regime. So far these have not been found in WTO itself, but rather in one or two of the new bilateral offers (notably the Africa Growth and Opportunity Act, or AGOA) that incorporate significant improvements in preferences for certain products where African LDCs have a comparative advantage. The drawback of these new opportunities is that they are unilateral, time limited, and hedged by conditions. As the WTO process falters and intratrading bloc competition increases, African governments should try to stimulate more such concessions and to obtain them in more permanent forms.

In sum, the challenge for Africa at the international level is to carve out a space within the emerging opportunities presented by value chain restructuring—such as achieving greater economies of scale while maintaining quality standards, diversifying customer bases, and leapfrogging intermediaries, as well as exploiting those specialty and fair trade markets where higher prices are available for quality content in the context of more manageable increases in entry barriers. Africa also needs to become more involved in steering a modification of current forms of regulation, not only in relation to WTO rules, but also in terms of promoting the equivalence of less demanding alternatives to current product and process standards. At the domestic level, the challenge is to devise institutional forms that promote private coordination in defense of public goods, to promote new forms of industrial policy, and to make chain participation more socially broad based.

## Trading Down?

The term *trading down* has a double meaning in relation to this book. First, it is shorthand for some of the precise processes lying behind Africa's experience of trade disintegration. As our analysis has shown, exclusion and marginalization have been experienced as a result of the failure of African farms and firms to meet new expectations concerning quality, lead times, volumes, and prices, and their failure in actively shaping new standards to their advantage—including ones related to social and environmental concerns raised by Northern NGOs. In some cases, exclusion and marginalization have even occurred as a result of the failure of Africa's farms and firms to continue meeting traditional expectations in relation to these dimensions, as the provision of public goods like quality control has collapsed. Where a presence has been retained in some GVCs, this has usually been associated either passively, with specialization in traditional varietal and/or quality profiles that happen to continue to attract premia, or actively by greater specialization than before in more price competitive offerings of products of basic quality. This latter process is illustrated in the relative success stories of Ugandan Robusta coffee and clothing exports to the U.S. market from rural South Africa. These may also be considered expressions of trading down, since their price competitiveness rests on foundations that are even more vulnerable than those of cheap labor alone. Ugandan coffee's long-term competitiveness in relation to other large-scale Robusta suppliers is questionable, and much of the price advantage enjoyed by Southern African clothing exports will disappear when quotas are removed from China and other countries in the coming years. Finally, and paradoxically, trading down processes have also occurred when higher quality standards have been achieved, but without attracting higher prices (or value added) for African producers.

A second, and quite distinct, meaning of trading down is a prescriptive one. The term can be used as a useful rhetorical corrective to those economic development narratives that recommend post-Fordist solutions for all countries, regardless of their factor endowments. Such narratives are commonly formulated in terms of trading up, in the form of programs promoting, among other things, flexible production systems, high-value niche exports, technological upgrading, employee multi-skilling, and collateralization of social capital as it is embodied in local networks of small- and medium-scale enterprises. In recent years, such programs have been sold by consulting companies to one developing country government after another, on the basis that they represent the only genuine alternative to the so-called race to the bottom entailed by trying to compete with China at its own game. The purchasers of these programs should ask themselves why, as a result of adopting them, they would be any more likely to be able to compete with countries—ranging from Germany to Taiwan—that institutionalized similar strategies years ago and have been able to devote high levels of resources to them.

In this rhetorical context, trading down can be used to sum up certain aspects of the practical policies followed by the small number of African-based enterprises which, in the chains considered here, have consolidated roles as second-tier suppliers or which have gained a foothold in relation to first-tier supplier status. Their emphasis has tended to be on economies of scale, relatively high levels of specialization, and simple and labor-intensive technologies. Flexibility has been pursued mainly in relation to price and lead time and on the basis of geographical spread of production. In some cases, the products traded can be regarded as high value, but almost without exception they have been aimed at mass markets, via large-scale retailers. Strategies of this kind take their point of departure in the realities of African resource endowments and have a proven track record. They indeed borrow from the Chinese experience, and in some cases are carried in Africa by businesspeople of Chinese extraction. As China itself becomes more economically mature, the prospects for Africa to build on this experience are reasonably promising.

## GVC Analysis and Future Research Directions

In this book, we have sought to specify the historical dynamics of the rise of buyer-driven GVCs in the context of changing regulatory environments and corporate strategies. We also examined how lead firms struggle to define and manage quality, and how this process shapes the functional division of labor and entry barriers along value chains. Furthermore, we explored how occupying lead firm status depends not only on economic attributes such as market share, but also on the diffusion among their suppliers of quality narratives defining, transmitting, and justifying the choice of specific standards for products and for production and process methods.

Historically, the GVCs analyzed in this book have witnessed the consolidation of a compromise between industrial and market quality conventions, against the background of a weakening of domestic conventions based on trust and repeated social interactions. The market-industrial compromise has been to some extent encroached on by domestic conventions based on region of origin and by civic conventions reflecting the concerns of specialty and ethical markets. So far, lead firms have been able to neutralize these threats through processes of standardization and codification that allow the absorption of features of domestic and civic conventions into the market-industrial fold. Alternatively, they have been able to develop and legitimize more intuitive processes of transmission of quality information that do not require the building of trust in classically prescribed ways.

Lead firms can use different strategies to maintain their position. Not all of these conform to the objective of externalizing an increasing number of functions—nor are these externalized functions necessarily low profit. The specific strategies that lead firms adopt depend on the following: how sensitive they are to pressures arising from maximizing shareholder value and to matching broader expectations concerning how firms should be organized to deliver in financial markets; what degree of internal coherence of reference values there is within these firms; and to what extent the regulatory framework (both national and international) facilitates the process of supply chain restructuring.

Despite these differences, it is clear that buyer-driven governance is becoming exercised increasingly through hands-off forms of coordination. In much of the postwar period, lead firms preferred hands-on forms of coordination with their immediate suppliers—especially vertical integration, but also "thick" social and/or contractual relationships (often exclusive) with dedicated suppliers. More recently, they have devised more hands-off forms, in tandem with institutionalizing a category of explicitly first-tier suppliers. These suppliers are encouraged to absorb an increasing number of functions, including the day-to-day coordination of operations further upstream. This often results in more hands-on forms of coordination between first-tier and second-tier suppliers and beyond. In this way, lead firms may drive a value chain without actually directly controlling it (or owning the functional capabilities to do so) in its entirety—or even in large segments.

Lead firms that have achieved this organizational model have often done so through the codification and standardization of quality and performance requirements, and through the adoption of third-party certification or monitoring (e.g., to manage socioeconomic and environmental concerns). When this is not possible, relatively hands-off forms of coordination have been achieved through informal learning processes in which suppliers are invited to understand the mindsets and operational culture of buyers. The need for standardization and codification of quality information rises not only from the need to externalize functions (and thus maximize shareholder value), but also from the imperative of product differentiation, which means achieving economies of scale *and* of scope. This entails providing a large range of different qualities and achieving economies of scale within several product lines at the same time. The more standardized each product or module for assembly is, the easier it is to reduce costs and deliver both variety and a competitive price.

In conclusion, we argue that the original distinction made in GVC analysis between buyer-driven and producer-driven forms of governance remains a key analytical contribution. This book is a step in the direction of unpacking the historical dynamics of the rise of buyer drivenness against the background of changing regulatory environments (both internationally and within individual countries) and the emergence of increasingly complex sets of standards. It is also an attempt to fine-tune the concept of buyer-driven governance by adding underlying components to its description and making predictions about the future based on historical dynamics—in line with the tradition of political economy. At the same time, we have insisted that GVC analysis needs to combine an understanding of the sources, exercise, and consequences of private economic power much more clearly with one of discourses about public regulation and consumption. This is particularly the case for agrofood products—where regulation has a potentially decisive role in lowering entry barriers for local producers and where consumption is changing rapidly. Further research and debate are also needed on clarifying the historical dynamics of GVCs in relation to normative and cognitive, and not only material, aspects of governance, the (changing) composition of quality conventions, and the role of consumers and civil society actors in defining long-term changes in how quality is defined and perceived. Finally, more efforts are needed in terms of better understanding the role of standards as a device of governance in GVCs.

# Notes

PREFACE

1. In this book, we refer to industrialized economies in North America and Europe, plus Japan, New Zealand, and Australia, as the North or Northern countries.

2. In GVC analysis, lead firms are a group of firms in a particular functional position (or positions) that are able to shape the division of labor, and therefore influence the distribution of value added, along a value chain (or along the most profitable parts of it). GVC analysis focuses its attention on the characteristics of these firms as a group, rather than on which individual firm is the market leader among others in the same functional position.

## CHAPTER 1

1. OECD is the club of the world's 20 wealthiest countries.

2. World GDP is usually defined as the aggregate value of goods and services produced by all nations within their national boundaries and regardless of the nationality of the entities producing them.

3. Data distinguishing components from the rest of this category do not feature in recent WTO international trade statistics.

4. The table contains information on 21 retailers because one of them has sometimes given different sales figures in different reports. Depending on which report is accepted, the retailer concerned falls within or just outside the top 20.

5. See also Reardon and Berdegué (2002); Reardon, Berdegué, and Farrington (2002); Reardon et al. (2003); and Weatherspoon and Reardon (2003).

6. Pension funds and investment trusts fall into two categories: those that are directly managed and those that are managed on a delegate basis and are engaged in competition with each other for subscriptions from directly managed funds, nonfinancial corporations, and wealthy individuals. Delegate funds operate on a global basis and aim at maximizing returns by moving funds very rapidly between different companies, markets, and types of financial instruments.

7. Other common uses of the term "financialization" refer to the increasing tendency for nonfinancial corporations to acquire financial assets and buy financial subsidiaries. However, these tendencies may be more an expression of the shareholder value doctrine than of financialization itself.

8. For a conceptual critique of the moral and functional claims of shareholder ideology, see Engelen (2002).

9. For a recent discussion of cash cow strategies in the mainland E.U. food manufacturing sector, see Perez and Palpacuer (2002). The cash cow argument is paralleled by business consultant prescriptions concerning core competences, although these are sometimes also interpreted simply as justifications for downsizing.

10. Gibbon (2002a) also describes contests within firms over different interpretations of how to improve margins within the framework of a cash cow strategy. He compares arguments with financialist rationales (emphasis on buying-in margin) to ones with "retailerist" rationales (emphasis on selling-out margin).

11. Whereas the share of GDP represented by the assets of institutional investors held in listed companies is over 100 percent in the United Kingdom and over 70 percent in the United States, in Austria, the Netherlands, Switzerland, and Sweden, it is in the range of 30 to 50 percent. In most other European countries, it is less than 20 percent (Guillén 2000).

12. In a comparison of U.S.- and E.U.-owned auto manufacturers, Dupuy and Lung (2001) report that whereas institutional investors held 59.3 percent of the stock of GM and 39.8 percent of Ford, their presence in E.U. ownership structures was in a range between 11 percent and 28 percent.

13. Some of these changes are seen as having been accelerated by Vodaphone's takeover of Mannesmann in 2000. Vodaphone's bid was construed as hostile up until the last moment, when Mannesmann's supervisory board suddenly reversed its position and agreed to the takeover. Later, it emerged that six former board members had received personal bonuses from Vodaphone totaling more than € 74 million. Subsequently, the former Mannesmann CEO Klaus Esser and five others, including Josef Ackermann, chairman of Deutsche Bank, were prosecuted for breach of shareholders' trust, a criminal offense. Although some in German industry have described the takeover as a wake-up call for German industry to get its act together, Ackermann with the backing of Deutsche Bank has gone much further. He claimed that the prosecution was motivated by "destructive social envy," which he compared with "the constructive readiness in the US and UK to emulate success" (*Financial Times*, February 9, 2003). An interim judgment issued in March 2004 found that there were insufficient grounds to pursue a criminal case against the accused, but that corporate law had been broken in awarding inappropriate bonuses.

14. Real GDP is GDP expressed in prices of a common base year rather than current prices, thus discounting the effects of inflation.

15. Using different time periods and a per capita measure does not alter the trend: global real GDP growth per capita was 2.9 percent in 1950 to 1973 and 1.3 percent in 1973 to 1998.

16. Rewe's takeover of Budgen's was also an instance of an international M&A. Another sharp increase in U.K. retail concentration occurred in 2004 with the takeover of Safeway by Wm Morrison.

17. When Royal Ahold experienced major problems in 2002–2003 (see later), its earlier Latin American acquisitions were redistributed mainly among its rivals. In Brazil, Wal-Mart acquired the Bompreco chain, thereby making it the country's third largest operator.

18. Tesco's recent M&As in Asia and central Europe include the purchase of C-Two Network in Japan and 13 hypermarkets in Poland from the German chain HIT. Its first entry into the central European market was in 1993, when it purchased a chain of hypermarkets in the Czech Republic and Slovakia set up by Kmart. In 2003, the share of non-U.K. sales in Tesco's total sales rose to 17.6 percent (Tesco plc 2003). Wal-Mart's expansion into Asia was on the basis of acquiring a 38 percent stake in the Japanese chain Seiyu.

19. According to Weatherspoon and Reardon (2003), South African and/or Kenyan FDI has led to the rise of supermarket chains, first in Zimbabwe, Zambia, Namibia, Botswana, and Swaziland, then in Mauritius, Madagascar, Angola, Mozambique, Tanzania, and Uganda. This spread of FDI in retailing is said to be tentatively moving into West Africa.

20. Many large Scandinavian supermarkets and hypermarkets also incorporate betting shops.

21. According to the market research group ABG, supermarkets and hypermarkets accounted for 77 percent of all U.K. food sales in 1997.

22. In the United States, excluding food sales via convenience store formats (a format where market concentration is low), the market share of the four largest players was 20.8 percent and of the eight largest 39.5 percent in 1997 (U.S. Census Bureau 2000).

23. Own-label products are those that are distributed by supermarkets under their name/label (or under a related product line label) rather than under the brand names owned by other industry actors.

24. See www.the-list.co.uk.

25. The crisis revolved partly around the fact that these had been recorded for accounting purposes as straight earnings rather than discounts and partly that these had been inflated by an unknown amount.

26. During a recent discussion in Denmark, it was asserted that a majority of the profits of leading Danish supermarkets derived from lump sum payments (*Politiken*, November 10, 2003).

27. It was on this basis that a large retailer (and user of these programs) described them in an interview with one of the authors as "a fool's paradise for suppliers."

28. In the words of an industry consultant (Dixon 1999):

It used to be [and still is for many] that . . . suppliers had representatives who called on customers, took orders and shipped materials to customer[s]. . . . Then, a few years ago, the concept of supplier-managed inventory appeared on the scene, making it commonplace for suppliers to carry out some level of planning and restocking of customer materials requirements. After "supplier-managed inventory" came "supplier commodity management," where suppliers take control and responsibility for a wide range of customers, doing planning, inventory control and even direct production sequencing and deliveries. Today we are beginning to see more advanced forms of supplier commodity management, whereby customers are asking—even demanding—that their suppliers manage products while also taking responsibility for products that they don't normally sell, eliminating the need for the customer to interface with large numbers of suppliers. Approaches to product delivery and control . . . have reached a point where the term "supplier" hardly applies. Instead it has been replaced by the new [type of actor] . . . the company that "does it all" for the customer.

29. On the "Third Italy," see, among others, Piore and Sabel (1984). There is no single definition of "Toyotaism," but a common feature of most definitions is just-in-time production on the basis of long-term subcontracting relations with core suppliers, with high sunk costs on both sides.

30. This, more generally, characterizes a hands-off type of governance, which seems to be emerging in a number of GVCs (see Chapters 3 and 6).

31. See the more detailed account of this path of upgrading and its limitations in Chapters 3 and 5.

32. This is said to be one of the main differences between U.S. electronics contract manufacturers and Far Eastern ones. The former use a base manufacturing process that can be applied to a broad product range; the latter uses one that can serve only the personal computer industry (Sturgeon 2002).

33. See the discussion of the WTO TRIMs agreement in Chapter 2.

34. In this book, downstream means closer to the consumer and upstream means closer to the producer.

35. The connection may run both ways. Bayer was forced to become a pharmaceutical specialist from 2001 onward. This followed its forced withdrawal of Lipobay, a blockbuster anticholesterol drug that became linked with fatal side effects, and the unrelenting pressure that it came under as a result.

36. Schreiber, whose turnover exceeds $2 billion a year, employs 4,200 persons globally in plants in the United States, Mexico, Brazil, France, Germany, Saudi Arabia, and India. Schreiber describes itself as "the largest customer brand cheese company in the world . . . providing products to the biggest names in fast food and . . . store-brand cheese products to grocery chains and wholesalers." It further offers "product innovation, category management, risk management, vendor managed inventory, supply chain management and many other value-added services" (www.sficorp.com).

37. Of these companies, only Fyffes relies on contract farming or direct purchases for more than 50 percent of its business. The others are essentially plantation companies (Rabobank 2001).

38. A similar picture applies in the case of a few fresh vegetable contract suppliers like Flamingo Holdings (see Chapter 5), but these are rather exceptional.

39. ACP stands for African, Caribbean, and Pacific, a group of 77 countries with special trade and aid arrangements with the E.U. codified in the Lomé Convention (1975) and later the Cotonou Agreement (2000; see Chapter 2). Under these agreements, ACP bananas entered the European Union at preferential tariff rates and on the basis of a tied licensing system, of which Geest was a beneficiary.

40. A distinct but related principle of differentiation can be found among contract food ingredient manufacturers. Here, a distinction can now be made between single ingredient suppliers and multi-ingredient suppliers (that is, suppliers of custom-made solutions (Rabobank 2002a). Interestingly, the food ingredient companies that sought to upgrade from single- or multi-ingredient supply into food ingredient branding have failed to do so (Rabobank 2002a).

41. "As regards practically all the finished products and services of industry and trade, it is clear that ... every manufacturer of gloves or shaving cream or handsaws has a small and precarious market which he [sic] tries—must try—to build up and to keep by price strategy, quality strategy – 'product differentiation' – and advertising. Thus we get a completely different pattern which there seems to be no reason to expect to yield the results of perfect competition and which fits much better into the monopolistic schema. In these cases we can speak of monopolistic competition" (Schumpeter 1943: 79, 98–103).

42. In the process, Unilever sold off its baking, sauce, and soup businesses.

43. Ketchup, sauces, and condiments.

44. Earthgrains had been spun off by the U.S. brewers Anheuser Bush only a short time earlier.

45. As a result, the combined U.S. market share of the two companies reached 40 percent. In the European Union, it is not far below this level (*Euromonitor*, October 30, 2002).

46. Among the most recent examples is Danone's acquisition of the organic dairy producer Stonyfield Farm, giving it an increase in U.S. dairy product market share from 30 percent to 34.5 percent (almost on a par with General Mills' Yoplait, with whom it constitutes a duopoly).

## CHAPTER 2

1. By contrast, the emergence after 1995 of the so-called post-Washington consensus has had apparently little impact on the negotiation or even the discussion of trade rules.

2. For shorthand purposes, *bilateral agreements* is used here to include plurilateral agreements, such as those between regional groupings or between a regional grouping and one country, and offers to restricted groups of countries by a single large trading country.

3. There are, for example, discrepancies of an order of 25–30 percent in the value of South African exports to the E.U. as reported by the South Africa Department of Trade and Industry and the presumably more accurate E.U. import data.

4. Angola, Cameroon, DR Congo, Rep. of the Congo, Côte d'Ivoire, Gabon, Ghana, Kenya, Liberia, Mali, Nigeria, Southern African Customs Union, Zambia, and Zimbabwe.

5. This argument is associated with a much broader debate about the African malaise and its appropriate forms of treatment. Sachs is part of a broader camp for whom reviving trade and boarding the globalization boat are central policy recommendations. Rodrik is part of a camp for whom a focus on growth as such takes precedence over one on trade.

6. Cameroon, DR Congo, Rep. Of the Congo, Côte d'Ivoire, Madagascar, Senegal, Ethiopia, Ghana, Kenya, Malawi, Mauritius, Nigeria, South Africa, Tanzania, Uganda, Zambia, and Zimbabwe.

7. Mauritius' official language is English, but the working language of both government and business is French.

8. LDCs are countries whose annual per capita GDP is lower than $900, and which fulfill certain other socioeconomic criteria defined by the UN system.

Currently, the following African countries are classified as LDCs: Mauritania, Chad, Sao Tome & Principe, Angola, Rwanda, Niger, Sudan, Guinea-Bissau, Burundi, Somalia, Benin, Gambia, Malawi, Ethiopia, Mali, Mozambique, Guinea, Togo, Tanzania, Burkina Faso, Madagascar, Uganda, Zambia, Sierra Leone, and Central African Republic.

9. Blackhurst and Lyakurwa (2000), using the same sample of twenty sub-Saharan African countries as Subramanian and Tamirisa (2001), show that eight agricultural primary commodities account for 73 percent of total African agricultural exports.

10. Tariff escalation refers to the levying of much higher tariffs on processed goods than those levied on primary commodities. The ostensible justification for tariff escalation is that high tariffs for processed goods reflect the fact that these are normally compounds of several primary products rather than primary products in a different form.

11. GATT and UNCTAD were not the only organizations backing such measures. In the 1960s and 1970s, both the IMF and the E.U. set up commodity price stabilization funds to provide developing countries with assistance to overcome shortfalls in export earnings arising from adverse market conditions.

12. The apparently outstanding success of INRA for producing countries perhaps is somewhat misleading. INRA's recommended price for natural rubber is not set oligopolistically, but is linked to the open market price for synthetic rubber.

13. The final eight calendar years of ICO activity were characterized by monthly nominal price variability of 14.8 percent. This indicator almost doubled to 37 percent in the 1990–1997 period (Gilbert, 1996) and then further increased to 43 percent in the 1998–2000 period (calculated from CSCE data). Fitter and Kaplinsky (2001: 77) show a similar trend using a different data set.

14. Cotton prices declined from a six-year average value of 84.7 percent of the 1990 price in 1984–1989 to a six-year average of 77.8 percent of this price in 1996–2001. During the middle period of six years (1990–1995), the cotton price actually rose to a value of 91.3 (GATT/WTO, various). During the first four years following the collapse of the tin and sugar agreements, price falls occurred that were of a similar nature to those described here for coffee and cocoa (Gilbert 1996).

15. The developed countries/country groups that implemented GSP were the following: Australia, Austria, Canada, the E.U., Finland, Japan, New Zealand, Norway, Sweden, Switzerland, and the U.S.

16. Over the whole period (1976–1995), GSP-qualifying trade grew from $10.4 billion to $109 billion (Arnau 2002).

17. The objective of STABEX was to stabilize developing country export earnings in periods of declining agricultural commodity prices. SYSMIN aimed at stabilizing mineral export earnings.

18. For some temperate-zone products admitted under seasonal quotas, there were also volume-related recommended prices within the E.U.

19. Different sources give the ACP countries an E.U. market share of respectively 8 percent and 6.7 percent in 1975–1976 and 3.4 percent and 3 percent in 1994–1995.

20. Panagariya (2002) argues that Côte d'Ivoire, Zimbabwe, and Jamaica were also net beneficiaries, but not to the same extent as Mauritius.

21. In the case of the Africa Growth and Opportunity Act (AGOA), it applies instead to the U.S.-defined category of low-income beneficiary country (countries whose per capita GDP fell below $1,500 in 1998).

22. The opportunity to (re)negotiate the Safeguards Agreement is sometimes mentioned by commentators as well.

23. Rulings are now adopted unless there is a clear consensus of opinion against them. Before, they could be blocked if there was no clear consensus for them.

24. In addition, some countries agreed to provide a minimum market access opportunity, such that the share of imports in domestic consumption of products then subjected to import restrictions would rise by 55 percent by 2000.

25. Safeguards are those exceptional actions that importing countries are allowed to take when faced by sudden surges of imports from specific countries.

26. The great majority of simulations of the effects of the successful conclusion of the ATC on the global geography of clothing production predict very strong gains by China, with India as the only other clear beneficiary. Most studies predict a fall in African clothing exports (for a summary, see Appelbaum 2003).

27. The Special 301 section of the Omnibus Trade and Competitiveness Act allowed the U.S. to use the DSM of GATT, but also authorized retaliatory action if the latter failed to address U.S. concerns. Between 1988 and 1994 the U.S. took unilateral action against Korea, India, Taiwan, and Thailand under this Act.

28. The precise level of protection to be given to geographical indications was not determined in the Uruguay Round and was still being negotiated at the time of writing.

29. Basically, this consists of the rights of farmers and breeders to multiply seeds or living organisms for their own use. However, to the extent that seed companies manage to introduce GM terminator seeds, farmers' rights become hollowed out.

30. It is generally recognized that pressure from the pharmaceutical industry was one of the main sources for the inclusion of references to securing adequate and effective international protection for intellectual property rights in the Special 301 section of the U.S. Omnibus Trade and Competitiveness Act of 1988. The reference to intellectual property rights in the Trade Act prefigured the WTO TRIPs Agreement of 1994.

31. Srinivasan, generally a keen WTO enthusiast, cites other economists to this effect, while himself reserving strong criticism for the Agreement.

32. According to UNCTAD, in recent years the U.S. alone has accounted for around 42 percent of all patents filed globally. The U.S. has granted 1.5 million patents in the last ten years, including patents for colors, noises, and smells (*Financial Times* April 30, 2003).

33. Members may set standards higher than those set by international bodies if they can provide scientific justification for doing so (the precautionary principle, often used by the E.U., is not considered sufficient on its own). They may also set their own standards for products where no international standard exists, providing that these have some scientific backing.

34. For example, Singapore is in the process of discussing bilateral arrangements with Japan, New Zealand, Switzerland, and the U.S. Japan is doing so with Korea, Mexico, and the Philippines. China and the ten ASEAN countries are planning to implement a free trade area by 2010, and India has entered negotiations with ASEAN for the same reason. In addition, there is the so-called APEC acceleration process (see later).

35. Moreover, import protectionist interests, especially agricultural ones, still dominate the U.S. Trade Advisory Committee system. Although agriculture represents only 3 percent of U.S. exports by value, it accounts for 25 percent of Advisory Committee membership. Textiles and clothing, nonferrous ores, and lumber and wood are also heavily overrepresented. See U.S. General Accounting Office (2002) and Kreuger (1996).

36. The E.U.'s offer to the Mercosur countries in April 2004 is an exception to this picture. The latter appear to have been offered specially favorable access for agricultural products in exchange for ceasing to press the EU for major concessions in this area within WTO (*Financial Times* April 15, 2004)

37. *Regional accumulation* means counting processes or value added from other beneficiary countries as if they had taken place in the exporting country. In the case of the E.U.–South Africa Free Trade Agreement, regional accumulation from ACP countries is allowed, but only if this is confined to one ACP country, if its value is less than the value added in South Africa, and if the components or raw materials involved themselves conform to E.U. rules of origin (McQueen 2002).

38. However, the E.U. indicated during the Phase I EPA negotiations that it was not willing to discuss arrangements for a general nonpunitive alternative to EPAs for these countries.

39. The Central America, Australia, and Morocco agreements had not been ratified by Congress at the time of writing. Negotiations with Egypt had been abandoned after the latter country withdrew its support for a U.S.-led WTO dispute over E.U. restrictions on genetically modified foods.

40. NAFTA includes a provision, which the U.S. government is now itself seeking to remove, providing companies with the right to sue host governments for actions "tantamount to expropriation." A number of U.S. companies have sued U.S. authorities (mostly state governments) under this provision for regulative interventions construed as affecting their profitability.

41. For example, the Agreement with Australia retains existing import quotas on Australian sugar and provides only slight increases in dairy and beef quotas (in the latter case, over eighteen years) (*Financial Times* February 11, 2004).

42. Clothing is considered to be a NAFTA product only if it has been made within the NAFTA yarn forward rule—that is, if spinning as well as knitting/weaving and assembly have been carried out in the exporting country or in another NAFTA member.

43. According to Arnau (2002), real GSP preference margins into the E.U. have fallen to 2.5 percent; into Japan, they stand at 2.4 percent; and into the U.S., they are only 1.8 percent.

44. This toughening of rules of origin is evident in relation to the issue of cumulation. Everything But Arms allows cumulation only from other LDCs or the E.U. itself. No cumulation at all is allowed for sugar, rice, and fish products.

45. This ratio was revised upward in 2002 from a cap originally set at 3.5 percent. A third version of the Act came into effect in 2004, extending the Act's coverage until 2013 and the suspension of the yarn forward rule of origin until 2007. Subsequently, Mauritius has been granted a 1-year derogation from the stricter rule of origin that applied to itself and South Africa.

46. Retailers appear to have assumed a place alongside high-technology sectors in the U.S. free trade lobby. The emergence of Wal-Mart as the United States' largest business contributor to the 2004 election campaign is said to follow from its recognition that "no company would be more hurt by a backlash against trade than Wal-Mart" (www.Politicalmoneyline.com).

## CHAPTER 3

1. For a detailed coverage of the *filière* literature, see Raikes, Jensen, and Ponte (2000).

2. For a similar approach, but with more explicit focus on issues of power in supply chain, see Cox et al. (2002).

3. To some extent, the gaps between GVC and similar approaches are less wide than portrayed in the literature, especially if recent work on GVCs is taken into consideration. Two examples may be helpful to illustrate this. First, Henderson et al. (2002, 446), in pointing out the limitations of GVC analysis from a production network perspective, argue that the "nature and articulation of firm-centered production networks are deeply influenced by the concrete sociopolitical contexts within which they are embedded." Yet, GVC *has* examined how the same GVC can be shaped differently by different constellations of actors in different countries—through regulation, business practices, and unorthodox alliances between firms and civil society groups (see, for example, contributions to Daviron and Gibbon 2002a; Ponte 2002c). Second, Raynolds (2004) explains governance in commodity networks as the relations through which key actors create, maintain, and transform network activities—in contrast to GVC, where governance is said to be a pre-existing structural feature. Again, much GVC work has underlined how the mechanisms of governance and its features change in time and are characterized by contested overlaps of quality conventions, rather than being pre-determined and immutable (see Daviron and Ponte 2005; Ponte 2003; and later, Chapter 6). It has also started to look at different business cultures and forms of legitimation and normative action that shape different configurations of governance (Messner 2002; Ponte 2003). In other words, there has already been a process of embedding GVC in relation to different forms of state regulation, business cultures, expectations, and values. In the last couple of years, the GVC literature has expanded considerably, both empirically and conceptually. Earlier case studies on manufacturing and high technology (on the auto industry, most recently, see Barnes, Kaplinsky, and Morris 2003; Humphrey 2003b) have been accompanied by case studies on agrofood commodities, services, transport, and logistics. Recent efforts have focused on two areas. The first is empirical observation and theoretical discussion of (different and changing) forms (and dimensions) of coordination and *governance* in GVCs (Gereffi 2003a; Gereffi, Humphrey, and Sturgeon 2004; Humphrey

and Schmitz 2003; Ponte 2003; Sturgeon 2001, 2002). The second is conceptual and policy-related analyses of paths of *upgrading* , with particular reference to developing country farms and firms (Gereffi 2003b; Gibbon 2001a; Humphrey 2003a; Kaplinsky and Morris 2002; Vargas 2001). Related discussions have taken place on the links between forms of governance and upgrading (Gibbon 2003; Humphrey and Schmitz 2002a), the relationship between GVCs and industrial clusters (Humphrey and Schmitz 2002b; Nadvi and Halder 2002; Palpacuer and Parisotto 2003), and learning processes and supply relations within GVCs (Humphrey 2003b; Schmitz 1999; Schmitz and Knorriga 1999). A more explicit effort has also been made to link issues of governance and upgrading with over-all regulatory structures (Gereffi, Spener, and Bair 2002; Gibbon 2003; Kessler 1999; Ponte 2002b, 2002c), with processes of globalization and international in-equality (Kaplinsky 2000; Talbot 2002), and with corporate concentration (Vorley 2003). Finally, there is an emergent literature analyzing the links between value chains, standards, certifications, and ethical trade issues (Barrientos, Dolan, and Tallontire 2003; Daviron 2002; Daviron and Ponte 2005; Messner 2002; Morris and Dunne 2004; Nadvi and Wältring 2002; Ponte 2002a; Quadros 2002; Vorley, Roe, and Bass 2002).

4. We owe this observation to Florence Palpacuer.

5. Gereffi (2001a, 2001b) entertained two other possibilities: first, that e-commerce and the internet may accelerate the tendency to make all chains more buyer-driven, or second, that e-commerce may be captured by established lead-ers in both producer-driven and buyer-driven chains, without changing the nature of leadership of these chains.

6. Actually, many of the technological innovations of the Fordist period were in fact more related to the organization of the labor process (e.g., Taylorism) rather than to technology as such (Daviron 2003).

7. For specific case studies on upgrading, see among others Vargas (2001) on the tobacco industry in Brazil, Kaplinsky and Morris (2002) on the wood furniture sector in South Africa, and Nadvi and Halder (2002) on surgical in-struments in Pakistan. See also the detailed discussion of upgrading within the chains examined in this book, in Chapter 5.

8. Another was that the leading U.K. designer George Davis, "who loved Mauritius" shifted his services from the solidly midmarket U.K. chain Next to the supermarket Asda, which was launching a high-volume clothing range. Asda were concerned to build on his local supply base and reproduce it in a cheaper environment.

## Chapter 4

1. Most of the researchers in the GLAF group were based at the Centre for Development Research, Copenhagen (now Danish Institute for Interna-tional Studies); others were affiliated to the Institute of Geography—University of Copenhagen, the Institute of Economics—Danish Royal Veterinary and Agricultural University (KVL), and the Department of Geography, University of Witwatersrand.

2. In addition, this chapter draws on parallel work on cocoa by a researcher based at CIRAD, Montpellier (Losch 2002), and on fresh vegetables by researchers at the Institute of Development Studies, University of Sussex (Dolan and Humphrey 2000). For GLAF studies examining cross-cutting themes, rather than single sectors/chains, see Daviron and Gibbon (2002a, 2002b); Gibbon (2000, 2001b); M.F. Jensen (2000a, b); Pedersen (2001, 2002); Raikes, Jensen, and Ponte (2000); and Raikes and Gibbon (2000).

3. Although these developments have potentially great trade integration effects on a global plane, they are likely to have intensified Africa's marginalization. Containerization has entailed demands for higher investment in ports and in freight handling capacity and creates a need for a higher level of administrative capacity, all areas where Africa lags behind. Also, no round-the-world route goes nearer to West Africa than southern Spain or nearer to East Africa than Dubai.

4. The U.K. market leader, Marks & Spencer (M&S), continued to work through exclusivity contracts with a handful of leading U.K. manufacturers until well into the 1990s.

5. Wal-Mart had over a million employees in 2003. Carrefour had almost 400,000 of whom 274,000 were in Europe, and Tesco had 221,000.

6. A stock-out is not having stock to sell when there is demand for it.

7. Stock-turn is the period taken to turn over an entire inventory once. In 2002, Wal-Mart was said to have achieved 7.8 stock-turns/year, in comparison with Target's 6.3 and Kmart's 3.6. (http://www.baseline.com/articles2/0.3959.37385.00asp)

8. Cross-docking means using delivery centers only as transfer points, rather than for warehousing.

9. Wal-Mart gives no breakdown of sales by product group, but most people in the clothing industry reckon its clothing sales represent around 8 percent of its total sales.

10. Carrefour's 2003 *Annual Report* mentions progress having been made in concentrating sourcing (not distribution) for its Brazilian operations to twelve regional centers.

11. This focus has been characteristic of Tesco since its foundation as a London street market trader during the First World War. The autobiography of its founder, Jack Cohen, was entitled *Pile It High and Sell It Cheap*. Nonetheless, Tesco has successfully avoided a purely hard discount image.

12. The other two are ensuring product availability and consumer communication.

13. Wilkinson (2002) provides an illuminating discussion of the emerging challenges faced by branded foods manufacturers in the context of diversification of demand, new content to demand, and increasingly powerful retailers. He argues that they face two main challenges from first, nutriceuticals and functional foods, and second, the reintroduction of agricultural products as final foods (as opposed to raw materials for processing foods). The final foods industry is seen as being squeezed between demand and supply: it is largely passive in relation to new biotechnologies and lacks the knowledge of final markets that retail has. Wilkinson shows that branded foods manufacturers have reacted to

these new challenges through product differentiation and diversification, offering of ready-to-heat and ready-to-eat products, and expanding their cold and frozen snack lines. Also, new competitive pressures for scale led to brand culling and focus on leading brands. Yet, retail seems to have achieved the upper hand over manufacturers. One indicator is the growth of generics and various forms of retailer's fees imposed on the food industry (ibid., 335). Another indicator is that the average turnover of the world's top ten retailers in 2000 was almost twice the turnover of the food and drinks sector (ibid.). The vulnerability of brands to consumer and nongovernmental organization (NGO) action adds to the problems of branded foods manufacturers.

14. Most where retailers are the lead agents; some where it is food manufacturers who play this role.

15. The term *first-tier supplier* was used first to describe a leading group of suppliers of parts and components to automobile manufacturers. This sector was also the first in which this group of suppliers took on system integrating functions.

16. This decree gave powers to local authorities to finance and build large regional fruit and vegetable markets and to determine their rules of operation to promote fair competition between buyer and seller. Wholesalers outside of these markets are not allowed to operate within 20 km. This provision was aimed at agglomerating the wholesale trade, thereby reducing transaction costs for retailers to source through them. Presently, there are around seventeen such markets, the largest of which are at Rungis (near Paris) and Lille. Most cover very large physical areas and handle around 250,000–300,000 tons of produce each year.

17. The order of exposition of GVCs in this chapter reflects the order used in Chapter 5 to discuss the two main stories arising from the analysis of entry barriers.

18. In this book, by *Arabica* we mean Mild Arabica (wet processed). The term *Robusta* is used to cover both Robusta and Hard Arabica (dry processed).

19. Good agricultural practices incorporate measures to ensure environmental and social responsibility (from monitoring of provision of basic physical and social services to farm workers to equitable reward systems).

20. Examples of this equipment are optic sizers (at a cost of about US$120,000 each) and handheld sugar content gauges.

21. In the case of clothing, some intermediaries are attempting to pass this function further upstream. When one of the authors revisited South African clothing exporters in May 2003, he was told that over the previous few months some U.K. trading houses had stopped issuing letters of credit. "These days they just give us the name of a bank and tell us to use their name as a reference."

## Chapter 5

1. Rules of origin have actually been tightened in recent agreements and offers tabled by the E.U. (see Chapter 2).

2. EUREP-GAP stands for European Retailer Group Good Agricultural Practices Protocol. This is a set of normative requirements suitable for enforcement

as internationally recognized certification criteria. It covers flowers, ornamentals, fruit, and vegetables and aims at reducing the risks of food safety lapses in agricultural production.

3. These practices conform to the U.K. private standard care levels for fresh produce. To qualify as a grower/exporter of semiprocessed fresh products, such as shucked peas, a more advanced high standard care group of practices has to be in place (B.N. Jensen 2002). On the impact of EUREP-GAP in selected African contexts, see also du Toit (2002), Freidberg (2003b), and Hughes (2001).

4. Cross-costing is the buyer practice of relaying information on given supplier prices to other suppliers to pressurize them to adopt more competitive prices.

5. In the citrus chain into the U.K., first-tier suppliers' active efforts at supplier development seem to be greatest where the end customer actively encourages competition between first-tier suppliers, and where one or two first-tier suppliers find themselves in weak positions. At the same time, first-tier suppliers' price pressure on second-tier suppliers appears to be greatest where the position of the first-tier supplier is most secure (Mather 2002b).

6. In illustration of these points, the entry strategy of a large global clothing sector intermediary (MAST Industries) in a new location (Southern Africa) can be referred to. In contrast to the procedure it adopts when entering locations that already occupied established positions in the global chain, the first personnel this intermediary sent to Southern Africa were not merchandisers but textile technicians. These were charged with locating blocks that mills in the region had worked with in the period 1950–1970 and that featured materials, constructions, and patterns that were of contemporary fashion relevance, and then matching the textile manufacturers concerned with clothing producers who could (on the basis of technical assistance) use these textiles for volume production of new styles.

7. An example of client-dedicated merchandizing is the provision of a distinct and exclusive account manager for the U.S. client.

8. An example of full fabric sourcing is identifying a suitable textile supplier and purchasing (on one's own account) fabric from this supplier.

9. Where clothing deliveries to developed countries are made to delivery centers (see Chapter 3), they require labeling down to the store level and need to arrive at the delivery center within twenty-four hours of intended arrival in the store of destination.

10. In the case of Uganda, exports were carried out by a state-run monopoly until the early 1990s.

11. It should be noted that this has been facilitated by the development of international courier services.

12. Mauritian clothing exports to the E.U. and U.S. were worth respectively $523 and $121 million in 1990, whereas South Africa's were worth $32 million and zero.

13. Besides labor costs, the other main components of price are quota costs (see later) and exchange rate levels. Although export prices are typically denominated in $ or €, buyers are granted discounts as a matter of course when local currencies depreciate against these denominations. Shifts in exchange rate can thus rapidly transform perceptions of the competitiveness of particular

producing countries. A second relevant aspect is the dollar-euro exchange rate. Since fabrics mostly originate in Asia, they are denominated in dollars, meaning that producers using Asian fabrics who sell into the E.U. market gain when the euro is appreciating but lose when it falls in value.

14. The Multifibre Arrangement quota system acts in contradictory ways in relation to price-related sourcing decisions. Directly, the existence of quotas increases prices from those countries that are quota bound, since the quota is tradable and commands a specific price. In the case of China, this can be the same or even higher than producer prices. Indirectly though, the existence of quotas mitigates price pressure since an exporter's possession of a quota removes risks for those buying from him/her that the purchased goods will be subject to market access problems in the U.S. or E.U.

15. An additional, highly resource-demanding, requirement was reported by a fresh vegetable exporter in Tanzania, who stated that they had established an operation in the country because their U.K. importer had told them that the supermarket end customer wanted all suppliers to be able to "put two countries on the shelf." The reason for this was to hedge against poor weather conditions or pest epidemics in the main country of operation.

16. Evidence on prices is less clear, and statistical comparisons are difficult because of differences in the traded crop subtypes.

17. Until 2001, the state marketing board had an official export monopoly. Since then, licensed private buyers, who were previously confined to primary purchasing, have been allowed to export 30 percent of their purchases directly. However, none appeared to have done so in 2002.

18. ADM recently acquired ED&F Man's cocoa wing, which is engaged in a major smallholder development project in Nigeria (Losch 2002).

19. Besides being unique in the sense that it has seen an increasing dominance of world markets by African countries, cocoa is also unique in being the only major crop whose international trade has seen a transition away from plantation and toward smallholder production in recent years.

20. A third player entered the market in the 2001 season.

21. Cotton is unique in Zimbabwe in that it is an export crop that is overwhelmingly produced by smallholders. Hence, it has not been subject to significant disruption by the land invasions that began in 2001. These have had devastating effects for other export crops and for interest in the country from foreign investors.

22. *Traded through Northern European ports* denotes sold through European-based international traders or (much less commonly) delivered directly to the few remaining European spinners. The Cotlook A index is based on prices for this part of the international trade only (see later).

23. *Job lots* refers to large-volume batches of specific styles offered by exporters or manufacturers. Importers acquire these speculatively when they have no order in advance for them from a retailer. Sales are typically on consignment, meaning that the exporter/manufacturer is paid only if the importer finds a buyer.

24. Having stood at 2 percent of the Cotlook A index in the mid-1990s, the spread between the A and B indexes has gradually widened to 10 percent,

whereas the premium commanded by extra-fine cottons has increased from 70 percent over the A index to 100 percent.

25. Product diversification into snow/snap peas also entails geographical expansion since the most suitable growing area for these crops is considered to be around Mount Kenya, whereas green bean (and cut flower) production conditions are considered to be most favorable around Lake Naivasha.

26. Mauritian-owned companies predominate only in export to the E.U. Export to the U.S. is dominated, as in South Africa and elsewhere in Africa, by overseas Chinese-owned firms.

## CHAPTER 6

1. See Busch and Tanaka (1996) and Nadvi and Wältring (2002) for other kinds of classifications of standards.

2. In some of the literature on conventions, a distinction is made between convention economics and convention theory as such. The distinction is also sometimes portrayed in terms of a strategic approach versus an interpretive approach to conventions (Batifoulier 2001). The former approach is said to be inspired by an instrumental view of conventions as coordinative actions that are motivated by personal interest and are based on the expectation of reciprocity. This has led to contributions engaging critically with game theory and that see conventions as the result of strategic interaction. Selected examples of the strategic approach to conventions (or convention economics) can be found in edited collections by Batifouier (2001, pt. 3), Favereau and Lazega (2002), and Orléan (2004); in relation to quality issues, see Gomez (1994). The interpretive approach is said to be inspired by a normative view of conventions as customs whose validity is approved within a group and is guaranteed by threats of general reprobation. In this approach, a convention is distinct from the rule of law, on the basis of the different nature of its associated sanction: rather than needing a juridical system of coercion, nonconformity entails the risk of something akin to a social boycott. The interpretive approach to conventions sees them as models of evaluation that allow the interpretation of rules (Batifoulier and de Larquier 2001). In this book, we refer to convention theory (i.e., the interpretive approach to conventions).

3. Initially, convention theory developed around the theme of the specificity of labor and analyzed the rules, norms, and conventions that formed the basis of qualifications in the labor market (Salais and Thévenot 1986). Later, this approach was extended to other commodities and to the analysis of economic exchange in general. For key contributions, see Batifoulier (2001), Boltanski and Chiapello (1999), Boltanski and Thévenot (1991), Favereau and Lazega (2002), Nicholas and Valceschini (1995), Orléan (2004), Sylvander (1995), and Valceschini (1993).

4. This leads to the paradoxical situation where product determinism obscures both the possibility of coexistence of different conventions within a firm in relation to a given product and the possibility that firms involved in producing or marketing products with different resource requirements may draw from a single overall convention.

5. *Spirit of capitalism* is defined as "the ideology that justifies people's commitment to capitalism, and which renders this commitment attractive" (Boltanski and Chiapello 2002, 2).

6. Freidberg (2003b) refers to the simple distinction (as in Sylvander 1995) between institutional means of quality assurance (certification schemes and labels; which in Boltanski and Thévenot 1991 would qualify as industrial) and transactional means (norms and practices underlining trust between buyer and seller; domestic in Boltanski and Thévenot; Freidberg 2003b, 99).

7. Commodity fetishism as a concept was introduced by Marx and can be defined as "the necessary masking of social relations under which commodities are produced from which capitalist commodity production gains much of its legitimacy" (Guthman 2002, 296; see also Hartwick 1998). Contemporary discussions of commodity fetishism also cover society-nature relations that can be equally concealed in commodity production (see Allen and Kovach 2000; Guthman 2002, 297) and the masking of social and environmental relations through standards and certifications (Freidberg 2003b; Daviron and Ponte 2005).

8. "The conventions providing information about the production process . . . serve to facilitate marketing because, like the transparent plastic box, they assure buyers . . . that all is clean, nothing hidden. But they are only effective if buyers value those conventions and, indeed, accept them at face value . . . [T]he conventions themselves have become fetishized commodities. Like the plastic box and other forms of packaging, labels and codes of conduct are produced for exchange . . . and invested with meanings" (Freidberg 2003b, 29).

9. Along with the embeddedness approach (Granovetter 1985; Polanyi 1957/2001) and evolutionary economics (Fullbrook 2002; Hodgson 2002; Nielsen 2001), convention theory attempts to go beyond the limitations of both reductionist theories, which unite individuals and aggregate them through structural determination, and methodological individualism, for which macro phenomena are the result of aggregate acts of many individuals (see Biggart and Beamish 2003).

10. It is not possible to cover the large literature on consumption here. We limit our coverage to approaches that more closely relate to convention theory and that can inspire GVC analysis more directly. For reviews of the consumption literature, see among others Crewe (2002), Fine (2002), Goodman (2002), Guthman (2002), Hartwick (1998), Lockie (2002), and Marsden and Wrigley (1995).

11. Callon and collaborators actually refer to lead firms as suppliers, because their reference point is consumers. To avoid confusion, we have corrected this in our exposition.

12. On the limitations of the economy of qualities approach, of GVC analysis, and the possible overlaps between the two, see Thompson (2003, 208).

13. Functional foods, also known as nutriceuticals, are products that bring food closer to medicine by claiming to have a special health quality status (Wilkinson 2002, 337–40).

14. Quality conventions and processes of standardization also help in understanding the institutional framework of a value chain through the analysis of the conditions under which subordinate actors in a value chain can upgrade and how (see Chapter 5).

15. *Handle* refers to the eye-catching look and feel of a product.

16. A further step may be taking place in the direction of "control of control of control": the International Social and Environmental Accreditation and Labeling (ISEAL) Alliance has recently published a "code of good practice for setting social and environmental standards" (see www.isealalliance.org).

17. However, it is not clear to what extent grinders have aimed at achieving unambiguous lead firm status, as opposed to sharing this status with branded chocolate manufacturers (see discussion on contract manufacturing in Chapters 1 and 3).

18. HACCP stands for Hazard Analysis and Critical Control Point, which is a quality assurance methodology intended to reduce the risk of microbial, chemical, and physical contamination in food. In some contexts, its use is mandatory for some industry functions. ISO 9000 and 14000 are systems of assurance of respectively total quality management and environmentally responsible management. Although they are not mandatory anywhere, these voluntary systems have extremely wide credibility.

19. In an unpublished paper recently referred to by Murdoch, Marsden, and Banks (2000), Thévenot (1998) is said to distinguish domestic and public conventions. The latter is said to be encompassing brands, trademarks, and packaging.

20. This is becoming the case for at least part of the mainstream coffee market, against a background of a collapse of quality control in several coffee-producing countries (Ponte 2002c). It has been the case for a long period for so-called commodity clothing items, such as men's socks and boxer shorts.

21. On the influence of interior designers and high-street flower bouquet designers in relation to retailers' quality considerations in the cut flower industry, see Hughes (2001).

# References

Akerlof, G. 1970. The Market for Lemons: Quality Uncertainty and the Market Mechanisms. *Quarterly Journal of Economics* 89:488–500.

Allaire, G., and R. Boyer. 1995a. Régulation et conventions dans l'agriculture et les ISS. In G. Allaire and R. Boyer, eds. *La Grande Transformation de l'Agriculture: Lectures Conventionnalistes et Regulationnistes.* Paris: INRA-Economica.

Allaire, G., and R. Boyer. 1995b. *La Grande Transformation de l'Agriculture: Lectures Conventionnalistes et Regulationnistes.* Paris: INRA-Economica.

Allen, P., and M. Kovach. 2000. The Capitalist Composition of Organic: The Potential of Markets in Fulfilling the Promise of Organic Agriculture. *Agriculture and Human Values* 17 (3): 221–32.

Appadurai, A. 1986. Introduction: Commodities and the politics of value. In A. Appadurai, ed. *The Social Life of Things: Commodities in Cultural Perspective.* Cambridge: Cambridge University Press.

Appelbaum, R. 2003. *Assessing the Impact of the Phase-out of the Agreement on Textile and Clothing on Apparel Exports from Developing Countries.* University of California at Santa Cruz: Center for Global Studies.

Arnau, J. 2002. *The Generalised System of Preferences and the World Trade Organisation.* London: Cameron May.

Audley, J., D. Papademetriou, S. Polaski, and S. Vaughan. 2003. *NAFTA's Promise and Reality.* Washington: Carnegie Endowment for International Peace.

Baas, H., A. van Potten, and A. Zwanenbery. 1998. *The World of Food Retailing: Developments and Strategies.* Utrecht: Rabobank.

Bain, J. 1956. *Barriers to New Competition.* Cambridge, MA: Harvard University Press.

Barham, E. 2002. Towards a Theory of Values-Based Labeling. *Agriculture and Human Values* 19 (4): 349–60.

Barnes, J., and R. Kaplinsky. 1999. Globalization and Trade Policy Reform: Whither the Automobile Components Sector in South Africa. Mimeo. Brighton, UK: Institute of Development Studies, University of Sussex.

Barnes, J., R. Kaplinski, and M. Morris. 2003. Industrial Policy in Developing Countries: Developing Dynamic Comparative Advantage in the South African Automobile Sector. Mimeo. Brighton, UK: Institute of Development Studies, University of Sussex.

Barrientos, S., C. Dolan, and A. Tallontire. 2003. A Gendered Value Chain Approach to Codes of Conduct in African Horticulture. *World Development* 31 (9): 1511–26.

Barzel, Y. 1997. *Economic Analysis of Property Rights.* 2nd ed. Cambridge: Cambridge University Press.

Bates, R. 1997. *Open-economy Politics: The Political Economy of the World Coffee Trade.* Princeton, NJ: Princeton University Press.

Batifoulier, P., ed. 2001. *Téorie des Conventions.* Paris: Economica.

Batifoulier, P., and G. de Larquier. 2001. Introduction–De la convention et de ses usages. In P. Batifoulier, ed. *Téorie des Conventions.* Paris: Economica.

Bhagwati, J., A. Panagariya, and P. Krishna, eds. 1999. *Trading Blocs: Alternative Approaches to Analysing Preferential Trade Agreements.* Cambridge, MA: MIT Press.

Biggart, N. W., and T. D. Beamish. 2003. The Economic Sociology of Conventions: Habit, Custom, Practice, and Routine in Market Order. *Annual Review of Sociology* 29:443–64.

Binswanger, H., and M. Rosenzweig. 1986. Behavioural and Material Determinants of Production Relations in Agriculture. *Journal of Development Studies* 22 (3): 503–39.

Blackhurst, R., and W. Lyakurwa. 2000. Markets and Market Access for African Exports: Past, Present and Future Directions. Mimeo. African Trade Project. Nairobi: African Economic Research Consortium.

Boltanski, L., and E. Chiapello. 1999. *Le Nouvel Esprit du Capitalisme.* Paris: Gallimard.

Boltanski, L., and E. Chiapello. 2002. The New Spirit of Capitalism. Paper presented at the Conference of Europeanists, Chicago.

Boltanski O., and L. Thévenot. 1991. *De la Justification. Les Économies de la Grandeur.* Paris: Gallimard.

Bonanno, A., and D. Constance. 1996. *Caught in the Net: The Global Tuna Industry, Environmentalism and the State.* Lawrence: University Press of Kansas.

Brenton, P., and T. Ikezuki. 2004. The Initial and Potential Impact of Preferential Access to the U.S. Market under the African Growth and Opportunity Act. *World Bank Policy Research Paper* 3262. Washington, DC: World Bank.

Busch, L. 2000. The Moral Economy of Grades and Standards. *Journal of Rural Studies* 16 (3): 273–83.

Busch, L. 2002. Virgil, Vigilance, and Voice: Agrifood Ethics in an Age of Globalization. *Journal of Agricultural and Environmental Ethics* 16: 459–77.

Busch, L., and K. Tanaka. 1996. Rites of Passage: Constructing Quality in a Commodity Subsector. *Science, Technology and Human Values* 21 (1): 3–27.

Callon, M., C. Méadel, and V. Rabeharisoa. 2002. The Economy of Qualities. *Economy and Society* 31 (2): 194–217.

Campa, J., and L. Goldberg. 1997. The Evolving Export Orientation of Manufacturing Industries: Evidence from Four Countries. *National Bureau for Economic Research Working Paper* 5919. Cambridge, MA: National Bureau for Economic Research.

Carrefour. 2003. *Annual Report* at www.carrefour.com

Castells, M. 1996. *The Rise of the Network Society.* Oxford: Blackwell.

Chamberlin, E. 1946. *The Theory of Monopolistic Competition: A Reorientation of the Theory of Value.* 5th ed. Cambridge, MA: Harvard University Press.

Clancy, M. 1998. Commodity Chains, Services and Development: Theory and Preliminary Evidence from the Tourism Industry. *Review of International Political Economy* 5 (1): 122–48.

Corporate Intelligence on Retailing, at www.cior.com

Cox, A., P. Ireland, C. Lonsdale, J. Sanderson, and G. Watson. 2002. *Supply Chains, Markets and Power: Mapping Buyer and Supplier Power Regimes*. London: Routledge.

Crewe, L. 2002. Geographies of Retailing and Consumption. *Progress in Human Geography* 24 (2): 275–90.

Cronon, W. 1991. *Nature's Metropolis: Chicago and the Great West*. New York: W.W. Norton.

Crotty, J. 2002. The Effects of Increased Product Market Competition and Changes in Financial Markets on the Performance of Non-financial Corporations in the Neo-liberal Era. *Political Economy Research Institute Working Paper* no. 44. Amherst: Department of Economics, University of Massachusetts at Amherst.

Daviron, B. 1993. Conflict et Cooperation sur le Marché International du Café: Une Analyse de Longue Periode. Thèse de Doctorat. Montpellier: Ecole Nationale Supérieure Agronomique de Montpellier.

Daviron, B. 1996. The rise and fall of governmental power on the international coffee market. In M. Griffon and P. Guillaumont, eds. *Economics of Agricultural Policies in Developing Countries*. Paris: Editions de la Revue Française d'Economie.

Daviron, B. 2002. Small Farm Production and the Standardization of Tropical Products. *Journal of Agrarian Change* 2 (2): 162–84.

Daviron, B. 2003. Explaining the Past Contrast and Current Convergence between Agricultural and Industrial Standardisation. Paper presented at the international workshop, Standards, Trade and Value-chains: What Role for Developing Countries? Copenhagen.

Daviron, B., and P. Gibbon, eds. 2002a. Global Commodity Chains and African Export Crop Agriculture. Special issue, *Journal of Agrarian Change* 2 (2). Oxford: Blackwell.

Daviron, B., and P. Gibbon. 2002b. Global Commodity Chains and African Export Crop Agriculture. *Journal of Agrarian Change* 2 (2): 137–61.

Daviron, B., and S. Ponte. 2005. *The Coffee Paradox: Global Markets, Commodity Trade and the Elusive Promise of Development*. London: Zed Books.

Dicken, P. 2003. *Global Shift: Reshaping the Global Economic Map in the 21st Century*. 4th ed. London: Sage.

Dixon, L. 1999. The New Age Supplier. *Purchasing*, 9 February.

Dolan, C., and J. Humphrey. 2000. Governance and Trade in Fresh Vegetables: The Impact of UK Supermarkets on the African Horticultural Industry. *Journal of Development Studies* 37 (2): 144–177.

Dore, R., B. Lazonick, and M. O'Sullivan. 1999. Varieties of Capitalism in the Twentieth Century. *Oxford Review of Economic Policy* 15 (4): 102–20.

du Toit, A. 2002. Globalizing Ethics: Social Technologies of Private Regulation and the South African Wine Industry. *Journal of Agrarian Change* 2 (3): 356–80.

DuPuis, M. 2000. Not in My Body: rBGH and the Rise of Organic Milk. *Agriculture and Human Values* 17 (3): 285–95.

Dupuy, C., and Y. Lung. 2001. *Institutional Investors and the Car Industry*. Document de travail 2001–2005. Inst. Fédératif de Recherches sur le Dynamiques Économiques, Univ. Montesquieu Bordeaux IV.

Durkheim, E. 1950; *The Rules of Sociological Method*. New York: Free Press.

Engelen, E. 2002. Corporate Governance, Property and Democracy: A Conceptual Critique of Shareholder Ideology. *Economy and Society* 31 (3): 391–413.

Ernst, D. 2000. Global Production Networks and the Changing Geography of Innovation Systems: Implications for Developing Countries. *East-West Centre Working Paper* 9. Honolulu: East-West Centre.

Euromonitor. 2002. Available at www.euromonitor.com

Eymard-Duvernay, F. 1989. Conventions de Qualité et Formes de Coordination. *Revue Economique* (40) 2: 329–59.

FAO. 1990. *Trade Yearbook*. Vol. 43, 1989. Rome: FAO.

FAO.2002. *Trade Yearbook*. Vol. 53, 1999. Rome: FAO.

Favereau, O., and E. Lazega, eds. 2002. *Conventions and Structures in Economic Organization*. Cheltenham: Edward Elgar.

Feenstra, R. 1998. Integration of Trade and Disintegration of Production in the Global Economy. *Journal of Economic Perspectives* 12 (4): 907–40.

Feenstra, R., and G. Hanson. 1999. Productivity Measurement and the Impact of Trade and Technology on Wages: Estimations from the US 1972-90. *Quarterly Journal of Economics* 114 (3): 907–40.

*Financial Times* (London). Various.

Fine, B. 2002. *The World of Consumption: The Material and Cultural Revisited*. 2nd ed. London: Routledge.

Finger, J., and J. Nogués. 2002. The Unbalanced Uruguay Round Outcome: The New Areas in Future WTO Negotiations. *World Economy* 25 (3): 321–40.

Fitter, R., and R. Kaplinsky. 2001. Who Gains from Product Rents as the Coffee Market Becomes More Differentiated? A Value-chain Analysis. *IDS Bulletin* 32 (3): 69–82.

Foer, A. 2001. *Divestiture and the Category Captain: New Considerations on Merger Remedies*. American Antitrust Institute, FTC Watch 577, 19 November. Available at www.antitrustinstitute.org/recent/153.cfm

Fold, N. 2000. A Matter of Good Taste? Quality and the Construction of Standards for Chocolate Products in the EU. *Cahiers d'Economie et Sociologie Rurales* 55–56: 92–110.

Fold, N. 2001. Restructuring of the European Chocolate Industry and Its Impact on Cocoa Production in West Africa. *Journal of Economic Geography* 1 (3): 405–20.

Fold, N. 2002. Lead Firms and Competition in "Bi-Polar" Commodity Chains: Grinders and Branders in the Global Cocoa-Chocolate Industry. *Journal of Agrarian Change* 2 (2): 228–47.

Fold, N. 2004. Spilling the beans on a tough nut: Liberalisation and local supply system changes in Ghana's cocoa and shea chains. A. Hughes. and S. Reimer, eds. *Geographies of Commodity Chains*. London: Routledge.

Fold, N., and M. N. Larsen, eds. Forthcoming. *Re-placing Africa in the Global Economy*. James Currey: Oxford.

Freidberg, S. 2003a. Cleaning Up Down South: Supermarkets, Ethical Trade and African Horticulture. *Social and Cultural Geography* 4 (1): 27–43.

Freidberg, S. 2003b. Culture, Conventions and Colonial Constructs of Rurality in South-North Horticultural Trades. *Journal of Rural Studies* 19 (1): 97–109.

Friedland, W. 1984. Commodity systems analysis: An approach to the sociology of agriculture. In H. K. Schwarzweller, ed. *Research in Rurval Sociology and Development*. Greenwich, CT: JAI Press.

Friedland, W. 2001. Reprise on Commodity Systems Methodology. *International Journal of Sociology of Agriculture and Food* 9 (1): 82–103.

Friedmann, H. 1993. The Political Economy of Food: A Global Crisis. *New Left Review* 197:28–59.

Friedmann, H., and P. McMichael. 1989. Agriculture and the State System: The Rise and Decline of National Agricultures, 1870 to the Present. *Sociologia Ruralis* 29:93–117.

Froud, J., C. Haslam, S. Johal, and K. Wiliams. 2000 Shareholder Value and Financialisation. *Economy and Society* 29 (1): 80–110.

Fullbrook, E., ed. 2002. *Intersubjectivity in Economics*. London: Routledge.

Gap Inc. 2004. *2003 Social Responsibility Report* Available at www.gapinc.com

GATT/WTO. Various. *International Trade Statistics*. Geneva: GATT/WTO.

Gereffi, G. 1994. The organization of buyer-driven global commodity chains: How US retailers shape overseas production networks. In G. Gereffi and M. Korzeniewicz, eds. *Commodity Chains and Global Capitalism*.Westport, CT: Greenwood Press.

Gereffi, G. 1995. Global production systems and Third World development. In B. Stallings, ed. *Global Change, Regional Response: The New International Context of Development*. Cambridge: Cambridge University Press.

Gereffi, G. 1999. International Trade and Industrial Up-Grading in the Apparel Commodity Chain. *Journal of International Economics* 48 (1): 37–70.

Gereffi, G. 2001a. Beyond the Producer-Driven/Buyer-Driven Dichotomy. The Evolution of Global Value Chains in the Internet Era. *IDS Bulletin* 32 (3): 30–40.

Gereffi, G. 2001b. Shifting Governance Structures in Global Commodity Chains, with Special Reference to the Internet. *American Behavioral Scientist* (44) 10: 1616–37.

Gereffi, G. 2003a. The global economy: Organization, governance, and development. In N. Smelser and R. Swedberg, eds. *Handbook of Economic Sociology*. Princeton, NJ: Princeton University Press.

Gereffi, G. 2003b. Global Value Chains and Industrial Upgrading: Current Challenges. Paper presented at the international workshop, Standards, Trade and Value-chains: What Role for Developing Countries? Copenhagen.

Gereffi, G., J. Humphrey, and T. Sturgeon. 2004. The Governance of Global Value Chains. *Review of International Political Economy*.

Gereffi, G., and M. Korzeniewicz, eds. 1994. *Commodity Chains and Global Capitalism*. Westport, CT: Greenwood Press.

Gereffi G., M. Korzeniewicz, and R. Korzeniewicz. 1994. Introduction: Global commodity chains. In G. Gereffi and M. Korzeniewicz, eds. *Commodity Chains and Global Capitalism*. Westport, CT: Greenwood Press.

Gereffi, G., D. Spener, and J. Bair, eds. 2002. *Free Trade and Uneven Development: The North American Apparel Industry after NAFTA.* Philadelphia: Temple University Press.

Gibbon, P. 2000. Back to the Basics through Delocalisation: The Mauritian Garment Industry at the End of the 20th Century. *CDR Working Paper* 00.7. Copenhagen: Centre for Development Research.

Gibbon, P. 2001a. Upgrading Primary Production: A Global Commodity Chain Approach. *World Development* 29 (2): 345–63.

Gibbon, P. 2001b. Agro-commodity Chains: An Introduction. *IDS Bulletin* 32 (3): 60–68.

Gibbon, P. 2002a. At the Cutting Edge? Financialisation and UK Clothing Retailers' Global Sourcing Patterns and Practices. *Competition and Change* 6 (3): 289–308.

Gibbon, P. 2002b. South Africa and the Global Commodity Chain for Clothing: Export Performance and Constraints. *CDR Working Paper* 02.7. Copenhagen: Centre for Development Research.

Gibbon, P. 2003. The African Growth and Opportunity Act and the Global Commodity Chain for Clothing. *World Development* 31 (11): 1809–27.

Gibbon, P. Forthcoming. Segmentation, governance and upgrading in global clothing chains: A Mauritian case study. In N. Fold and M. N. Larsen, eds. *Re-placing Africa in the Global Economy.* James Currey: Oxford.

Gibbon, P. and L. Thomsen. 2002. Scandinavian Clothing Retailers' Global Sourcing Patterns and Practices. *CDR Working Paper* 02.14. Copenhagen: Centre for Development Research.

Gilbert, C. 1996. International Commodity Agreements: An Obituary Notice. *World Development* 24 (1): 1–19.

Giovannucci, D., and S. Ponte. 2004. Standards as a New Form of Social Contract? Sustainability Initiatives in the Coffee Industry. *Food Policy.*

Giovannucci, D., and T. Reardon. 2000. *Understanding Grades and Standards and How to Apply Them.* Washington, DC: World Bank.

Glover, D., and K. Kusterer. 1990. *Small Farmers, Big Business: Contract Farming and Rural Development.* London: MacMillan.

Gomez, P. Y. 1994. *Qualité et Théorie des Conventions.* Paris: Economica.

Goodman, D. 2002. Rethinking Food Production-Consumption: Integrative Approaches. *Sociologia Ruralis* 42 (4): 271–77.

Goodman, D. 2003. The "Quality Turn" and Alternative Food Practices: Reflections and Agenda. *Journal of Rural Studies* 19:1–7.

Goodman, D. 2004. Rural Europe Redux? Reflections on Alternative Agro-food Networks and Paradigm Change. *Sociologia Ruralis* 44 (1): 3–16.

Grahl, J. 2001. Globalised Finance: The Challenge to the Euro. *New Left Review* 8:23–47.

Granovetter, M. 1985. Economic Action and Social Structure: The Problem of Embeddedness. *Americal Journal of Sociology* 91 (3): 135–54.

*Guardian* (London). Various.

Guillén, M. 2000. Corporate Governance and Globalisation: Is There a Convergence Across Countries? Advances in international competitiveness management programme. The Wharton School and Department of Sociology, University of Pennsylvania.

Guthman, J. 2002. Commodified Meanings, Meaningful Commodities: Rethinking Production-Consumption Links through the Organic System of Provision. *Sociologia Ruralis* 42 (4): 295–311.

Guthman, J. 2003. Fast Food/Organic Food: Reflexive Tastes and the Making of "Yuppie Chow." *Social and Cultural Geography* 4 (1): 45–58.

Hall, R., and D. Soskice, eds. 2001. *Varieties of Capitalism: The Institutional Foundations of Comparative Advantage.* Oxford: Oxford University Press.

Harrison, B. 1994. *Lean and Mean: The Changing Landscape of Corporate Power in the Age of Flexibility.* New York: Basic Books.

Hartwick, E. 1998. Geographies of Consumption: A Commodity Chain Approach. *Environment and Planning D: Society and Space* 16:423–37.

Heijbroek, A., and R. Konjin 1995. *The Cocoa and Chocolate Market.* Utrecht, Netherlands: Rabobank.

Henderson, J., P. Dicken, M. Hess, N. Coe, and H. Wai-Chung Yeung. 2002. Global Production Networks and the Analysis of Economic Development. *Review of International Political Economy* 9 (3): 436–64.

Henson, S., and R. Loader. 2001. Barriers to Agricultural Exports from Developing Coutnries: The Role of Sanitary and Phytosanitary Requirements. *World Development* 29 (1): 85–102.

Hermann, R., K. Burger, and H. P. Smit. 1993. *International Commodity Policy: A Quantitative Analysis.* London: Routledge.

Hirst, P., and G. Thompson. 1996. *Globalisation in Question.* London: Polity Press.

Hodgson, G. M., ed. 2002. *A Modern Reader in Institutional and Evolutionary Economics.* Cheltenham: Edward Elgar.

Hoekman, B. 1996. Assessing the general agreement on trade in services. In W. Martin and L. Winters, eds. *The Uruguay Round and the Developing Countries.* Cambridge: Cambridge University Press.

Hoekman, B., and K. Anderson. 2001. Developing Country Agriculture and the New Trade Agenda. *Economic Development and Cultural Change* 49 (1): 171–80.

Hone, A. 1973. The Primary Commodities Boom. *New Left Review* I/81:82–92.

Hopkins, T. K., and I. Wallerstein. 1986. Commodity Chains in the World Economy Prior to 1800. *Review* 10 (1): 157–70.

Hopkins, T. K., and I. Wallerstein. 1994. Commodity chains: Construct and research. In G. Gereffi and M. Korzeniewicz, eds. *Commodity Chains and Global Capitalism.* Westport, CT: Greenwood Press.

Hughes, A. 2000. Retailers, Knowledges and Changing Commodity Networks: The Case of the Cut Flower Trade. *Geoforum* 31:175–90.

Hughes, A. 2001. Global Commodity Networks, Ethical Trade and Governmentality: Organising Business Responsibility in the Kenyan Cut Flower Industry. *Transactions of the Institute of British Geographers* 26:39–406.

Humphrey, J. 2003a. Upgrading in Global Value Chains. Background paper for the World Commission on the Social Dimensions of Globalisation. Brighton, UK: Institute of Development Studies, University of Sussex.

Humphrey, J. 2003b. Globalisation and Supply Chain Networks. The Auto Industry in Brazil and India. *Global Networks* 3 (2): 121–42.

Humphrey, J., and H. Schmitz. 2002a. Developing Country Firms in the World Economy: Governance and Upgrading in Global Value Chains. *INEF Report* 61/2002. Duisburg, Germany: INEF-University of Duisburg.

Humphrey, J., and H. Schmitz. 2002b. How Does Insertion in Global Value Chains Affect Upgrading in Industrial Clusters? *Regional Studies* 36:1017–28.

Humphrey, J., and H. Schmitz. 2003. Chain governance and upgrading: Taking stock. In H. Schmitz, ed. *Local Enterprises in the Global Economy: Issues of Governance and Upgrading*. Cheltenham: Edward Elgar.

Jaffee, S. 1994. Contract farming in the shadow of competitive markets: The experience of Kenyan horticulture. In P. Little and M. Watts, eds. *Living under Contract: Contract Farming and Agrarian Transformation in Sub-Saharan Africa*. Madison: University of Wisconsin Press.

Jaffee, S. 2003. From Challenge to Opportunity: Transforming Kenyan Fresh Vegetable Trade in the Context of Emerging Food Safety and Other Standards. *Agriculture and Rural Development Working Paper* 10. Washington, DC: World Bank.

Jensen, B. N. 2002. Standarder og Markedskrav: Implikationer for Markedsstruktur og Markedsadgang, Exempliciferet ved Tanzanias Eksport af Grøntsager til EU Markedet. Master's thesis, Department of Geography and International Development Studies, Roskilde University, Denmark.

Jensen, M. F. 2000. Standards and Smallholders: A Case Study from Kenyan Export Horticulture. Paper for the joint CDR-CIRAD workshop, on the coordination of African-based agrocommodity chains, Copenhagen: Centre for Development Research.

Jensen, M. F. 2002a. Reviewing the SPS Agreement: A Developing Country Perspective. *CDR Working Paper* 02-3. Copenhagen: Centre for Development Research.

Jensen, M. F. 2002b. African Exports and the Organisational Challenges Arising from Food Safety Requirements: What Can Be Expected from Changes in EU Food Safety Policies? Paper presented at the CDR workshop on global commodity chains, Copenhagen: Centre for Development Research.

Jürgens, U. 2002. "The German Car Industry," Corporate Governance, Innovation and Economic Performance in the EU. Research project working paper.

Kädtler, J., and H-J. Sperling. 2002. The Power of Financial Markets and the Resilience of Operations: Arguments and Evidence from the German Car Industry. *Competition and Change* 6 (1): 81–94.

Kaplinsky, R. 2000. Spreading the Gains from Globalization: What Can Be Learned from Value Chain Analysis? *IDS Working Paper* 100. Brighton, UK: Institute of Development Studies, University of Sussex.

Kaplinsky, R., and M. Morris. 2002. The Globalization of Product Markets and Immiserizing Growth: Lessons from the South African Furniture Industry. *World Development* 30 (7): 1159–77.

Kenney, M., and R. Florida. 1994. Japanese Maquiladoras: Production Organization and Global Commodity Chains. *World Development* 22 (1): 27–44.

Kessler, J. A. 1999. The North American Free Trade Agreement, Emerging Apparel Production Networks and Industrial Upgrading: The Southern California/Mexico Connection. *Review of International Political Economy* 6 (4): 565–608.

Keynes, J. M. (1942/1980) The international regulation of primary products. In D. Moggridge, ed. *Collected Writings of J. M. Keynes*. Vol. 27. London: Macmillan.

Klein, N. 2000. *No Logo*. Toronto: Knopf.

Kreuger, A., ed. *The Political Economy of US Trade Policy*. Cambridge, MA: National Bureau of Economic Research.

Lancaster, K. J. 1966. A New Approach to Consumer Theory. *Journal of Political Economy* 74:132–57.

Langlois, R. 2003. The Vanishing Hand: The Changing Dynamics of Industrial Capitalism. *Industrial and Corporate Change* 12 (2): 351–85.

Larsen, M. N. 2002. Is Oligopoly a Condition of Successful Privatization? The Case of Cotton in Zimbabwe. *Journal of Agrarian Change* 2 (2): 185–205.

Larsen, M. N. 2003a. Re-regulating a Failed Market: The Tanzanian Cotton Sector 1999–2002. *DIIS Working Paper* 03.2. Copenhagen: Danish Institute for International Studies.

Larsen, M. N. 2003b. Quality Standard-setting in the Global Cotton Chain and Cotton Sector Reform in Sub-Saharan Africa. *DIIS Working Paper* 03.07. Copenhagen: Danish Institute for International Studies.

Latour, B. 1987. *Science in Action: How to Follow Scientists and Engineers through Society*. Cambridge, MA: Harvard University Press.

Latour, B. 1998. To Modernise or ecologise? That is the question. In B. Braun and N. Castree, eds. *Remaking Reality: Nature at the Millennium*. London: Routledge.

Lazonick, B., and M. O'Sullivan. 2000. Maximising Shareholder Value: A New Ideology of Corporate Governance. *Economy and Society* 29 (1): 13–35.

Leslie, D., and S. Reimer. 1999. Spatialising Commodity Chains. *Progress in Human Geography* 23 (3): 401–20.

Leslie, D., and S. Reimer. 2003. Fashioning Furniture: Restructuring the Furniture Commodity Chain. *Area* 35 (4): 427–37.

Levitt, T. 1983. The Globalisation of Markets. *Harvard Business Review*, May-June: 92–102.

Levy, T. 2002. The theory of conventions and a new theory of the firm. In E. Fullbrook, ed. *Intersubjectivity in Economics*. London: Routledge.

Lewis, D. K. 1969. *Convention: A Philosophical Study*. Cambridge, MA: Harvard University Press.

Lockie, S. 2002. "The Invisible Mouth": Mobilizing "the Consumer" in Food Production-Consumption Networks. *Sociologia Ruralis* 42 (4): 278–94.

Losch, B. 2002. Global Restructuring and Liberalisation: Côte d'Ivoire and the End of the International Cocoa Market? *Journal of Agrarian Change* 2 (2): 206–28.

Lundvall, B. A., ed. 1992. *National Systems of Innovation: Towards a Theory of Innovation and Interactive Learning*. London: Pinter.

Lüthje, B. 2001. Electronics Contract Manufacturing: Global Production and the International Division of Labour in the Age of the Internet.

Frankfurt, Germany: Institut für Sozialforschung, Johan Wolfgang Goethe Universität.

Maddison, A. 2001. *The World Economy: A Millennial Perspective*. Paris: OECD.

Marsden, T., J. Banks, and G. Bristow. 2000. Food Supply Chain Approaches: Exploring Their Role in Rural Development. *Sociologia Ruralis* 40 (4): 424–38.

Marsden, T., A. Flynn, and M. Harrison. 2000. *Consuming Interests: The Social Provision of Foods*. London: UCL Press.

Marsden, T., R. Munton, N. Ward, and S. Whatmore. 1996. Agricultural Geography and the Political Economy Approach: A Review. *Economic Geography* 72 (4): 361–75.

Marsden, T., and N. Wrigley. 1995. Regulation, Retailing, and Consumption. *Environment and Planning A* 27:1899–912.

Mather, C. 2002a. A Note on Capespan and the Citrus Cooperatives. Mimeo. Department of Geography, Witwatersrand University, Republic of South Africa.

Mather, C. 2002b. A Note on the UK and Japanese Chains for Citrus. Mimeo. Department of Geography, Witwatersrand University, Republic of South Africa.

Mather, C. 2002c. Citrus Commodity Chains. Mimeo. Department of Geography, Witwatersrand University, Republic of South Africa.

Mather, C. 2002d. Regulating South Africa's Citrus Export Commodity Chain(s) after Liberalisation. Paper presented at the International Geographical Union conference on changing economic spaces, Johannesburg.

Mather, C. 2004. Citrus, apartheid and the struggle to (re)present outspan oranges. In A. Hughes and S. Reimer, eds. *Geographies of Commodity Chains*. London: Routledge.

Mather, C., and S. Greenberg. 2003. Market Liberalisation in Post-apartheid South Africa: The Restructuring of Citrus Exports after "Deregulation." *Journal of Southern African Studies* 29 (2): 393–412.

McCalman, P. 2000. Who Enjoys TRIPs abroad? An Empirical Analysis of Intellectual Property Rights in the Uruguay Round. Mimeo. Department of Economics, University of California at Santa Cruz.

McQueen, M. 2002. The EU's Free Trade Agreements with Developing Countries: A Case of Wishful Thinking? *World Economy* 25 (9): 1369–84.

Messner, D. 2002. The Concept of the "World Economic Triangle": Global Governance Patterns and Options for Regions. *IDS Working Paper* 173. Brighton: Institute of Development Studies, University of Sussex.

Michalopolous, C. 2001. *Developing Countries in the WTO*. London: Palgrave.

Milberg, W. 2003. The Changing Structure of Trade Linked to Global Production Systems: What Are the Policy Implications? Paper prepared for ILO. New York: New School University.

Milgrom, P., and J. Roberts. 1986. Price and Advertising Signals of Product Quality. *Journal of Political Economy* 94 (4): 796–821.

Miller, P. 1998. The margins of accounting. In M. Callon, ed. *The Laws of the Markets*. Oxford: Blackwell.

mm.eurodata. Available at www.mm.eurodata.com

Morin, F. 2000. A Transformation in the French Model of Shareholding and Management. *Economy and Society* 29 (1): 36–53.

Morris, M., and N. Dunne. 2004. Driving Environmental Certification: Its Impact on the Furniture and Timber Products Value Chain in South Africa. *Geoforum* 35:251–66.

Morrissey, O. 2000. Investment and Competition Policy in Developing Countries: Implications of and for the WTO. Research Paper 00/2. Centre for Research in Economic Development and International Trade, University of Nottingham, UK.

Morrissey, O., and Y. Rai. 1995. The GATT Agreement on TRIMs: Implications for Developing Countries and Their Relationships with Transnational Corporations. *Journal of Development Studies* 31 (5): 702–24.

Mshomba, R. 2000. *Africa in the Global Economy*. Boulder, CO: Lynne Rienner.

Murdoch, J. 1995. Actor Networks and the Evolution of Economic Forms: Combining Description and Explanation in Theories of Regulation, Flexible Specialization, and Networks. *Environment Planning A* 27:731–57.

Murdoch, J., T. Marsden, and J. Banks. 2000. Quality, Nature and Embeddedness: Some Theoretical Considerations in the Context of the Food Sector. *Economic Geography* 76:107–25.

Murdoch, J., and M. Miele. 1999. "Back to Nature": Changing "Worlds of Production" in the Food Sector. *Sociologia Ruralis* 39 (4): 465–83.

Nadvi, K., and G. Halder. 2002. Local Clusters in Global Value Chains: Exploring Dynamics Linkages between Germany and Pakistan. *IDS Working Paper* 152. Institute of Development Studies, University of Sussex.

Nadvi, K., and F. Wältring. 2002. Making Sense of Global Standards. *INEF Report* 58/2002. Duisburg, Germany: INEF-University of Duisburg.

Nestlé SA. 2002. *Management Report*. Available at www.nestle.com

Ng, F., and A. Yeats. 2001. On the Recent Trade Performance of Sub-Saharan African Countries: Cause for Hope or More of the Same? Mimeo. Trade Research Team. Washington, DC: World Bank.

Nicholas, F., and E. Valceschini. eds. 1995. *Agro-alimentaire: Une Économie de la Qualité*. Paris, INRA/Economica.

Nielsen, C. P. 2003. *Regional and Preferential Trade Agreements: A Literature review and Identification of Further Steps*. Report no. 155. Copenhagen: Food Economics Institute.

Nielsen, K. 2001. Institutionalist Approaches in the Social Sciences: Typology, Dialogue, and Future Challenges. *Journal of Economic Issues* 35 (2): 505–16.

North, D. C. 1990. *Institutions, Institutional Change and Economic Performance*. Cambridge: Cambridge University Press.

OECD. 1995. The Changing Role of Telecommunications in the Economy: Globalisation and Its Impact on National Telecommunications Policy. OECD/GD(95) 116, available at http://www.oecd.org/dataoecd/11129/2091257.pdf

OECD. 2001. *Agricultural Policies in OECD Countries: Monitoring and Evaluation*. Paris: OECD.

Ohmae, K. 1990. *The Borderless World*. New York: Collins.

Orléan, A. 2004. L'économie des conventions: Définitions et résultats. Preface to the 4th edition of A. Orlean, ed. *Analyse Économique des Conventions*. Paris: Presses Universitaires de France.

Page, S., and A. Hewitt. 2002. The New European Trade Preferences: Does Everything But Arms Help the Poor? *Development Policy Review* 20 (1): 91–102.

Palpacuer, F. 2000. Characterising Governance in Value Chain Analysis. Paper prepared for the IDS/Rockefeller Foundation meeting on global value chains, Bellagio, Italy.

Palpacuer, F., P. Gibbon, and L. Thomsen. 2005. New Challenges for Developing Country Suppliers in Global Clothing Chains: A Comparative European Perspective. *World Development* 33 (2).

Palpacuer, F., and A. Parisotto. 2003. Global Production and Local Jobs: Can Global Enterprise Networks Be Used as Levers for Local Development? *Global Networks* 3 (2): 1470–2266.

Panagariya, A. 2002 EU Preferential Trade Arrangements and Developing Countries. *World Economy* 25 (10): 1415–32.

Pedersen, P. O. 2001. Freight Transport under Globalisation and Its Impact on Africa. *Journal of Transport Geography* 9:85–99.

Pedersen, P. O. 2002. The Logistical Revolution and the Changing Structure of Agriculturally Based Commodity Chains in Africa. *CDR Working Paper* 02.12. Copenhagen: Centre for Development Research.

Perez, R., and F. Palpacuer. 2002. Mutations des Modes de Gouvernance, Dynamiques de Compétitivé et Management Stratégique des Firmes: Le Cas des Firmes Multinationales Alimentaires en Europe. Commissariat Général au Plan, Service des Etudes et de la Recherche, EFRI, Université de Montpellier.

Piore, M., and C. Sabel. 1984. *The Second Industrial Divide: Possibilities for Prosperity.* New York: Basic Books.

Polanyi. K. 1957/2001. *The Great Transformation: The Political and Economic Origins of Our Time.* Boston: Beacon Press.

Politicalmoneyline. Available at www.Politicalmoneyline.com

*Politiken* (Copenhagen). Various.

Ponte, S. 2001a. Behind the Coffee Crisis. *Economic and Political Weekly* 36 (46–47): 4410–7.

Ponte, S. 2001b. Coffee Markets in East Africa: Local Responses to Global Challenges or Global Responses to Local Challenges? *CDR Working Paper* 01.5. Copenhagen: Centre for Development Research.

Ponte, S. 2001c. The "Latte Revolution"? Winners and Losers in the Restructuring of the Global Coffee Marketing Chain. *CDR Working Paper* 01.3. Copenhagen: Centre for Development Research.

Ponte, S. 2002a. Standards, Trade and Equity: Lessons from the Specialty Coffee Industry. *CDR Working Paper* 02.13. Copenhagen: Centre for Development Research.

Ponte, S. 2002b. The "Latte Revolution"? Regulation, Markets and Consumption in the Global Coffee Chain. *World Development* 30 (7): 1099–1122.

Ponte, S. 2002c. Brewing a Bitter Cup? Deregulation, Quality and the Re-organization of Coffee Marketing in East Africa. *Journal of Agrarian Change* 2 (2): 248–72.

Ponte, S. 2003. Quality Conventions and the Governance of Global Value Chains. Paper prepared for the conference, Conventions et Institutions: Approfondissements théoriques et contributions au débat politique, Paris.

Ponte, S. 2004a. Standards and Sustainability in the Coffee Sector: A Global Value Chain Approach. Winnipeg, Manitoba, Canada: IISD and UNCTAD.

Ponte, S. 2004b. The Politics of Ownership: Tanzanian Coffee Policy in the Age of Liberal Reformism. *African Affairs*. 103 (413): 615–633.

Porter, G., and K. Phillips-Howard. 1997. Comparing Contracts: An Evaluation of Contract Farming Schemes in Africa. *World Development* 25 (2): 227–38.

Porter, M. 1985. *Competitive Advantage*. New York: Free Press.

Porter, M. 1987. Changing patterns of international competition. In D. J. Teece, ed. *The Competitive Challenge: Strategies for Industrial Innovation and Renewal*. Cambridge, MA: Ballinger.

Porter, M. 1990. *The Competitive Advantage of Nations*. Cambridge, MA: Harvard Business School Press.

Poulton, C., P. Gibbon, J. Kydd, M. N. Larsen, A. Osorio, and D. Tschirley. 2004. Competition and Coordination in Liberalized African Cotton Market Systems. *World Development* 32 (3): 519–36.

Power, M. 1997. *The Audit Society: Rituals of Verification*. Oxford: Oxford University Press.

Prebisch, R. 1950. *The Economic Development of Latin America and Its Principal Problem*. Santiago, Chile: UNECLA.

Pritchard, B., and D. Burch. 2003. *Agri-food Globalization in Perspective: International Restructuring in the Processing Tomato Industry*. Aldershot, UK: Ashgate.

Quadros, R. 2002. Global Quality Standards, Chain Governance and the Techological Upgrading of Brazilian Auto-Components. *IDS Working Paper* 156, Brighton, UK: Institute of Development Studies, University of Sussex.

Rabach, E., and E.M. Kim. 1994. Where is the chain in commodity chains? The service sector nexus. In G. Gereffi and M. Korzeniewicz, eds. *Commodity Chains and Global Capitalism*. Westport, CT: Greenwood Press.

Rabobank. 2001. Fruit Traders in Trouble. Industry Note, Food and Agribusiness Research, 002–2001.

Rabobank, 2002a. Is Ingredient Branding the Way to Escape Commoditised Food Ingredient Markets ? Industry Note, Food and Agribusiness Research, 042–2002.

Rabobank. 2002b. *Identification and Assessment of Proposals by the International Coffee Sector Regarding the Poor Income Situation of Coffee Farmers*. Report commissioned by DGIS. Available at www.minbuza.nl/default.asp? CMS_ITEM=MB2455065#P127-2959

Raghavan, C. 2000. *The EC's Snail Pace Textile and Clothing Liberalisation*. Third World Network. Available at www.twnside.org.sg/title/snail.htm

Raikes, P., and P. Gibbon. 2000. Globalisation and African Export Crop Agriculture. *Journal of Peasant Studies* 27 (2): 50–93.

Raikes, P., M. F. Jensen, and S. Ponte. 2000. Global Commodity Chain Analysis and the French Filiére Approach: Comparison and Critique. *Economy and Society* 29 (3): 390–417.

Rammohan, K. T., and R. Sundaresan. 2003. Socially Embedding the Commodity Chain: An Exercise in Relation to Coir Yarn Spining in Southern India. *World Development* 31 (5): 903–23.

Raynolds, L. T. 2002. Consumer/Producer Links in Fair Trade Coffee Networks. *Sociologia Ruralis* 42 (4): 404–24.

Raynolds, L. 2004. The Globalization of Organic Agro-Food Networks. *World Development* 32 (5): 725–43.

Reardon, T., and J. A. Berdegué. 2002. The Rapid Rise of Supermarkets in Latin America: Challenges and Opportunities for Development. *Development Policy Review* 20 (4): 371–88.

Reardon, T., J.A. Berdegué, and J. Farrington. 2002. Supermarkets and Farming in Latin America: Pointing Directions for Elsewhere. *Natural Resource Perspectives* no. 81 (December).

Reardon, T., J. M. Codron, L. Busch, J. Bingen, and C. Harris. 2001. Global Change in Agrifood Grades and Standards: Agribusiness Strategic Responses in Developing Countries. *International Food and Agribusiness Management* 2 (3): 421–35.

Reardon, T., C. P. Timmer, C. B. Barrett, and J. A. Berdegué. 2003. The Rise of Supermarkets in Asia, Africa and Latin America. *American Journal of Agricultural Economics* 85:1140–46

Reinart, K. 2000. Give Us Virtue, But Not Yet: Safeguard Actions under the ATC. *World Economy* 23 (1): 25–55

Renard, M. C. 2003. Fair Trade: Quality, Market and Conventions. *Journal of Rural Studies* 19:87–96.

Retail Forward. 2002. *The Age of Wal-Mart*. Columbus, OH: Retail Forward.

Robinson, J. 1953. Imperfect Competition Revisited. *The Economic Journal* 63:579–93.

Rodrik, D. 1999. *The New Global Economy and Developing Countries: Making Openness Work*. London: Overseas Development Institute.

Rose, N., and P. Miller. 1992. Political Power beyond the State: Problematics of Government. *British Journal of Sociology* 43 (2): 173–205.

Sachs, J., and A. Warner. 1997. Sources of Slow Growth in African Economies. *Journal of African Economies* 6:335–76.

Salais, R. 1989. L'Analyse Économique des Conventions de Travail. *Revue Economique* 40 (2): 199–240.

Salais, R. 2002. The Contours of a Pragmatic Theory of "Situated" Institutions and Its Economic Relevance. Mimeo. IDHE, Ecole Normale Supérieure de Cachan.

Salais, R., and M. Storper. 1992. The Four "Worlds" of Contemporary Industry. *Cambridge Journal of Economics* 16:169–93.

Salais, R., and L. Thèvenot, eds. 1986. *Le Travail, Marché, Règles, Conventions*. Paris: INSEE-Economica.

Sapir, A. 2000. EC Regionalism at the Turn of the Millennium: Toward a New Paradigm. *World Economy* 23 (9): 1135–48.

Schaffer, G. 2003. How to make the WTO dispute settlement system work for developing countries: Some proactive developing country strategies. In V. Mosoti, ed. *Towards a Development-supportive Dispute Settlement System at the WTO*. Geneva: ICSTD.

Schmitz H. 1999. Global Competition and Local Cooperation: Success and Failures in the Sinos Valley, Brazil. *World Development* 27 (9): 1627–50.

Schmitz, H., and P. Knorriga. 1999. Learning from Global Buyers. *IDS Working Paper* 100. Brighton, UK: Institute of Development Studies, University of Sussex.

Schumpeter, J. 1943. *Capitalism, Socialism and Democracy*. London: Unwin University Books.

Shoch, J. 2001. *Trading Blows: Party Competition and US Trade Policy in a Globalizing Era*. Chapel Hill: University of North Carolina Press.

Shore, C., and S. Wright. 2000. Coercive accountability: The rise of audit culture in higher education. In M. Strathern, ed. *Audit Cultures: Anthropological Studies in Accountability, Ethics and the Academy*. London: Routledge.

Singer, H. 1950. The Distribution of Gains between Investing and Borrowing Countries. *American Economic Review* 40:473–85.

Smith, A., A. Rainnie, M. Dunford, J. Hardy, R. Hudson, and D. Sadler. 2002. Networks of Value, Commodities and Regions: Reworking Divisions of Labour in Macro-Regional Economies. *Progress in Human Geography* 26 (1): 41–63.

Srinivasan, T. 1998. *Developing Countries and the Multilateral Trading System: From the GATT to the Uruguay Round and the Future*. Boulder, CO: Westview.

Sterns, P. A., and L. Busch. 2002. Standard Setting in the African Horticultural Export Market: A Bottom-Up or Top-Down Approach? *Journal of Economic Issues* 38 (2): 527–37.

Stevens, C., and J. Kennan. 2001. The Impact of the EU's Everything But Arms Proposal: A Report to Oxfam. Oxford, UK: Oxfam.

Storper, M., and R. Salais. 1997. *Worlds of Production: The Action Frameworks of the Economy*. Cambridge, MA: Harvard University Press.

Strathern, M., ed. 2000. *Audit Cultures: Anthropological Studies in Accountability, Ethics and the Academy*. London: Routledge.

Sturgeon, T. J. 2001. How Do We Define Value Chains and Production Networks? *IDS Bulletin* 32 (3): 9–18.

Sturgeon, T. 2002. Modular Manufacturing Networks: A New American Model of Industrial Organisation. *Industrial and Corporate Change* 11 (3): 451–96.

Sturgeon, T., and R. Lester. 2002. Upgrading East Asian Industries: New Challenges for Local Suppliers. Paper prepared for World Bank project on East Asia's economic future. Industrial Performance Center, Massachusetts Institute of Technology, Cambridge, MA.

Subramanian, A., and N. Tamirisa. 2001. Africa's Trade Revisited. *IMF Working paper* WP/01/35. Washington, DC: International Monetary Fund.

Sylvander, B. 1995. Convention de qualité, concurrence et coopération: Cas du label rouge dans la filière volaille. In G. Allaire and R. Boyer, eds. *La Grande Transformation de l'Agriculture*. Paris: INRA-Economica.

Talbot, J. M. 2002. Tropical Commodity Chains, Forward Integration Strategies and International Inequality: Coffee, Cocoa and Tea. *Review of International Political Economy* 9 (9): 701–34.

Tang, X. 2000. The ATC and related trade policy developments. In UNCTAD (ed.) *A Positive Agenda and Future Trade Negotiations*. Geneva: UNCTAD.

Tesco plc. 2003. *Annual Report*, London.

Tharakan, D. 2002. The EU and Preferential Arrangements. *World Economy* 25 (10): 1387–98.

Thévenot, L. 1995. Des marchés aux normes. In G. Allaire and R. Boyer, eds. *La Grande Transformation de l'Agriculture: Lectures Conventionnalistes et Regulationnistes.* Paris: INRA-Economica.

Thévenot, L. 1997. Un gouvernement par les normes: Pratiques et politiques des formats d'information. In C. Bernard and L. Thévenot, eds. *Cognition et Information en Societé.* Paris: Ed. de l'Ecole des Hautes Etudes en Sciences Sociales.

Thévenot, L. 1998. Innovating in "Qualified Markets": Quality, Norms and Conventions. Paper presented at conference on systems and trajectories of innovation, Institute of International Studies, University of California, Berkeley.

Thévenot, L. 2002. Conventions of co-ordination and the framing of uncertainty. In E. Fullbrook, ed. *Intersubjectivity in Economics.* London: Routledge.

Thévenot, L., M. Moody, and C. Lafaye. 2000. Forms of valuing nature: Arguments and modes of justification in French and American environmental disputes. In M. Lamont and L. Thévenot, eds. *Rethinking Comparative Cultural Sociology: Repertoires of Evaluation in France and the United States.* Cambridge: Cambridge University Press.

Thompson, G. 2003. *Between Hierarchies and Markets: The Logic and Limits of Network Forms of Organization.* Oxford: Oxford University Press.

Tirole, J. 1988. *The Theory of Industrial Organization.* Cambridge, MA: MIT Press.

Tyson, T. 2000. A Contract for the Future. *Pharmaceutical Manufacturing International.* Available at http://www.worldpharmaceutical.net.eds

UK Competition Commission. 2000. *Supermarkets: A Report on the Supply of Groceries from Multiple Stores in the United Kingdom.* London: Department of Trade and Industry.

UNCTAD Common Fund for Commodities. 2001. *The Role of Commodities in Least Developed Countries.* UNCTAD/DITC/COM/32.

Unnevehr, L. 2000. Food Safety Issues and Fresh Food Product Exports from Least Developed Countries. *Agricultural Economics* 23:231–40.

U.S. Census Bureau. 2000. *1997 Economic Census. Retail Trade Establishment and Firm Size.* EC 97 R445-52. Washington, DC: U.S. Census Bureau.

U.S. Government Accounting Office. 2002. *International Trade: Advisory Committee System Should Be Updated to Better Serve US Policy Needs.* Report no. GAO-02-786. Washington, DC: U.S. Government Accounting Office.

Valceschini, E. 1993. Conventions Économiques et Mutation de l'Économie Contractuelle dans le Secteur des Légumes Transformés. *Economie Rurale* (Novembre-Decembre): 19–26.

Valceschini, E., and F. Nicholas, 1995. La dinamique économique de la qualité agro-alimentaire. In F. Nicholas and E. Valceschini, eds. *Agro-alimentaire: Une Économie de la Qualité.* Paris, INRA/Economica.

van Dijk, J. B., D. H. M. van Doesburg, A. M. A. Heijbroek, M. R. I. A. Wazir, and G. S. M. de Wolff. 1998. *The World Coffee Market.* Utrecht, Netherlands: Rabobank.

Vargas, M. A. 2001. Forms of Governance, Learning Mechanisms and Upgrading Strategies in the Tobacco Cluster in Rio Pardo Valley—Brazil. *IDS Working*

*Paper* 125, Brighton, UK: Institute of Development Studies, University of Sussex.

Vitols, S. 2002. Shareholder Value, Management Culture and Production Regimes in the Transformation of the German Chemical-pharmaceutical Industry. *Competition and Change* 6 (3): 309–25.

Vorley, B. 2003. *Corporate Concentration from Farm to Consumer*. Report for the UK Food Group. London: IIED.

Vorley, B., D. Roe, and S. Bass. 2002. *Standards and Sustainable Trade*. Report for the proposed Sustainable Trade and Innovation Centre. London: IIED.

Wal-Mart. 2003. *Annual Report*.

Watts, M. 1994. Life under contract: Contract farming, agrarian restructuring and flexible accumulation. In P. Little and M. Watts, eds. *Living under Contract: Contract Farming and Agrarian Transformation in Sub-Saharan Africa*. Madison: University of Wisconsin Press.

Weatherspoon, D., and T. Reardon. 2003. The Rise of Supermarkets in Africa: Implications for Agrifood Systems and the Rural Poor. *Development Policy Review* 21 (3): 333–55.

Weber, M. 1978. The types of legitimate domination. In G. Roh and C. Wittich, eds. *Economy and Society*. Berkeley: University of California Press.

Weiss, L. 1998. *The Myth of the Powerless State*. Ithaca: Cornell University Press.

Weiss, L. 1999. Globalisation and National Governance: Antinomy or Interdependece? *Review of International Studies* 25 (5): 59–88.

Whatmore, S., and L. Thorne. 1997. Nourishing networks: Alternative geographies of food. In D. Goodman and M. Watts, eds. *Globalising Food: Agrarian Questions and Global Restructuring*. London: Routledge.

Whitley, R. 1999. *Divergent Capitalisms: The Social Structuring and Change of Business Systems*. Oxford: Oxford University Press.

Wilkinson, J. 1997. A New Paradigm for Economic Analysis? *Economy and Society* 26 (3): 305–39.

Wilkinson, J. 2002. The Final Foods Industry and the Changing Face of the Global Agro-Food System. *Sociologia Ruralis* 42 (2): 329–46.

Williams, K. 2000. From Shareholder Value to Present-day Capitalism. *Economy and Society* 29 (1): 1–12.

Williamson, O. E. 1979. Transaction-Cost Economics: The Governance of Contractual Relations. *Journal of Law and Economics* 22:233–61.

Williamson, O. E., and S.E. Masten, eds. 1995. *Transaction Cost Economics*. Aldershot, UK: Edward Elgar.

Wilson, J. S., and V. O. Abiola, eds. 2003. *Standards and Global Trade: A Voice for Africa*. Washington, DC: World Bank.

Wolinsky, A. 1983. Prices as Signals of Product Quality. *Review of Economic Studies* 50:647–56.

WTO. 2002. *International Trade Statistics*. Geneva: WTO.

www.the-list.co.uk

# Index

**Peter Gibbon** is a Senior Researcher at the Danish Institute for International Studies. Among his earlier publications is *A Blighted Harvest: The World Bank and African Agriculture in the 1980s*. He has also edited numerous books.

**Stefano Ponte** is a Senior Researcher at the Danish Institute for International Studies. He is the author of *Farmers and Markets in Tanzania: How Market Reforms Affect Rural Livelihoods in Africa* and co-author (with Benoit Daviron) of *The Coffee Paradox: Commodity Trade and the Elusive Promise of Development*.